ABOLITIONISM

SOCIAL MOVEMENTS PAST AND PRESENT

Irwin T. Sanders, Editor

American Temperance Movements: Cycles of Reform
by Jack S. Blocker Jr.

The Antinuclear Movement
by Jerome Brian Price

The Charismatic Movement: Is There a New Pentecost?
by Margaret Poloma

Civil Rights: The 1960s Freedom Struggle
by Rhoda Lois Blumberg

The Conservative Movement
by Paul Gottfried and Thomas Fleming

*Family Planning and Population Control:
The Trials of a Successful Movement*
by Kurt W. Back

Let the People Decide: Neighborhood Organizing in America
by Robert Fisher

The Rise of a Gay and Lesbian Movement
by Barry D Adam

ABOLITIONISM
A REVOLUTIONARY MOVEMENT

Herbert Aptheker

Twayne Publishers • Boston
A Division of G. K. Hall & Co.

Abolitionism: A Revolutionary Movement
Herbert Aptheker

Copyright 1989 by G. K. Hall & Co.
All rights reserved.
Published by Twayne Publishers
A Division of G. K. Hall & Co.
70 Lincoln Street, Boston, Massachusetts 02111

Copyediting supervised by Barbara Sutton.
Book production by Janet Z. Reynolds.
Typeset by Compset, Inc., of Beverly, Massachusetts.

Printed on permanent/durable acid-free paper
and bound in the United States of America.

First Printing 1989

Library of Congress Cataloging-in-Publication Data

Aptheker, Herbert, 1915–
    Abolitionism : a revolutionary movement / Herbert Aptheker.
        p.   cm.—(Social movements past and present)
    Bibliography: p.
    Includes index.
    ISBN 0-8057-9702-5.   ISBN 0-8057-9730-0 (pbk.)
    1. Slavery—United States—Anti-slavery movements.
  2. Abolitionists—United States—History. I. Title. II. Series
E449.A156   1989
326′.0973—dc19   88-29461
                                                                        CIP

There are innumerable battles yet to be fought for the right . . . and those who shall hereafter go forth to defend the righteous cause, no matter at what cost or with what disparity of numbers, cannot fail to gain strength and inspiration from an intelligent acquaintance with the means and methods used in the Anti-Slavery movement.

—William Lloyd Garrison to Edmund Quincy and others, 17 March 1873, in W. P. Garrison and F. J. Garrison, Garrison, *4:258*

Contents

About the Author   ix
Acknowledgments   x
Introduction   xi

Chapter One
Early Seeding of Abolitionism   1

Chapter Two
Jefferson's "Fire Bell in the Night"   7

Chapter Three
Revolutionary Consciousness: Supporters and Opponents   15

Chapter Four
Social Class, Labor, and Abolitionism   35

Chapter Five
Organization of the Abolitionist Movement   50

Chapter Six
Abolitionism, Racism, and the Afro-American People   58

Chapter Seven
Women and Abolitionism   77

Chapter Eight
Political Prisoners and Martyrs   94

Chapter Nine
John Brown and Revolution   123

Chapter Ten
**The Civil War as Revolution: Abolitionism's
Culmination**   143

Notes and References   163
Bibliographic Essay   183
Index   186

About the Author

Herbert Aptheker has been on the faculties of Bryn Mawr College, City University of New York, Yale University, University of California at Berkeley, Santa Clara University, Humboldt University (Berlin, GDR), and since 1977, the Law School, University of California at Berkeley.

His articles and reviews have appeared in scholarly journals since 1937. His first publication was *The Negro in the Civil War* (1938), followed by *The Negro in the Abolitionist Movement* (1941). His *American Negro Slave Revolts* was first issued by Columbia University Press in 1943. Among other relevant publications are *A Documentary History of the Negro People in the United States* in three volumes (1951–74), the thirty-eight volumes of *The Collected Published Writings of W. E. B. Du Bois* (1973–86), three volumes of *Du Bois's Correspondence* (1973–78), and certain volumes by Du Bois not published during his lifetime, including *Education for Black People* (1975) and *Against Racism: Essays and Papers 1887–1961* (1985).

Acknowledgments

I offer my sincere thanks to my mentors: W. E. B. Du Bois, Carter G. Woodson, Charles H. Wesley, Lorenzo J. Greene, Louis E. Burnham, Henry Winston, Claude Williams, Elizabeth Lawson, Helen Boardman, and William L. Patterson.

I also wish to thank my younger friends who have been most helpful: Paul Kranz, Robert Kaufman, and David Fathi. To my daughter, Bettina Aptheker, and to Irwin T. Sanders, who improved the manuscript, I am indebted. And, as ever, I am especially grateful to Fay P. Aptheker.

Introduction

In the first six decades of the nineteenth century, the malignancy of slavery affected every facet of life in the United States. Constant ferment marked its existence; countervailing forces were finally sufficiently potent to overcome it, but only after a fierce war had taken hundreds of thousands of lives and the survival of the Republic had been in doubt.

Leading the momentous struggle against slavery, informing it, inspiring it, was the Abolitionist movement—the second successful revolutionary movement in the history of the United States.

The bulk of the vast literature on Abolitionism treats it as simply one of numerous reform movements of the pre–Civil War era; in this sense the literature ignores the question of its revolutionary character. Occasionally, however, one will find the same historian both denying and affirming that it was revolutionary. An example is David Brion Davis, writing in the textbook, *The Great Republic*. On one page he writes, "Nor could abolitionists think of themselves as revolutionaries; by historical definition, the evangelical conscience was an antidote to revolution"— which would have surprised David Walker and other outstanding Abolitionists such as William Lloyd Garrison, Wendell Phillips, Frederick Douglass, and Lydia Maria Child, not to mention John Brown. Then on a later page Davis observes that the Abolitionists had "a revolutionary purpose—a purpose that threatened one of the nation's chief capital investments as well as a national system for racial control."[1]

The fact is that many, perhaps most, of the Abolitionists were revolutionists in their own minds, and the movement as a whole was a revolutionary one in every respect. Lewis Perry has taken essentially this position regarding the left wing of Abolitionism. Its adherents, he remarks, "would usually have agreed that the abolition of slavery presupposed a revolution in power relationships in America," and says later, "The institution of slavery was a major component of the social order in the United States, and to attack slavery was inescapably to call for extensive social change."[2]

Among the "classical" historians, one sometimes finds an appreciation of the revolutionary quality of Abolitionism. For example, James Ford Rhodes, himself a teenager at the time of the Civil War, comments that "merchants, manufacturers, and capitalists were against the movement, for trade with the South was important." He adds that though those who founded the American Anti-Slavery Society in 1833 were "of good character, pure morals, and . . . law-abiding," still their meeting "was regarded by all Southern people, and by nearly all at the North, in much the same way as we should now look upon an assemblage of anarchists."[3]

The term *revolutionary movement* is used in this work in its precise sense. That is, the Abolitionists sought the uncompensated emancipation, at once, of the slaves. This meant the confiscation of billions of dollars worth of private property, the ownership of which constituted the power of, and defined the nature of, the slave-owning class, which predominated in the South and nationally, in the latter case until the mid-1850s. It was the ruling class. In its ownership of the slaves, the best land, the animals and tools to make that land productive, and the crops thereby realized, the slaveholding class possessed wealth far in excess of any other property-owning class prior to the Civil War. Fundamentally because of this economic dominance, slaveholders controlled both political parties—usually favoring one, but dominating the other, too. It also controlled thereby the executive, legislative, and judicial arms of the federal government and so dominated its domestic and foreign policy. This economic and political predominance assured the slaveholding class effective control, too, over the ideological structure of the society. The slaveholding influence was decisive in publishing—books, periodicals, and newspapers; in education—texts, faculties, and administrators; and in religion—preferred texts and personnel.

The Abolitionists led a movement whose basic aim was the termination of the base of this power, the slaveholding system. It meant the overthrow of the propertied ruling class in the only way such a class can be overthrown—by the elimination of the property upon which its power rests.

Here two fundamental components of Abolitionism will be emphasized: (1) its revolutionary nature, and (2) its organization. Abolitionism was a highly organized movement, with local, sectional, and national associations, constitutions, organs of publications, duly admitted members, elected and/or appointed leaders, and full-time activists—professional revolutionaries.

Given its fundamental aim, one would expect this second revolution to be more truly democratic than was the first American Revolution, with its less profound property challenge and its less ambitious transformation of society. Indeed it was more democratic: it was a black-white movement much more fully than its predecessor; it was a male-female movement much more fully than its predecessor; it was more fully conscious of its challenge to property rights. Moreover, that challenge was a fundamental characteristic of the second revolution, whereas it was only at the fringes of the first—in some attacks on feudal vestiges and royal privileges, for example.

Although a salient feature of the Abolitionist movement was its black-white character, it is important to emphasize the overwhelming consequence of its black component. Slavery was the unique experience of black people in the United States (although some Native Americans were enslaved and there was an important biological mix of blacks and Native Americans as slaves). They alone endured it, survived it, and combated it. They were the first and most lasting Abolitionists. Their conspiracies and insurrections, individual struggles, systematic flights, maroon communities, efforts to buy freedom, cultural solidity, creation of antislavery organizations and publications—all preceded the black-white united efforts. They developed a convention movement, with delegates from many states meeting annually from 1830 to the Civil War and collectively deciding on priorities and strategies for their people. They rejected colonizationism. Without the initiative of the Afro-American people, without their illumination of the nature of slavery, without their persistent struggle to be free, there would have been no national Abolitionist movement. And when the movement did appear, the participation of black people in every aspect was indispensable to its functioning and its eventual success.

More conscious of its challenge to property rights than was the first revolution, the Abolitionist movement was also characterized by a class cohesiveness, something approaching modern class consciousness. Its leadership and membership were derived from several classes, but the heaviest weight, especially in the membership, was among largely non-propertied elements—farmers, mechanics, artisans, workers, and the members of their families. Although there was some ambiguity in the relationship between Abolitionism and the young labor movement, especially in the generation prior to the Civil War, the relationship became increasingly close and explicit. This was true both in the United States and abroad.

In their international qualities, the two revolutions were comparable. Each consciously sought assistance from abroad, and each had a profound impact upon individuals, organizations, and governments outside the United States.

Both the Revolutionary War and the Abolitionist movement succeeded in their fundamental goals: national independence and a republican form of government in the first; an end to chattel slavery in the second. Neither, of course, established the millennium. The signal failure of the first—the retention of slavery—offered the main task of the second. The signal failure of the second—the persistence of racism—left much work to be done, and still to be done, by ensuing generations.

Although the Abolitionist movement did not succeed in extirpating racism, one of its fundamental commitments was the undertaking of that formidable task. Racism permeated slavery in the United States—characterized it, justified it, and sustained it. In another manifestation, in somewhat altered form, racism rationalized the genocidal policy practiced toward the indigenous population, the Native Americans. And it spilled over, of course, in the treatment accorded free blacks, both in the South and in the North. To attack slavery, then, was to attack racism. But this does not mean that all the whites who participated in the attack were themselves free of racism. Many were not. But many others were, and all of them, in different degrees of consciousness, insofar as they battled slavery weakened racism.

In this sense, abolitionism is one proof of the error of U. B. Phillips's view that the maintenance of white supremacy was the central theme of southern history, some later suggesting that this might well be amended to read that the maintenance of white supremacy was the central theme of *American* history.[4]

The central commitment of the Abolitionist movement—its struggle against racism—was directed not only at enslavement but at all manifestations of the poison. Where individual participants in Abolitionism failed in this commitment—and there was failure—they were hurting the movement of which they were a part (thus again confirming that one of the defining qualities of Abolitionism was antiracism). It also is true, as

Richard H. Sewell in particular has made clear,[5] that many leaders and adherents of the Free Soil and Republican parties took advanced positions on the political and civil rights of blacks, as well as trying to prevent the expansion of slavery. Opposition to slavery, itself, as well as to its expansion, was basic to both parties. And as Sewell also demonstrated, a number of white people in both organizations rejected altogether the idea of black inferiority.

Comprehension of the basic significance of antiracism (as opposed to merely antislavery) marked the thinking of several leading Abolitionists and affected their struggles to realize the full revolutionary potential of the Civil War. For example, Wendell Phillips, probably the outstanding orator of the pre–Civil War era, prophesied in December 1860: "For a hundred years, at least, our history will probably be a record of the struggles of a proud and selfish race to do justice to one that circumstances had thrown into its power. The effects of slavery will not vanish in one generation, or even in two. It were a very slight evil if they could be done away with more quickly."[6]

The argument that the exigencies of war allowed and required an emancipationist policy was urged by antislavery politicians from John Quincy Adams to Charles Sumner and formed the rationale for Lincoln's Emancipation Proclamation—although even that wartime order did invoke the word *justice*. But Abolitionists like Phillips, Parker Pillsbury, Gerrit Smith, and Lydia Maria Child were worried by the general failure to demand emancipation on ethical grounds. Child wrote to Smith on 7 January 1862: "This entire absence of a moral sense on the subject has disheartened me more than anything else. Even should they be emancipated, merely as a 'war necessity,' everything *must* go wrong, if there is no heart or conscience in the subject." Child continued, as prophetically and truly as had Phillips, "It is evident that a great moral work still needs to be done."[7]

A little later, Frederick Douglass, the greatest of the black Abolitionists, uttered the same warning in a speech given at Cooper Union in New York City on 6 February 1862 and reported in the *New York Tribune* two days later:

Much as I value the present apparent hostility to slavery at the North, I plainly see that it is less the outgrowth of high and intelligent moral conviction against slavery as such, then because of the trouble its friends have brought upon the country. I would have slavery hated for that and more. A man that hates slavery for what it does to the white man stands ready to embrace it the moment its injuries are confined to the black man, and he ceases to feel those injuries in his own person.[8]

Abolitionism, as a revolutionary movement, resulted in serious victimization for many of its adherents; the victimization was endured both in the causes of antislavery and its twin, antiracism.

The experience of slavery and the struggle against it were also profoundly affected by religion. In its priestly guise, religion was an important bulwark of the institution, but in its prophetic aspect, it served as a goad and inspirer of Abolitionism. Jefferson Davis and John Brown, John C. Calhoun and Nat Turner, were all religious men, but the lessons they learned show their religiousness certainly differed. The religion of Abolitionism as manifested in the writings of David Walker and William Lloyd Garrison differed little from what today is called the theology of liberation. The sense of enlightenment, perfectionism, and revivalism that helped induce profound efforts at social renovation also induced critical approaches to theology in general. This helps explain the attacks against Abolitionists like Garrison as an apostate or an agnostic, if not an atheist. And it helps explain the profound questioning of traditional religious practice that marked Frederick Douglass and that led to a rejection of religion altogether and the appearance of a significant atheist presence in pre–Civil War United States, an atheism that normally affirmed a hatred of slavery.

It is significant, also, that Abolitionism helped stimulate other socially progressive ideas and movements. It accompanied women's awakening consciousness of their oppression. It fed concern for civil liberties, as freedoms of speech, petition, assembly, mail were increasingly assaulted by proslavery forces. It fostered consideration of the place and dignity of labor and of democracy in general, as both were attacked by the servants of the slavocrats. The entire experience of Abolitionism—especially its confrontration with property ownership and its mounting allegiance to egalitarianism—fed currents of socialist thought. This is related to Du Bois's penetrating suggestion that the Emancipation Proclamation is one of the most important documents in labor history, as well as Marx's proposition that labor in a white skin could not be free so long as labor in a black skin was branded.

A central problem in comprehending Abolitionism—as is the case with any successful revolutionary effort—is to explicate its success. It was combating the most powerful single force in the nation, a force that had largely made in its own image the country's political and ideological features. The success is attributable to the mounting collision of slavery and nonslavery interests. Becoming ever more apparent was the basic contradiction between slavery as such and eighteenth- and nineteenth-century values inherent in the best theological and secular traditions, as expressed in the more elevated Judeo-Christian teachings and the secular Enlightenment themes captured in the Declaration of Independence and the Preamble to the U.S. Constitution. Lincoln's observation that if slavery was not wrong, nothing was wrong, was uttered in another way and an earlier time when Jefferson excoriated slavery's devastating impact upon human conduct and character and suggested to Gov. James Monroe that when he was dealing with slave rebels, he should exercise mercy within the limits of his office. Said the author of the Declaration of Independence: "The other states & the world at large will forever condemn us if we indulge a principle of revenge or go one step beyond absolute necessity. They cannot lose sight of the rights of the two parties, & the object of the unsuccessful one."[9]

The system of slavery not only had legal, religious, and moral needs that conflicted with enlightened views and practices and thus provoked resistance. It also had economic characteristics and compulsions that conflicted with those of nonslaveholders. This was notably true in the oligarchic character of the slaveholding system, which induced pressures toward reducing the percentage of the white population who had direct interest in slave ownership. It was true, also, in other compulsions of the slaveholding system, compulsions of both an economic character—to maintain and raise the level of profits—and a policing character—to prevent the accumulation in a limited (and closed) space of a relatively high percentage of slaves.

Increasingly these needs induced class conflict within the South, a condition that became aggravated in the ten or fifteen years prior to secessions and played an important role in the decision to secede. Further, the expansionism and the particular desires of the slaveholding class—the Mexican War was a prime example of the former, and opposition to protective tariffs and to free-labor settlement of the West were examples of the latter—induced serious economic and political differences with the swiftly growing areas outside of slavery. The resulting clashes threw into increasing doubt for wider and wider circles of the population the utility of the slave system. The distance between doubting slavery's utility and questioning its morality was not great. This development increased the actual number of Abolitionists, and even more important, it diminished the hostility toward Abolitionists that had characterized the movement's first two decades.

As we have noted, slavery increasingly undercut the civil liberties of white people, first in the South and then outside it. Also troublesome to many outside the Abolitionist circle was the tendency of the advocates of slavery not only to intensify their political and economic demands but also to move their ideological positions further and further to the right: from a tentative suggestion that slavery was necessary, if not exactly wholesome, to an insistence that slavery was ideal, divinely sanctioned, the Republic's bulwark. Their arguments took their most extreme form in the suggestion that slavery was really the natural condition not only of blacks but of all working people, and that it was a solution, indeed, the only practical solution, to the chronic class struggle that was tearing apart European and northern culture. Such propaganda accompanied political and judicial actions that seemed aimed at nationalizing slavery and making its active support a duty of the entire citizenry.

This progression of arguments helped solve the key problem posed by some Abolitionists in the 1830s and 1840s—namely, how to persuade the general nonslaveholding white population that its own interests were harmed by slavery. But such a development requires hard efforts to be effective. This was the function first of the Afro-American population whose struggles never let the question of slavery subside and second, in an intertwined fashion, of the organized opposition to slavery of blacks and whites that was Abolitionism.

Chapter One

Early Seeding of Abolitionism

Almost all the leaders of the American Revolution—from George Washington and John Adams to Thomas Jefferson and Thomas Paine—indicated their hostility to slavery, some of them, such as Jefferson and Paine, in language whose severity was not exceeded by David Walker or William Lloyd Garrison. Further, a substantial number among them—especially those north of the main slaveholding areas such as Benjamin Franklin, John Jay, and Alexander Hamilton—held leading offices in various emancipationist organizations, with Franklin in particular, as both printer and statesman, playing very active roles therein.[1]

Moreover, as Dwight Lowell Dumond has shown in detail, from about the 1790s to the 1820s, scores, probably hundreds, of southern whites opposed to slavery were forced by repressive acts of churches and states to migrate into the North.[2] This resulted from the growing commitment by the slaveholding class to maintain its dominance, especially as the significance of slavery increased after 1790. An outcome of this commitment was the increasing harassment of antislavery men and women, the curbing of their freedoms of speech, press, and petition, and, increasingly, the endangerment of not only their livelihood but their lives. As Dumond wrote, "The idea that the South was turned away from emancipation and toward a defense of slavery by the abolition movement of the North is a monstrous fiction" (p. 87).

Among the prominent figures forced to migrate because of their antislavery sentiments and activities in this generation prior to the 1830s was David Barrow, a Baptist preacher (1753–1819) active in North Carolina and Virginia, who moved to Kentucky in 1798 and published anti-slavery tracts until his death. William Hickman and George Smith, both of Virginia, followed similar paths into Kentucky in this period. Other antislavery activists in Kentucky at that time were John Sutton, Joshua Carman, and Carter Tarrant. Another significant figure in this era was James Galliland, a South Carolina preacher who moved to Ohio in 1805 where he remained for over thirty years. He participated in the later, national Abolitionist movement, becoming a vice president of the American Anti-Slavery Society when it was organized in 1833.

Samuel Doak, a contemporary of Galliland, also left the South, in this case, Virginia, because of his hostility to slavery. He too moved to Ohio and continued to publicize his antislavery views. His son-in-law, John Rankin, originally from Tennessee, was especially well known in Ohio's antislavery circles. Rankin's *Letters on American Slavery* (1823) had considerable impact; like Galliland, he lived into the period of the organized Abolitionist movement and was a lecturer for the American Anti-Slavery Society.

Other leading exiles from the slave South included Levi Coffin, who left North Carolina in 1789 and settled in Indiana for a lifetime of personally dangerous but effective work against slavery, and Gideon Blackburn, who left Virginia in 1772 and traveled from Tennessee to Kentucky and finally to Illinois where he became an ally of the martyred Lovejoy. Thomas Morris, a bricklayer, migrated from Virginia to Ohio in 1776, became a lawyer, and was the state's chief justice from 1830 to 1833 and then, for six years, a U.S. senator. While in the Senate Morris was a pioneer in the politicization of the antislavery movement. Edward Coles of Virginia, who had been private secretary to President James Madison, migrated to Illinois and became an outstanding Abolitionist. Among the prominent Lane Seminary rebels were several from southern slaveholding families, notably William T. Allan of Alabama and James Thome of Kentucky.

Alexander Campbell was another who followed the path from Virginia to Kentucky to Ohio; he became vice president of that state's antislavery society and was elected to the U.S. Senate. George Bourne traveled from England to Virginia to Pennsylvania; his Virginia experiences with slavery moved this Presbyterian minister to migrate to a free state and to publish there, in 1816, his significant *The Book and Slavery Irreconcilable*.

In a direct line to Benjamin Lundy—whose influence upon Garrison was decisive—were two Tennessee natives, Charles Osborn, who moved to Ohio where he issued in 1817 an antislavery paper, the *Philanthropist,* and Elihu Embree, who published the *Emancipator* in Tennessee in 1820, which not only advocated emancipation but denounced racism itself with vigor.

Benjamin Lundy (1789–1839), one of the key figures in the history of antislavery agitation, does not fit this pattern of those born and raised in the South. A native of New Jersey, he was reared in a Quaker family. By 1809 he was living in Wheeling, Virginia (now West Virginia), and earning his way as a saddler. Although living outside the plantation area, he was in a slave state and was deeply affronted by the frequent slave coffles, or trains of blacks fastened together, that passed through his town. He migrated to Ohio and there began his lifelong, heroic, antislavery and antiracist work.

In 1816 Lundy founded the Union Humane Society in Mount Pleasant, Ohio, and obtained employment in the office of a local newspaper, the *Philanthropist.* Wanting a paper with a clearer focus, he set up in the same town his *Genius of Universal Emancipation* in 1821. When this attracted the attention of the Tennessee Manumission Society, which offered to print it, Lundy moved to Greenville in that state. But he remained there only briefly, moving to Baltimore with its better facilities in 1824. In the Maryland city, the paper gained a cadre of supporters and salespeople; it also acquired the official assistance of the American Convention for Promoting Abolition of Slavery. By the next year, Lundy's *Genius* was appearing in both weekly and monthly editions; the two together had almost eleven hundred subscribers.

One of Lundy's persistent themes was not only the sinfulness of slavery and its wastefulness in economic terms but also the danger it represented to the lives of Americans and the preservation of the Union. He also continued to denounce the concept of racial inferiority, a position that distinguished him from the colonizationists to whom he was otherwise attracted. A pacifist, he was impressed with the argumentation of Elizabeth Heyrick's *Immediate, Not Gradual Emancipation,* first published in the author's homeland, England, in 1826 and repeatedly reissued in the United States.

Lundy established the National Anti-Slavery Tract Society in Baltimore in 1828 and carried his message to nineteen northern states for the next two years. During one such tour, Garrison heard Lundy speak. It was a decisive factor in Garrison's assuming his lifelong work, beginning with his joining Lundy in editing the *Genius* in Baltimore. Lundy was subsequently elected a manager of the American Anti-Slavery Society two years before his death. Through his early seeding, his antiracism, his warnings of slavery's expansionist nature, and his decisive influence upon Garrison, Lundy had achieved a major position among effective protagonists of liberation.[3]

Much of the forced migration from the South of antislavery whites occurred among those adhering to such egalitarian faiths as those espoused by Quakers, Baptists, and Methodists. Lesser known is the role of the Unitarian church, which was active in the 1820s in the Carolinas, Virginia, Kentucky, Tennessee, Florida, Alabama, Mississippi, and Louisiana. Clarence Gohlen many years ago called attention to the significant activity of Unitarianism as an important component of what he called "Southern liberalism." He noted, too, that when "King Cotton established his sovereignty" and when Unitarians in the North became prominent for their antislavery partisanship, their southern challenge to orthodoxy was suppressed.[4]

The emergence of the mature Abolitionist movement was furthered by notable developments on the national level. Among these, and of decisive consequence, was the first major confrontation in the nineteenth century involving the fundamental question of the disposition of federal territories that were not yet states. This economic-political issue posed a serious threat to the Union, so much so that forty years later it had helped bring the nation to the point of civil war.

The base for the confrontation was laid by the extraordinary growth of the significance of slavery during the first three decades of the nineteenth century. Indeed from 1800 to 1810 alone, cotton production doubled in South Carolina and Georgia, tripled in Tennessee, became appreciable in Louisiana (one million pounds in 1810), and increased by 60 percent in Virginia and almost 80 percent in North Carolina. Where a border state like Kentucky had counted 12,000 slaves in 1790, the figure had risen to 165,000 in 1830; Louisiana's slave population rose from 35,000 in 1810 to 110,000 in 1830. The areas that would become Alabama and Mississippi had 3,500 slaves in 1800; thirty years later the total was 183,000. Overall, in 1807 the number of slaves totaled 1 million and cotton production, about 50 million pounds; thirty years later, the number of slaves had doubled and the cotton production had multiplied ten times.

This growth in slavery's importance in the South occurred during a period that David B. Davis has said "may well have been America's critical decade of economic transformation" overall. The 1820s was a decade, Davis continues, that "marked the beginning of rapid urbanization, a decisive shift toward nonagricultural employment, and perhaps the fastest economic growth of the pre–Civil War era."[5] One result was the political revolution known as the Jacksonian Era, which was marked by enormous stimulation in national political activity and accompanied by religious revivalism and the "social Gospel" associated with Charles G. Finney, early mentor of Theodore Weld. Indeed, Weld's most recent biographer remarked that

the 1820's were preeminently exciting years precisely because the shape of America's future had not yet been set. The generation that came to maturity in this decade had been left the task of making good on the Revolutionary promise bequeathed to them by the founding fathers—to translate general principles of democracy and republican virtue into an ongoing social order.[6]

These swift socioeconomic developments helped bring about, on the political front, the first major national governmental crisis involving the question of slavery. They also ushered in a wave of social and reform activity. Springing up during the 1820s were the American Society for the Promotion of Temperance, the American Home Missionary Society, and various tract societies, peace societies, and movements to assist seamen, to help the mentally ill, and to abolish imprisonment for debt. The decade witnessed also the establishment of significant trade union and political labor organizations. All these movements were reform efforts; only that to abolish slavery was a revolutionary one.

Central to the period was the system of slavery, its enormous and growing power, its expansion, its tightening ideological, legal, and political repressiveness. Elsewhere, movements to abolish slavery were growing in Great Britain and France, in their colonies, in Mexico and Latin America, and revolutionary movements were defying monarchies and oligarchies from Czarist Russia (including Poland) to Greece, and from Greece to France.

While the Constitutional Convention was meeting in 1787, the U.S. Congress (operating under the Articles of Confederation) passed the Northwest Ordinance, largely at the inspiration of Jefferson and with the approval of Washington. This measure—consented to by all Southern members—prohibited slavery from what became the states of Ohio, Indiana, Illinois, Michigan, Wisconsin, and Iowa. The articles of this ordinance were preceded by a preamble affirming their adoption in the name of "extending the fundamental principles of civil and religious liberty."

The sixth article dealt with slavery and read (in language to be copied by the Thirteenth Amendment) "There shall be neither slavery nor involuntary servitude, otherwise than in the punishment of crimes, whereof the party shall have been duly convicted." But, the article continued in terms similar to the third paragraph of the second section of Article IV of the Constitution, "that any person escaping into the same, from whom labor or service may be lawfully claimed, in any one of the original States, such person may be lawfully reclaimed, and conveyed to the person claiming his or her labor in service, as aforesaid." Here clearly the power of the federal government over the institution of slavery was affirmed.

The same power was affirmed again when—as several times occurred—territorial government was organized by the federal government and slavery was permitted. Thus, when in 1802 Georgia ceded to the federal government the territory that was to become the states of Mississippi (1817) and Alabama (1819), it specifically declared that the 1787 ordinance was applicable, "that article only excepted which forbids slavery." Washington accepted the cession with that proviso.

From Jefferson's Louisiana Purchase there resulted the admission of three slave states—Louisiana (1812), Missouri (1821), after much debate, to be analyzed shortly, and Arkansas (1836). Although in terms of the original purchase in 1803, it was clearly stipulated that "the inhabitants of the ceded territory . . . shall be maintained in the free enjoyment of their liberty, property, and the religion which they profess," the word *inhabitants* was defined so loosely that forty thousand slaves who inhabited the territory were excluded.

When Florida was purchased from Spain in 1819, substantially the same undertaking regarding its "inhabitants" was agreed to by the United States. Again, however, the "inhabitants" no more included slaves than it did cattle. Florida as a territory had slavery and entered the Union as a slave state in 1845. Texas too was admitted as a slave state the same year, but it joined the Union not as a territory but as a sovereign state—having broken with Mexico.

Chapter Two

Jefferson's "Fire Bell in the Night"

When Missouri's admission to the Union came before Congress, the issue of slavery had reached such a critical juncture that the debate on its statehood heralded a new era in the nation's history.

Beginning in 1817, congressional debates concerning slavery became tinged with the urgency and bitterness that had been foreshadowed in the 1790 debates on the anti–slave trade petitions, and this atmosphere became manifest in the 1819–21 Missouri debates. Those of 1817, continuing sporadically to 1819, revolved around proposals for amending the 1793 Fugitive Slave Act. The amendments offered by some northern representatives would have provided apprehended blacks with the protection of habeas corpus. Southern representatives rejected this out of hand and insisted on the priority of the property rights of slave owners even if this might occasionally endanger the rights of blacks actually free or make outright kidnapping easier. No amendments of any kind resulted from this debate.

It had been brought on by the growing antislavery agitation in the South and the North and by the mounting incidence of successful flights to freedom by slaves and resistance to recapture by blacks in the North. But one result, as Thomas D. Morris concluded, was that many people— black and white—decided that for free black people in the North the only possible "protection . . . existed in the laws of the [northern] states, to which antislavery reformers now increasingly turned their attention." The enactment of so-called personal liberty laws was to follow in the 1820s.[1]

It was against this background that great excitement arose when, in 1819, the question of the admission of Missouri Territory as a state reached the floor of Congress. The consequence of the debate was particularly intense because at the time the Union contained twenty states, with ten slave and ten free. The imbalance that would result if Missouri were admitted as slave or free was resolved only when it became possible to admit Maine—hitherto part of Massachusetts—as a state. The admission of both in 1820–21 made possible, briefly, the maintenance of an equilibrium in the number of slave and nonslave states.

The question in 1819, then, of the presence or absence of slavery in Missouri was a central one. At the same time, the proposed constitution of the new state contained a provision to bar from migration into Missouri any free black people. Although the first question has received most of the attention of later historians, the latter provoked as much bitter contemporary debate as did the question of slavery itself. In the resolution of the matter, the heart of the so-called Missouri Compromise was to admit the territory as a slave state but to exclude slavery from the remainder of the Louisiana Territory north of it—that is, north of the latitude 36' 30". To this was added Maine's admission to the Union—without slavery, of course.

Both acts involved basic constitutional questions—the implications of slavery's westward migration and that of the federal citizenship of free black people who, in several northern states, enjoyed either all or most of the rights attached to citizenship. By the plain language of the Constitution: "The citizens of each state shall be entitled to all privileges and immunities of citizens in the several States" (III, 2, 1). Neither here, nor in any other passage of the original Constitution, is any distinction made because of color or race nor is either word mentioned in that document.

In the related but separate congressional debates of 1817–19 on amending the 1793 Fugitive Slave Act, the question revolved around the effort by southern representatives to permit the delivery of fugitives even if this endangered free blacks and assisted kidnappers. Northern representatives were bitterly opposed to such an amendment—and none was passed—on the ground of the sanctity of the writ of habeas corpus. Again this involved a defense of the Constitution's clear language: "The privilege of the writ of habeas corpus shall not be suspended, unless when in cases of rebellion or invasion the public safety may require it" (I, 9, 2). The proposals to amend the 1793 act, and in doing so to undercut so vital a right as that of habeas corpus, helped persuade Abolitionists to give greater attention to the laws of the states. A result was agitation for and, in several cases, passage of personal liberty acts in some northern states, beginning in 1826. This was to be in subsequent years a major source of confrontation between pro- and antislavery forces.

In 1818 Missouri residents began serious agitation for entry into the Union; a bill for this purpose first reached the floor of the House in February 1819. James Tallmadge of New York, a future president of New York University, then serving his only term in the House, moved an amendment prohibiting slavery's introduction and calling for the emancipation at the age of fifteen of all who might be born slaves after Missouri's admission. A sharp debate of short duration followed: Henry Clay of Kentucky opposed the amendment; John W. Taylor, Tallmadge's colleague from New York, spoke in its favor. The amendment passed the House four days after being introduced (17 February 1819) and went on to the Senate. There it was referred to a committee headed by Charles Tait of Georgia, where it lost.

The Missouri bill (along with Maine's proposed entry) appeared again before the House in December 1819 and was hotly debated before crowded galleries—including, it was observed, black people—and finally was approved 20 March 1820. Among those speaking for the Missouri proposals were William Pinkney of Maryland and Spencer Roane of Virginia; Harrison Gray of Massachusetts and Rufus King of New York opposed it. In the gallery sat John Quincy Adams, then Monroe's secretary of state. He thought that King's speech of 11 February was a good one but that it might well have been stronger, although he wrote in his diary on that date that "the speech was called by Southerners seditious and inflammatory." Adams confided to the same source that "it would be better to destroy the Union than to permit the spread of slavery"—strong language for anyone in 1820 and quite extraordinary for a secretary of state.

John C. Calhoun—Adams's fellow cabinet member serving as secretary of war—discussed with him the debate and the whole question of slavery on 24 February 1820. Adams noted in his diary that Calhoun "did not think it [the slave question] would produce a dissolution of the Union." Calhoun added, however, according to Adams, that it might have such a result and that "if it should, the South would be from necessity compelled to form an alliance, offensive and defensive, with Great Britain." Adams at once commented, "that would be returning to the colonial state." Calhoun agreed—surprisingly, one is moved to add, remembering that this conversation occurred only five years after the second war with

Britain, the War of 1812, and but a generation after the Revolution had been concluded. Calhoun's defense was that "it would be forced upon us." Adams chose "to press the conversation no further" when his fellow cabinet member projected the possibility that secession would involve producing a society whose "communities [were] all military." Adams did record in his diary—although he did not express this thought to Calhoun—that "it is as obvious as anything that can be foreseen of futurity, that it must shortly afterwards be followed by the universal emancipation of the slaves"—an extraordinary piece of prophecy, even for John Quincy Adams.

Adams and Calhoun could not drop this question—not now that the Missouri debate had forced it open. On 3 March Adams recorded renewed discussion with the South Carolinian who remarked that enslaving the black made possible the freedom of the white and that in any case manual labor belonged only to slaves and was otherwise degrading. Here Calhoun opened the door to the later widespread position that, in reality, workers as a whole, whatever their complexion, were in effect in slavery, no matter what euphemism might be used to cover the fact. Adams replied he "could not see things in the same light," that it was a "perverted sentiment" that mistook "labor for slavery, and dominion for freedom."

How deep and how urgent was this question of slavery—over a decade prior to Garrison's *Liberator*—and how vivid was its revolutionary implications are further shown by the remarks Adams put to paper on the third of March after he had parted from Calhoun. Slavery, he wrote,

perverts human reason, and reduces man endowed with logical powers to maintain that slavery is sanctioned by the Christian religion, that slaves are happy and contented in their condition . . . while at the same time they vent execrations upon the slave-trade, curse Britain for having given them slaves, burn at the stake Negroes convicted of crimes for the terror of the example, and writhe in agonies of fear at the very mention of human rights as applicable to men of color. The impression produced upon my mind by the progress of this discussion is, that the bargain between freedom and slavery contained in the Constitution of the United States is morally and politically vicious, inconsistent upon which alone our Revolution can be justified. [The whole arrangement is] grossly unequal and impolitic, by admitting that slaves are at once enemies to be kept in subjection, property to be secured or restored to their owners, and persons not to be represented themselves, but for whom the masters are privileged with nearly a double share of representation. The consequence has been that this slave representation has governed the Union.

The entire outlook of the Abolitionist movement was reflected in this diary entry by a cabinet member soon to be president and thereafter a representative whose last efforts would constitute a dagger at the hearts of the slave owners but who, nevertheless, was himself not an Abolitionist.

Adams here came very close to one of the terminal points of Abolitionism—"No union with slaveholders"—for he admitted that he had "favored this Missouri compromise, believing it all that could be effected under the present Constitution, and from extreme unwillingness to put the Union at hazard." But, he went on, perhaps it would have been wise to have rejected the compromise and to have moved for "a convention of the States to revise and amend the Constitution." This would have meant dissolution of the present Union, no doubt, but, thought Adams, it "would have produced a new Union of thirteen or fourteen States unpolluted with slavery, with a great and glorious object to effect, namely, that of rallying to their standard the other States by the universal emancipation of their slaves."

Adams—anticipating Garrison by twenty years, but making the position still conditional—said also, "If the Union must be dissolved, slavery is precisely the question upon which it ought to break." He concluded the day's entry with its only erroneous projection: "For the present, however, this contest is laid asleep."

That this prediction was mistaken soon became apparent to Adams himself. In the next session of this same Congress objection arose to the admission of Missouri as a slave state because it became clear that Missouri's constitution not only provided for slavery but also prohibited the migration into Missouri of free blacks from other states.

In his diary of 29 November 1820, Adams told of a visit with Henry Baldwin, then a representative from Pennsylvania (in 1830 appointed an associate justice of the U.S. Supreme Court by President Jackson). Baldwin reported that because of the antimigration provision, some members of the House wanted to reopen the question of Missouri's admission as a state. Adams remarked that he thought this had small chance of success and so was "unjustified." He added, however, a long and passionate critique of the measure, and in doing so he again forecast, quite remarkably, future developments.

Adams thought that if Missouri were permitted to enter the Union with its antimigration provision, this would distress other states for it would constitute an "outrage" upon a portion of their citizens who would be in effect "cast out from the pale of the Union." He continued that, were he

a member of Massachusetts's legislature, he would feel "bound to vindi-
cate them by retaliation." This, he said, should take the form of a "de-
claratory act" affirming that so long as Missouri violated the citizenship
rights of inhabitants of Massachusetts, "so long the white citizens of the
State of Missouri should be held as aliens within the Commonwealth of
Massachusetts." Indeed, Adams said, he would go further and declare
that Congress, having violated the Constitution by permitting Missouri
to enter the Union with such a provision, had thereby joined in offending
"a portion of the citizens of Massachusetts." The latter state should retaliate by denying that any person could be considered a slave within its
territory and that, therefore, "I would prohibit by law the delivery of any
fugitive slave upon the claim of his master."

Adams affirmed that he would pursue this course even though it was
likely that Missouri "and the other slave-holding States" would retaliate.
All this might well lead, said Adams, to "the dissolution 'de facto' of the
Union," but in his view, Missouri's act had already dissolved that Union
"by robbing thousands of citizens of their rights" and, adding to the criminality of the act, the rights of "the poor, the unfortunate, the helpless."
How frightful, he said, was this act—"this barbarous article [which] de-
prives them of the little remnant of right yet left them—their rights as
citizens and as men."

John Quincy Adams—here in 1820—went on to declare that he would
pursue this course and defend these rights even if "the dissolution of the
Union be the consequence," for the real source of such a possible dissolution would be the "barbarous article" itself. He continued with this
astonishing paragraph:

If slavery be the destined sword in the hand of the destroying angel which is to
sever the ties of this Union, the same sword will cut in sunder the bonds of
slavery itself. A dissolution of the Union for the cause of slavery would be followed by a servile war in the slave-holding States, combined with a war between
the two severed portions of the Union. It seems to me that its result must be
the extirpation of slavery from this whole continent; and calamitous and desolat-
ing as this course of events in its progress must be, so glorious would be its final
issue, that, as God shall judge me, I dare not say that it is not to be desired.

John Quincy Adams in these sentences projected the passage of personal liberty laws by several states, beginning in 1826, the history of
which is closely tied to the developing movement to end slavery. He also
provided the text for the strikingly similar passage in Abraham Lincoln's

second inaugural address on 4 March 1865 as the second American revolution moved to a close:

Fondly do we hope—fervently do we pray—that this mighty scourge of war may speedily pass away. Yet if God wills that it continue, until all the wealth piled by the bondman's two hundred and fifty years of unrequited toil shall be sunk, and until every drop of blood drawn with the lash, shall be paid by another drawn with the sword, as was said three thousand years ago, so still must it be said, "the judgments of the Lord, are true and righteous altogether."[2]

Another immortal, the seventy-seven-year-old Jefferson—himself, of course, unlike Adams, a slave owner—reacted in a similarly alarmed and prophetic way to the Missouri debate. In a letter dated 22 April 1820, which contains the "fire bell in the night" phrase that has been quoted so often, Jefferson said more:

I had for a long time ceased to read newspapers, or pay any attention to public affairs, confident that they were in good hands, and content to be a passenger in our bark, to the shore from which I am now not distant. But this momentous question, like a fire bell in the night, awakened me and filled me with terror. I considered it at once the knell of the Union. But this is a reprieve only, not a final sentence. A geographical line, coinciding with a marked principle, moral and political, once conceived and held up to the angry passions of men, will never be obliterated; and every new irritation will mark it deeper and deeper.[3]

The international ramifications of a Republic born in a Declaration of Independence now, with the Missouri debate, considering slavery's expansion were not missing. This question of international "embarrassment" because of the position of the Afro-American—so enduring a feature of U.S. history—was articulated, for example, in the first session of the Sixteenth Congress by Timothy Fuller, a representative from Massachusetts. "All Europe," he declared, "the whole civilized world, are spectators of the scene. Our Declaration of Independence, our Revolution, our State institutions, and, above all, the great principles of our Federal Constitution, are arrayed on one side, and our legislative acts and national measures, the practical specifications of our real principles, on the other."[4]

This embarrassment intensified, as the international quality of the movement against chattel slavery expanded in the 1820s. A result was the emancipation of slaves in portions of Latin America, notably in Mexico, and the termination of the institution in the British West Indies in the

1830s. Indeed, thereafter in much of Western Europe, especially in Great Britain, antislavery became, prior to the Civil War, a movement that matched in scope and fervor the antiapartheid movement of the late twentieth century. The populace of Great Britain became a significant force in the antislavery movement in the United States; leaders in both countries cooperated with one another in the effort to end slavery in the States.

Here the presence and agitation of Abolitionists from the United States within Great Britain and Ireland—especially of black men and women— was of major consequence. So, too, was the literature of Abolitionism, notably Douglass's *Autobiography* and, especially, Harriet Beecher Stowe's *Uncle Tom's Cabin*, translated into every language of the European continent. The internationalism of this revolutionary movement is vividly illustrated by the close bond between progressive and democratic-minded peoples in Europe and like-minded men and women in the United States.

Chapter Three

Revolutionary Consciousness: Supporters and Opponents

Abolitionists and their foes agreed that the movement to emancipate the slaves, immediately and without compensation to the masters, was a revolutionary one. Thus William Lloyd Garrison repeatedly referred to "our revolutionary struggle" and to Abolitionism as "the new revolution for liberty."[1] Edmund Quincy put the matter succinctly: "Slavery exists, mainly, because it puts the entire political power of this great nation into the hands of a small oligarchy, the title of which is derived from the ownership of human flesh" (*Liberator,* 23 October 1846). Hence, he entitled his essay, "Revolution, the Only Remedy."

In Douglass's *North Star,* 19 January 1848, Henry Highland Garnet, one of the most effective and radical of the black Abolitionists, pointed out that he was writing in "a revolutionary age," having in mind the events then rocking Europe. He thought "revolution after revolution will undoubtedly take place until all men are placed upon equality." Citing the writings of Gerrit Smith, Garnet agreed that not only was slavery to be abolished but also great inequalities of wealth—especially in land ownership—would have to be terminated before one could possibly see something approximating human freedom. Garnet cited in particular Ireland where chattel slavery did not exist, "but the oppressions of Land Monopolists have engendered a lack and haggard famine."[2]

William Goodell, an effective writer and organizer in the Abolitionist movement, albeit one who differed with its Garrisonian wing, expressed a vivid appreciation of the revolutionary quality of the movement in his

15

widely read study *Slavery and Anti-Slavery: A History of the Great Struggle in Both Hemispheres,* published in 1852. This work, of over six
hundred pages, is of great general interest; it is permeated by a revolutionary consciousness. Illustrative of its breadth and depth is this paragraph from its first chapter:

The grand problem of the age is that of a more extended and better defined
freedom, especially for the lowest and most degraded portion of the species.
Ours is an advanced period in the struggle for human freedom. It is not to the
contest of the barons against an unlimited autocrat that we are summoned—nor
to the struggle of the middle classes against the barons; nor to the question of
taxation without representation; nor to the question of religious liberty, for those
who are regarded as human beings. The demands of liberty strike deeper, now,
and reach the ground tier of their humanity, hid under the rubbish of centuries
of degradation—classes who have scarcely been thought of as human and to
whom no Magna Carta . . . no organization of a House of Commons, no Declaration of Independence, have brought even a tithe or foretaste of their promised
blessings. The horseless, the landless, the homeless—the operatives of Manchester and Birmingham, the tenantry of Ireland, the Russian serfs,—above all
the North American Slaves—what have Christian civilization and democratic liberty and equality in reserve for these? And what are the responsibilities of Christians, of philanthropists, of statesmen, and of republican citizens, in respect to
them? These questions to be properly decided, must be studied, must be
understood.

In the same year that witnessed publication of Goodell's book, another
leading Abolitionist—but unlike Goodell, a Garrisonian in outlook—
offered an analysis of Abolitionism that emphasized its revolutionary
character. Wendell Phillips spoke to a Boston gathering of Abolitionists,
with Garrison on the platform:

Every thoughtful and unprejudiced mind must see that such an evil as slavery
will yield only to the most radical treatment. If you consider the work we have
to do, you will not think us needlessly aggressive, or that we dig down unnecessarily deep in laying the foundation of our enterprise. A money power of two
thousand millions of dollars, as the prices of slaves now range, held by a small
body of able and desperate men; that body raised into a political aristocracy by
special constitutional provisions, cotton, the product of slave labor, forming the
basis of our whole foreign commerce, and the commercial class so subsidized,
the press bought up, the pulpit reduced to vassalage, the heart of the common
people chilled by a bitter prejudice against the black race; our leading men bribed,
by ambition, either to silence or open hostility; in such a land, on what shall an

Abolitionist rely? Slavery has deeper roots here than any aristocratic institution has in Europe, and politics is but the common pulse-beat, of which revolution is the fever spasm . . . the old jest of one who tried to lift himself in his own basket is but a tame picture of the man who imagines that, by working solely through existing sects and parties, he can destroy slavery. Mechanics say nothing, but an earthquake strong enough to move all Egypt can bring down the Pyramids.[3]

A final illustration of this revolutionary consciousness on the part of the Abolitionist leadership itself is the classical passage from Frederick Douglass's great speech delivered 3 August 1857 in Canandaigua, New York:

Let me give you a word on the philosophy of reform. The whole history of the progress of human liberty shows that all concessions yet made to her august claims, have been born of earnest struggle. The conflict has been exciting, agitating, all-absorbing, and for the time being, putting all other tumults to silence. It must do this or it does nothing. If there is no struggle there is no progress. Those who profess to favor freedom and yet depreciate agitation, are men who want crops without plowing up the ground; they want rain without thunder and lightning. They want the ocean without the awful roar of its many waters.

This struggle may be a moral one, or it may be a physical one, or it may be both moral and physical, but it must be a struggle. Power concedes nothing without a demand. It never did and it never will. . . . Men may not get all they pay for in this world, but they most certainly pay for all they get. If we ever get free from the oppressions and wrongs heaped upon us, we must pay for their removal. We must do this by labor, by suffering, by sacrifice, and if needs be, by our lives and the lives of others.[4]

The personification of Douglass's analysis, John Brown, was to act out its content within two years. His enunciation of the revolutionary essence of the movement for which he died will be discussed later.

As the repressiveness of the slave states intensified with the deepening of the social crisis and challenge, the behavior of the Abolitionists took on more and more the pattern of classical revolutionary activity. Illustrative not only of their behavior but of the revolutionary consciousness it evoked is the following passage from a letter Wendell Phillips wrote to the British antislavery leader Elizabeth Pease on 9 March 1851:

The long evening sessions—debates about secret escapes—plans to evade where we can't resist—the door watched that no spy may enter—the whispering consultations of the morning—some putting property out of their hands, planning to incur penalties, and planning also that, in case of connection, the Government may get nothing from them—the doing, and answering no questions—intimates forbearing to ask the knowledge which it may be dangerous to have—all remind me of those foreign scenes which have hitherto been known to us, transatlantic republicans, only in books.[5]

Opponents of emancipation, too, sensed the revolutionary implications of the effort. Its challenge to private property, to sanctity of contract, to the dominant social order, to postulates not only of racism but of all forms of elitism, was explicitly affirmed and rejected in the name of law and order, civilization versus chaos, the stability of the social fabric. Attacking slavery was equated with levelism, agrarianism, anarchism, socialism, communism—the villains changed as the times changed.

In what apparently was the first North American defense of slavery, published in 1701, Judge John Saffin of Massachusetts, replying to Samuel Sewall's *The Selling of Joseph,* warned in his *Brief and Candid Answer* to Sewall (also published in 1701) that the latter's attack on slavery carried dangerous implications. To affirm an equal right to liberty of all made in God's image "seems to doubt the order that God hath set in the world, who hath ordained different degrees and orders of men, some to be high and honorable, some to be low and despicable . . . yea, some to be born slaves, and so to remain during their lives. . . . if this position of parity should be true, it would then follow that the ordinary course of Divine Providence of God in the world should be wrong and unjust (which we must not dare to think, much less to affirm)."

This argument, plus the idea of the inviolable character of private property, recurs in the literature rejecting antislavery. Alexander McDonnell, for example, in his *Considerations on Negro Slavery* published in London in 1824, defended its existence in the West Indies, insisted that ending slavery meant "barbarism," and warned that if property could be taken from slave owners, it could be taken from owners of other property. An earlier reflection of this awareness was expressed in a letter of 11 March 1798 from the influential Kentucky slave owner John Breckinridge to Isaac Shelby. Having in mind the agitation against slavery already underway, Breckinridge noted that if those opposed to slavery "can by one experiment emancipate our slaves, the same principle pursued will enable them at a second experiment to extinguish our land titles."[6]

Governor Stephen D. Miller of South Carolina made the related argument in 1829 that slavery induced significant political benefits, since it disenfranchised the poor in general which meant greater security to the elite's property.[7] The same point was a theme of Calvin Colton, the leading Whig pamphleteer and biographer of Henry Clay. In his anonymously published *Abolition Sedition* (Philadelphia, 1839), he called Abolitionism a form of levelism which therefore was profoundly "seditious."[8] And John C. Calhoun, in defending in the Senate in 1836 the destruction by mob action of Abolitionist literature in South Carolina the previous year, warned:

A very slight modification of the arguments used against the institutions which sustain the property and security of the South [would] make them equally effectual against the institutions of the North. . . . It would be well for those interested to reflect whether there now exists, or ever has existed, a wealthy and civilized community in which one portion did not live on the labor of another.[9]

Calhoun's biographer, Charles M. Wiltse, observed that when certain contemporaries—like Orestes Brownson—coupled "socialist" and "abolitionist," they understood that both were "expressions of the same mass movement whose philosophy was equality and whose political base was the preponderance of numbers."[10]

Calhoun, as the most profound and most influential of the officeholders and ideologists of the slaveholding class, deserves extended notice. Although the editor of Calhoun's *Papers* (which, as of the date of writing, has reached sixteen of a projected twenty volumes) rejects Richard Hofstadter's characterization of Calhoun as "the Marx of the Master Class,"[11] this ironic description does capture Calhoun's passionate class partisanship and his comprehension of the deeply conservative nature of a slaveholding society and the revolutionary implications of the Abolitionist movement.

One finds in Calhoun's speeches and writings an insistence upon rejecting egalitarianism, upon equating wealth with what he calls "civilization," and upon viewing chattel slavery as simply one form of the universal attributes of a "civilized" society. In Calhoun's civilization, the few are propertied and dominant and the many are propertyless and subordinate, the latter condition reflected in one or another guise of servility. He saw slavery as an ideal solution to the inexorable and increasingly dangerous problem (outside the slave South) of the class struggle—ideal because in a system of slavery, labor and capital become one, labor itself being capitalized. (Very significant in Calhoun's prose was the especially satisfactory situation of slavery in the South insofar as the slaves, being deeply and indelibly inferior to the masters, were in a *natural* condition;

this happy circumstance did not rule out, in his view, the advisability and necessity of slavery, by whatever disguise, in a "civilized" society.)

In Calhoun's language no distinction is apparent between slave property and any other kind of property. Therefore attacking slavery was profoundly subversive. It was deeply subversive of the South's civilization, since not only was the society based on slave property, but also that form of property was decisive to the southern community, to the South's way of life, to the very essence, the soul of what "the South" meant. Thus attacking slavery was attacking property *and* was challenging the entire substance of what southern life meant.

Calhoun emphasized that all property owners—merchants, manufacturers, landowners ("civilized" people)—were threatened, whether or not they knew it, by the Abolitionists' insistence that a particular form of private property was subject to elimination because it affronted religion or democratic theory or human considerations or social needs. Calhoun therefore insisted on the absolutely subversive, deeply revolutionary quality of Abolitionism. He also believed that Abolitionism was treasonous, this in line with his affirmation that it was supported by Great Britain as part of that nefarious power's desire to weaken the United States and, in fact, to challenge the dominant socioeconomic order in continental Europe. But in a seeming contradiction, he projected the idea that Abolitionism was part of anticolonialism (a direct threat, especially to Great Britain). He saw colonialism as a form of enslavement and therefore pointed to a connection between movements threatening imperial domination and those challenging slavery.

Calhoun also articulated the idea of the slaveholding South as the bulwark of conservatism in the nation; that as other property-holding classes in the rest of the nation found "civilization" threatened they could always count upon the slave South to oppose leveling, agrarian, democratic movements. Overall, slavery was indispensable to a viable social order, to the safety of the Republic, to a sane view of religion. It was, briefly, a supreme good whose elimination was simply unthinkable, especially given the "special circumstances" in the South—that is, with an inferior people as slaves. Therefore Abolitionism could come only from traitors, from fanatics like those who conducted the Inquisition; from altogether deranged minds.

These views became the dominant ones in the slave South and were institutionalized in the effort to create the Confederate States of America. Many of them persisted after the latter was routed; some still persist and add to the relevance of analyzing Abolitionism.

Calhoun epitomized the slaveholding South, was its most enduring and powerful spokesperson, its most persuasive and learned exponent, and its most revered figure. His words capture the prevailing mood of the slave South and convey both consciousness of the revolutionary character of Abolitionism on the part of its most committed opponents and a sense of the kind of implacable hostility those Abolitionist subversives faced:

The war which the abolitionists wage against us . . . is a war of religion and political favoritism . . . waged, not against our lives, but our character. . . . We cannot remain here in an endless struggle in defense of our character, our property, and institutions. (Senate speech, 9 March 1836)

Of all questions, which have been agitated under our government, abolition is that in which we of the South have the deepest concern. It strikes directly and fatally, not only at our prosperity, but our existence, as a people. (Letter, 5 August 1836)

Earlier, in the Senate, 7 January 1836, arguing against receiving petitions praying for an end to slavery in the District of Columbia submitted by Thomas Morris of Ohio, Calhoun had insisted that the very act of debating the subject of slavery had "a tendency to break asunder this Union." In any case, Calhoun held that agitating the question was useless because, he said,

The fifth amendment of the Constitution offers an insuperable barrier, which provides, among other things, that "no person shall be deprived of life, liberty, or property, without due process of law; nor shall private property be taken for public uses without just compensation." Are not slaves property? And if so, how can Congress any more take away the property of a master in his slave, in this District, than it could his life and liberty?

Calhoun was here quoting a section of the Constitution that, like its Preamble, was most often cited by antislavery advocates trained in the law—like William Goodell and Lysander Spooner—to buttress their insistence that, contrary to the view of Garrison, the Constitution not only failed to mention slavery as such but contained clearly antislavery sentiments.

In citing the Fifth Amendment, Calhoun was insisting that the human beings who were his slaves were not "persons" but were only and purely property—commodities to be owned precisely as one might own a cow or a piece of real estate or a farming implement. Those opposed to slavery would argue, on the contrary, that the impermissibility and illegality of his "owning" people were affirmed in plain English in the very language Calhoun quoted. Further, were the "property" component of these "persons" to be eliminated for what "public uses" would such transformation take place? Would not such elimination simply confirm the nonproperty essence of persons, thus restored to their personhood? Calhoun insisted that the language of the petitions, in many cases, slandered the slave owners. When pressed to offer an example of such slander, Calhoun pointed especially to certain of the petitioners referring to slavery as having created a "shambles."[12]

This word was used, too, by Thomas Mann Randolph, who, speaking in Virginia's House of Delegates early in 1832, said that slave sales from Virginia to the lower South came to about eighty-five hundred men, women, and children, each year, for the preceding twenty-year period. Randolph said: "It is a practice, and an increasing practice in parts of Virginia to rear slaves for market. How can an honorable mind, patriot and lover of his country, bear to see this ancient dominion converted into one grand menagerie where men are to be reared for market, like oxen for this shambles?"[13]

While arguing against the reception of Senator Morris's petition, Calhoun added that abolition of slavery not only undercut the sacredness of private property, consequential as that was, but also involved revolutionizing the hierarchical relationship of two distinct "races, of nearly equal numbers"; this would "subvert the relation, social and political" that characterized the South. Abolitionists sought to uproot, to transform an entire social order, said Calhoun; they who lived in the eye of this threat had to resist it. "Furthermore," he added, "just in slave property" alone what was at stake was some $950 million. Abolition would mean the end of this form of wealth and would deal a "fatal blow . . . to the productions of the great agricultural staples, on which the commerce, the navigation, the manufacturers and the Revenue of the country, almost entirely depend." In any case, Abolitionism was not only subversive; it was insane, for—as Calhoun's ideological descendants were to insist twelve decades later—"social and political equality between them [black and white] is impossible. No power on earth can overcome the difficulty."

Finally, talking directly to his fellow property owners from other sections of the Union, who made up the U.S. Senate, he completed his argument:

The sober and considerate portions of citizens of non-slaveholding States, who have a deep stake in the existing institutions of the country, would have little forecast not to see, that the assaults, which are now directed against the institutions of the Southern States, may be very easily directed against those, which uphold their own property and security. A very slight modification of the arguments used against the institutions which sustain the property and security of the South, would make them equally effectual against the institutions of the North including Banking, in which so vast an amount of property and capital is invested. . . .

Let those who are interested remember, that labor is the only resource of wealth, and how small a portion of it, in all old and civilized countries, even the best governed, is left to those by whose labor wealth is created. Let them also reflect, how little volition, or agency the operatives in any country have in the question of distribution—as little, with few exceptions, as the African of the slaveholding States has in the distribution of the proceeds of his labor. Nor is it the less oppressive, that in the one case it is effected by the stern and powerful will of the government, and in the other, by the more feeble and flexible will of the master. If the one be an evil so is the other. The only difference is the amount and the mode of exaction and distribution, and the agency by which they are effected.

In developing his arguments against Abolitionism Calhoun also began claiming that the right of petition encompassed only the right to *present* a petition, not to have its substance considered. And he insisted that consideration of its substance—the propriety of slavery—was outside the competence of Congress; in his words: "Our true position, that which is indispensable to our defense here, is that Congress has no legitimate jurisdiction over the subject of slavery, either here or elsewhere" (Senate speech, 9 March 1836).

He reiterated on this occasion, as often on other occasions, that the interest of Senate members from the nonslaveholding states in this question should be as keen as his own, for "if the tide continues to roll on its turbid waves of folly and fanaticism, it must in the end prostrate in the North all the institutions that uphold their peace and prosperity, and ultimately overwhelm all that is eminent, morally and intellectually." Presently, he continued, the United States seemed happily exempt "from those dangers originating in a conflict between labor and capital, which at this time threatens so much danger to constitutional government," but clearly, he maintained, this good fortune would not endure and the logic of Abolitionism was to hasten its end.

Calhoun had already defended the denial of freedoms of the mail and of the press in his ardent defense of the acts of a Charleston mob—of distinguished personages—who had burned alleged Abolitionist publications at the city's post office. Indeed, the president of the United States—then no friend of Calhoun's—had also done so in 1835, and Calhoun was delighted to commend his wisdom. Now, in 1836, he was attacking the right of petition and would soon put forth the conclusion that such a right was of little consequence where people were allegedly sovereign; petitioning, thought Calhoun, befitted *subjects*—particularly of tyrannical governments—not *citizens* of a republic. (This would eventuate in the gag rule of Congress, which was to produce the eventually successful crusade for freedom of petition led by John Quincy Adams who was assisted by Abolitionist Theodore Dwight Weld. That crusade was of great consequence in expanding the influence of Abolitionism, for it persuaded many that slavery's security seemed to require their own freedom's vitiation.)

Indeed, spurred by the Abolitionist upsurge of the 1830s, and the argumentation of President Jackson and Senator Calhoun, the legislatures of the Carolinas and of Georgia and Alabama called upon the legislatures of the nonslaveholding states "to suppress, by law, abolition publications." Senator John Ruggles of Maine presented on 8 April 1836 the resolution adopted by his state's legislature affirming its conviction—as Calhoun had insisted—that the federal government had no authority over slavery in the states. But Maine's legislature did feel it was "inexpedient to legislate on the subject of abolition publications." It chose, however, not to base this mere "inexpediency" on a defense of freedom of the press. Rather it affirmed the inexpediency of violating such freedom in this instance, because, it announced, "there is no abolition publication printed within the State and because all discussion on the subject has been arrested by the decided expression of public disapprobation."

But Calhoun was not satisfied, nor was his class. Although he seems not to have been able to present the Senate with an example of an antislavery publication with a Maine imprint, he did have—and showed the Senate—positive proof of the existence of a Maine Abolition Society, and he wanted it suppressed. "The point is," he said on 12 April 1836, "we need a law which would prohibit the circulation of 'incendiary publications' [whose precise definition clearly would be difficult] through the mails of the United States, despite its endangering freedom of the press."

Two principles buttressed this suggested legislation, said Calhoun: (1) "the subject of slavery is under the sole and exclusive control of the States where the institution exists," and (2) it was the "duty of the general government . . . to pass such laws as may be necessary to make it obligatory on its officers and agents to abstain from violating the laws of the [slaveholding] States, and to co-operate, as far as may consistently be done, in their execution."

But, he said, "the fact is our just hopes have not been realized. The legislatures of the South . . . have called upon the non-slaveholding States to repress the movements made within the jurisdiction of those States against their peace and security." This had not been done and until it was, southerners would complain. In effect, those of the slaveholding class, Calhoun was demanding, wanted the sanctity of slave property to be as zealously respected in the North as in the South. In the latter region this had entailed the curbing of freedom of speech, press, petition, and assembly, insofar as the security of slavery (defined by slaveowners) was concerned. The same condition had to exist in the North if the South was to be satisfied—and if the Union was to persist. Otherwise, said Calhoun, those of the slaveholding States had "a right to interpose" and they would do so.

Here was spelled out rationalization for the mob assaults, the gag rules, the Seamen's Acts violation of the right of northern (and British) seamen, the clash with the personal liberty laws of the North, the Fugitive Slave Act of 1850, the Kansas confrontation, and, finally, the Dred Scott decision, which affirmed as the law of the land the two principles enunciated by Calhoun on 12 April 1836.

Calhoun expatiated on these points and added others as the years went by and the Abolitionist movement not only did not abate but intensified. He regularly voiced with clarity and depth the interests of his class; in doing so his remarks illuminated the revolutionary quality of Abolitionism. In a debate on the Senate floor, 18 December 1837, Henry Clay of Kentucky had ventured the opinion that Abolitionism should be met by logic and reason. Calhoun would have none of this; he offered an interesting analogy to Clay, but received (and probably expected) no reply: "Suppose a petition were sent here to burn the manufactories of the North; would the Senator stop to reason about such a petition? Or that the property of the rich should be given to the poor; would he reason about that?"

On 27 December 1837, Calhoun moved for consideration by the Senate of five resolutions on abolition and the Union. Those held that the U.S. government was a federal one, created by states who joined "as free, independent and sovereign" entities, and did so in order to assure themselves of greater security against all dangers "*domestic* as well as foreign" (the emphasis is Calhoun's). These states "retained, severally, the exclusive and sole right over their own domestic institutions and police, and are alone responsible for them." Furthermore the federal government was "bound so to exercise its powers as to give, as far as may be practicable, increased security and stability to the domestic institutions of the States that compose the Union." Slavery existed prior to and at the time of the Constitution's adoption, and attacks upon it constituted "a violation of the most solemn obligations, moral and religious," the last words throwing down the gauntlet to those arguing the immorality of slavery and its violation of basic religious teachings such as the Ten Commandments and the Sermon on the Mount. Any effort to terminate slavery in the states, the District of Columbia, or the territories or the passage of any measure to this effect "would be a direct and dangerous attack on the institutions of all the slaveholding States." Finally, in a long passage challenging the Missouri Compromise of 1820 and prophesying its supercession by the legislation of the 1850s was the assertion that the Union rested upon the equality of all the states and that, therefore,

to refuse to extend to the southern and western States any advantage which would tend to strengthen, or render these more secure, or increase their limits or population by the annexation of new territory or States, on the assumption or under the pretext that the institution of slavery, as it exists among them, is immoral or sinful, or otherwise obnoxious, would be contrary to that equality of rights and advantages which the Constitution was intended to secure alike to all the members of the Union, and would, in effect, disfranchise the slave-holding States, withholding from them the advantages, while it subjected them to the burdens of government.

Only the final two resolutions touching the District of Columbia and the untrammeled right of slavery's expansion failed to receive a majority of the Senate's vote. To implement all of them was the central effort of the slaveholding class in the subsequent decades; all gained approval by the administration of James Buchanan. All were to be undone, in blood, by the revolutionary war for the Union and the end of slavery, and by Lincoln's time the inseparability of both had become apparent.

In the debate on his resolutions, held in January 1838, Calhoun accused Abolitionists of the same "blind, fanatical zeal" that had strengthened the tormentors of the Inquisition. He emphasized that whereas in the past "many in the South" had believed slavery to be "a moral and political evil," now he was sure "that folly and delusion are gone."[14] On the contrary, white southerners, he insisted (one suspects the insistence was to reassure not only himself but all other white southerners), now saw slavery "in its true light," namely, "as the most safe and stable basis for free institutions in the world."

Slavery had achieved this marvelous character because, said Calhoun, in his society there could not occur "the conflict . . . between capital and labor, which makes it so difficult to establish and maintain free institutions in all wealthy and civilized nations where such institutions as ours do not exist." "Each plantation," said Calhoun, "is a little community" whose "master . . . concentrates in himself the united interests of capital and labor." Hence the state under such circumstances was "perfectly harmonized" and the society was stable and subject to disturbance only by outsiders—a veritable land of milk and honey, magnolias and moonlight.

Further, "the blessing of this state of things extends beyond the limits of the South" for it made of that section the greatest conservative power, which prevented other portions, less fortunately constituted, from rushing into conflict. This "conflict in the North between labor and capital, which is constantly on the increase" found the slave South a great restrainer of excesses which had served and would continue to serve as a preserver of "our free institutions" so long as Abolitionists—"madmen"—were restrained. Precisely such restraint was the "highest and most solemn obligation that can be imposed on us as men and patriots."

It was during a later debate on the right of petition in the Senate (13 February 1840) that Calhoun came closest to explicitly abandoning if not condemning the right of petition. He asserted then that "the very essence of a right of petition implies a request from an inferior to a superior." Sen. Daniel Webster of Massachusetts ventured to disagree; indeed he thought the right of petition, affirmed in the Bill of Rights, "was peculiar to free government."

Shortly thereafter one of those events took place that never failed to recur and to push the question of slavery to the forefront of public attention. Early in 1840 the U.S. brig, *Enterprise,* facing heavy seas and in danger of sinking, put in to the Bahamas. It was, of course, given succor by the British authorities and its cargo secured for the American owners. Part of what the owners thought to be cargo, however, was not so considered by the authorities, Britain having completed the end of slavery in its West Indian colonies by 1838. The slaves, therefore, were held to be free by British law and a long diplomatic confrontation ensued (the slaves were not returned). On 8 April 1840, Calhoun, provoked by this episode, offered a major speech on the Senate floor. Somewhat new here was Calhoun's insistence that, Britain being the world's leading colonial power, it ill became her to pursue an antislavery line. This was true, Calhoun held, because colonialism did not differ from slavery. Specifically:

If it be contrary to the laws of nature or nations for man to hold man in subjection individually, is it not equally contrary for a body of men to hold another in subjection? And if that be true, is it not so much so for one nation to hold another in subjection? If there be a difference, is not the right the more perfect in a people or a nation than in the individuals who compose it?

One might expect Calhoun to have cited the experience of the United States vis-à-vis Great Britain. He refrained, however, perhaps because the language of the Declaration of Independence embarrassed him and his class and reflected the unfortunate "French extremism" that had afflicted Thomas Jefferson. He cited, rather, the dependency of India, Canada, and Ireland upon Great Britain as illustrating his point. He, indeed, went further and applied the principle of dependency to internal British politics, suggesting it was redolent of the realities of slavery. "If the right of self-government," he asked, "forbids the subjugation of one man to another, does it not equally forbid that of a small portion of the community over the residue?" Specifically, he warned the rulers of Great Britain—and, by extension, his Senate colleagues: "You cannot make a monopoly of a principle so as to bend it for your benefit. It will be carried out to its ultimate results, when its reaction will be terrific on your social and political condition."

Calhoun warned that the Chartist movement, then shaking England, was the logical fruit of democracy. Talk in favor of and movements for independence, he continued, were threatening West Indian colonies, while intellectuals in Europe—France especially—were beginning to equate the absence of democracy with the presence of slavery. Calhoun's point was that all this was logical. He warned that the London government in throwing diplomatic support on the side of antislavery "wars against herself." Calhoun insisted: "The maxim she now pushes against others will, in turn, be pushed against her. She is preparing the way for universal discord within and without." As for the Abolitionists at home, Calhoun dismissed them; they, he said, "have lost every feeling belonging to an American, and transferred their allegiance to a foreign power."

Potent as were Calhoun's theoretical arguments, he did not confine himself to that category. On the contrary, in his economic program, especially that opposing a policy of protective tariffs as likely to inhibit foreign trade, Calhoun emphasized the basic consequence of slave-grown produce in that regard. It was, as I have indicated, this economic thrust that was to have a strong influence nationally on the slave institution.

For example, in a Senate debate on tariff proposals on 16 March 1842, Calhoun presented elaborate tables specifying year by year from 1820 through 1840 the dollar value of exports of three main slave-grown crops—cotton, tobacco, and rice (omitting others, like sugar and hemp, that were not grown in his region of the South). Here it appeared, when one adds up his data, that in the years indicated exports of cotton were valued at $807,369,061; tobacco at $141,214,027; and rice at $44,042,958 for a total of $992,626,046—or just short of $1 billion, a colossal sum for that period. Indeed, a research assistant for Calhoun remarked that "more than three-fourths of the Domestic Exports of the U.S., therefore, are productions of slave labor."

Wilfred Carsel has shown that the counterattack by ideologists of the slaveholding class had reached this consensus by 1860: the condition of the so-called free workers in industrial society was abominable and was deteriorating; in actuality this free worker was enslaved at least as firmly as the South's chattel slaves; and that, in fact, in terms of sheer existence "wage slavery was infinitely worse for the worker than chattel slavery." He showed, also, the insistence by leading southern politicians—from Calhoun to James Hammond to Jefferson Davis—and leading southern ideologists—from George Fitzhugh to Edmund Ruffin—that the logic of Abolitionism was levelism, the annihilation of civilization defined as the private ownership of the means of production. Therefore, it was hoped that possessors of property—all forms of property—would unite to beat back the forces of anarchy. In such an effort the slave-owning system would be a basic ally of conservatism.[15]

F. W. Pickens, a representative from South Carolina, speaking in the House in 1836, declared that the few who dominated the social order were the "peculiar receptacles of the favors and blessings of an all-wise and all-pervading Providence." All societies, he felt, consisted of those who owned the means of production and those who did not, and the latter, whether called laborers or slaves, were in fact in a condition of servitude. He concluded: "If laborers ever obtain the political power of a country, it is in fact in a state of revolution, which must end in substantially transferring property to themselves . . . unless those who have it shall appeal to the sword and a standing army to protect it."[16]

In the 1850s, this class position had become a commonplace of slavocratic propaganda. William Harper, a leading proslavery advocate, in his book published in Charleston in 1852, *Pro Slavery Argument,* said, "It is as much in the order of nature that men should enslave each other as that animals should prey upon each other." This idea permeated the thinking of George Fitzhugh, one of the most influential of proslavery ideologists. Thus, for example, he wrote in *Sociology for the South* (Richmond, 1854), "Slavery will everywhere be abolished, or everywhere be re-instituted." The *Richmond Enquirer,* two years later, unburdened itself in paragraphs that Abolitionist and Republican party partisans were to reprint endlessly: "The great evil of Northern free society is that it is burdened with a servile class of mechanics and laborers unfit for self-government, and yet clothed with the attributes and powers of citizens. . . . Slavery is the natural and normal condition of the laboring man, whether white or black."

By the late 1840s and throughout the 1850s the slavocratic argument had reached the point where it was maintaining that chattel slavery was relative freedom and wage employment was true enslavement. Hence, James H. Hammond would assert, with a straight face, that if Great Britain placed its working class in the condition of the slaves in the South, this "would be . . . a most glorious act of *emancipation.*"[17] Statements of this kind were what William Lloyd Garrison had in mind, when he wrote in a letter, 25 January 1858, that slavery was held to be by its defenders "the normal condition of the laboring classes without regard to race or complexion."[18]

Certainly, the 1857 Dred Scott decision of the U.S. Supreme Court not only denied citizenship to Afro-Americans as a principle of U.S. law but also nationalized slavery's existence. With this accomplishment, the suppression of antislavery efforts in Kansas was secured—in Washington's opinion. The Lecompton Constitution, fraudulently framed in Kansas in that same year, contained a provision that "the right of property is before and higher than any constitutional sanction, and the right of the owner of a slave to such slave and its increase is the same and as inviolable as the right of the owner of any property whatsoever." The same document affirmed that its provisions might be amended after 1864 by a two-thirds vote, "But no alteration shall be made to affect the right of property in the ownership of slaves."[19]

This position was not held by "Border-State Ruffians" and proslavery fanatics only; it was the position of the Buchanan administration, too. (In 1856, of Buchanan's 174 electoral votes, 119 came from slave states.)

Buchanan's newspaper, the *Washington Union,* declared editorially on 17 November 1857 that the protection of slave property was "the duty of Congress and the Legislatures." Hence, concluded the administration's organ, "Every citizen of one State coming into another State has, therefore, a right to the protection of his person, and that property which is recognized as such by the Constitution of the United States, any law of a State to the contrary notwithstanding."[20] This meant that not only were all laws or proposals geographically limiting the bounds of slavery illegal but that all state laws that in the past emancipated slaves were confiscatory and unconstitutional and that all laws then in force prohibiting slavery *within* a particular state were unconstitutional.

The conclusion this argument led to was spelled out by Sen. Stephen Douglas of Illinois—whose political life depended upon the viability of each state's controlling institutions within its borders. It meant, he said in a major speech in the Senate on 22 March 1858, that a citizen of a slave state had the right to move into a free state like Illinois, bring his slaves with him, and settle with them therein. It meant the nationalizing of slavery; it meant an end to states' rights; it meant that white people outside the South (as well as inside the South) were forbidden to interfere with the existence of slavery inside their own state. All this meant, said Douglas, that "a fatal blow [was] being struck at the sovereignty of the States of this Union, a death blow to States' Rights, subversive of the Democratic platform." Thus, ironically, Seward's "higher law," said Douglas, was being used not to choke slavery but to extend it, to make it inviolable, and to make unconstitutional all efforts to check its spread or to curtail its existence. Thus, mimicking Calhoun, Douglas now found himself saying, "I do not recognize the right of the President or his Cabinet, no matter what my respect may be for them, to tell me my duty in the Senate chamber."

It was exactly the permanence and inviolability of chattel slavery that was inscribed in the Confederate Constitution. This was hailed by the Confederacy's vice president; speaking in 1861, Alexander Stephens of Georgia said:

The new [Confederate] Constitution has put at rest forever all the agitating questions relating to our peculiar institutions—African slavery as it exists among us—the proper status of the negro in our form of civilization. . . . Our new Government is founded . . . upon the great truth that the negro is not the equal of the white man. That slavery—subordination to the superior race—is his natural and normal condition.

Stephens added, "We are now the nucleus of a growing power, which . . . will become the controlling power on this continent."[21]

The latter remark was in keeping with the diplomacy and filibustering activities of partisans of slavery where its expansion was the central goal. The leading ideologist of secession, the Virginian Edmund Ruffin, in *The Political Economy of Slavery* (Washington, D.C., 1853), commented upon "the expediency and propriety of not only maintaining and preserving inviolate the existing condition of African slavery, but of its being extended to wherever the condition of the earth and its inhabitants would be manifestly improved thereby," like "nearly all Spanish America." Thus Lincoln in his "a house divided" speech of 16 June 1858 and Seward in his "irrepressible conflict" address of 25 October 1858 were referring to what by then had become the well-known theme of the most fervent proslavery advocates which was applied to the Republic itself—either all slave or all free.[22]

Abolitionists themselves were aware of their opponents' property-defense stance, and several responded to it in militant terms. One of the most articulate on this matter, as on so much else, was Wendell Phillips; his perceptions of this crucial question of property rights were sharpened by his experiences in Europe. Such travel had a similar impact upon others, including Garrison and Douglass. Typical was Phillips's letter to Garrison from England (published in the *Liberator,* 6 May 1841) to the effect that the wealthy were likely to find their property rights "infringed upon . . . whenever the owner allows the siren voice of his own tastes to drown out the cries of another's necessities."

Some Abolitionists—John A. Collins and Adin Ballou are examples—allowed their Abolitionism to be swallowed up in a generalized concern about the impoverished. Both became utopian socialists, the first founding a colony in upstate New York and Ballou following suit in Connecticut. Thus, by the mid-1840s, both had withdrawn from effective participation in Abolitionism. Others, however, remained very effective leaders of Abolitionism while their growing awareness of the generalized question of property and of the economic grounding of effective freedom, as well as a class consciousness, moved them toward socialism. This kind of development was reflected in the thinking, for instance, of Wendell Phillips, Lydia Maria Child, Theodore Weld, and George W. Julian.

In the case of Lydia Maria Child one finds her writing, in a letter dated 5 June 1861, "that carpenters, weavers, etc., are often real princes in disguise. The longer I live," she continued, "the more entirely and intensely do my sympathies go with the masses." She saw the Civil War itself increasingly in class terms (as did Harriet Beecher Stowe) with those supporting the Confederacy wanting "a demarcation of classes so strong, that the common people should be allowed to know only just enough to serve the aristocracy faithfully." Again, a little later, on 1 September 1861: "Aristocracy is *always* my aversion, whether in the form of English noble, Southern planter, or Boston respectable. . . . I honestly *believe* in the dignity of labor." Toward the close of her life, Child became a partisan of what she called "co-operation," which she thought, writing on 10 August 1880, was "the *only* way to solve the troublesome problem between labor and capital." Sharing the profits of production had to replace wage labor, she decided.[23]

By 1863, Theodore Weld was affirming that his opposition to chattel slavery had matured into opposition against "aristocracy, caste, monopoly, exclusive privilege and prerogative." And William Henry Seward, the New York Republican party leader, said in 1860, a year before becoming Lincoln's secretary of state, "It is an eternal question between classes— between the few privileged and the many unprivileged—the eternal question between aristocracy and democracy."[24]

Characteristic of Abolitionist belief on the nature of the Civil War was Douglass's remark that so far as the Confederacy was concerned, its leaders wanted slavery to be national and "freedom nowhere"; they wanted a society "in which the capitalist shall own the laborer" and non-slaveholders would be dismissed as "poor white trash."[25]

The continuity between Abolitionism and consequent forms of struggle against propertied privilege was expressed with sparking clarity by George W. Julian of Ohio, one of the most influential of political Abolitionists, in a statement published by the *Chicago Tribune,* 16 June 1874: "The abolition of poverty is the next work in order and the Abolitionist who does not see this fails to grasp the logic of the Anti-Slavery movement, and calls a halt to the inevitable march of progress." Julian went on: "African slavery was simply one form of domination of capital over the poor. . . . The system of Southern slavery was the natural outgrowth of that generally accepted political philosophy which makes the protection of property the chief end of government." Julian specifically urged the "working classes" to "wage war against the new forms of slavery which are everywhere insidiously entrenching themselves behind the power of combined capital, and barring the door against the principle of equal rights."[26]

Wendell Phillips also saw clearly the connection between attacking the ownership of slaves and attacking the ownership of the means of production in general. Thus, in the *National Anti-Slavery Standard,* 21 November 1868, Phillips proposed not so much an income tax as a system of taxation on capital itself that was confiscatory. He suggested it would be salutary if there were adopted a system whose result would be to "tax every man who owns more than three hundred acres at a rate doubling and trebling for each additional three hundred; tax every man who has more than one hundred thousand dollars at a rate doubling and quadrupling for every additional one hundred thousand, until the Treasury bursts with the means to clean off the debt in twenty years." For the post–Civil War South, Phillips proposed not only an egalitarian and politically democratic social order; he also suggested during and immediately after the war, a constitutional amendment making adequate and universal education a responsibility of the federal government, permanently disenfranchising all leading secessionists, and confiscating the plantations and dividing the land among the freed people and among immigrants. He wanted an educated, politically empowered, and economically secure mass population in the South—and in the North. [27]

Phillips's radical postwar projections were not only anticipated by his thoroughgoing radicalism expressed with increasing intensity in the 1840s and 1850s but made explicit during the war years, when his influence in particular and that of Abolitionism in general was at its height. In his "war for the Union" speech (Boston, 8 December 1861), he warned: "An aristocracy rooted in wealth, with its network spread over all social life, its poison penetrating every fibre of society, is the hardest possible evil to destroy." He was sure, this early in the war, that its essence was "the great struggle between the disguised aristocracy and the democracy of America." [28]

Chapter Four

Social Class, Labor, and Abolitionism

Although a considerable portion of the leadership of the Abolitionists was made up of fairly well-to-do people, like Arthur and Lewis Tappan, Wendell Phillips, Maria Weston Chapman, Gerrit Smith, others, like William Lloyd Garrison, Lucretia Mott, and Lydia Maria Child, were not. Practically all the black leaders were nonpropertied people. This was true of such former slaves as Frederick Douglass and Sojourner Truth, although a few who had always been free, like Robert Purvis and James Forten, were comparatively well off.

But the rank and file, both white and Afro-American, who made up the bulk of the original few thousands and then the tens and hundreds of thousands who formed the membership of the Abolitionist movement, were neither of the bourgeoisie nor among wealthy professionals.

Abolitionists, basing their judgments on their experiences, often made sharp distinctions in their attitudes toward the efforts of rich and poor. Lydia Maria Child was explicit on this point. Writing to her brother on 25 September 1835, she said, "We should be little troubled with mobs if people called respectable did not give them their sanction," an observation confirmed, as we shall see, by later investigators. A little later, on 19 December, to the same correspondent, she wrote:

What is the root of the difficulty on this great question of abolition? It is not with the farmers, it is not with the mechanics. The majority of their voices would be on the right side if the question were fairly brought before them; and the consciousness that such would be the result creates the earnest desire to stop discussion. No. No! It is not these who are to blame for the persecution suffered by the abolitionists. Manufacturers who supply the South, merchants who trade with the South, ministers settled at the South, and editors patronized by the South, are the ones who really promote mobs. Withdraw the aristocratic influence, and I should be perfectly easy to trust the cause to the good feeling of the people.[1]

Douglass, accepting an invitation in 1852 from the Garrisonian Western Anti-Slavery Society and seeking to allay differences between himself and Garrison, urged the need for unity, despite particular differences, in the antislavery crusade. "Both men and women," he said, must exert the utmost energy:

It is the poor man's work. The rich and noble will not do it. I know what it is to get a living by rolling casks on the wharves, and sweeping chimneys, and such like, and this makes me able to sympathize with the poor, and the bound everywhere. It is not to the rich that we are to look but to the poor, to the hardhanded working men of the country; these are the men who are to come to the rescue of the slave.[2]

This point was made not only by Abolitionists but also by respectable figures like Daniel Webster, U.S. senator from Massachusetts, whose own retainers from wealthy constituents reinforced his awareness of the power of economic interest. Speaking in the Senate on 7 March 1850, Webster noted that in the late eighteenth and early nineteenth centuries slavery was frequently denounced by leading southern personalities, whereas "it has now become an institution, a cherished institution there; no evil, no scourge, but a great religious, social, and moral blessing." How account for this dramatic change? "I suppose this, sir, is owing to the sudden uprising and rapid growth of the cotton plantations of the South." Whereas sixty years ago, he continued, cotton exports from the United States were "hardly more than forty or fifty thousand dollars a year," they had now reached about "a hundred millions of dollars." This, together with the millions represented by the cotton manufacturers and shipping interests of the North, had produced an economic interest of transcendent influence.

James H. Hammond of South Carolina, a major slaveholder, powerful politician, and ideologist for his class, commented in 1845 on the extreme bitterness marking the exchanges between slaveholders and Abolitionists:

But if your course was wholly different—if you distilled nectar from your lips and discoursed sweetest music, could you reasonably indulge the hope of accomplishing your object by such means? Nay, supposing that we were all convinced, and thought of Slavery precisely as you do, at what era of "moral suasion" do you imagine you could prevail on us to give up a thousand millions of dollars in the value of our slaves, and a thousand millions of dollars in the depreciation of our lands, in consequence of the want of laborers to cultivate them?[3]

In the North, there were both manufacturers who used slave-grown cotton in their businesses and the merchant bourgeoisie whose interests were centered in such ports as Baltimore, Philadelphia, and, especially, New York. Their ships hauled not only the cotton but also the rice, sugar, hemp, and tobacco wrung from the slaves' labor. Thus, most of these merchants in the decades before the Civil War allied themselves with the immediate exploiters of the Afro-American people. So it was that a partner in a large New York mercantile house summoned the outstanding Garrisonian Samuel J. May to him in 1835 and, according to the latter, said that he and his colleagues understood that slavery was, of course, "a great evil and a great wrong." But, he continued, it seemed to have been consented to by the founders of the Republic and to have been "provided for in the Constitution of our Union"—a point hotly contested by non-Garrisonian Abolitionists. The main point was this, said the merchant:

A great portion of the property of the Southerners is invested under its sanction, and the business of the North as well as of the South, has become adjusted to it. There are millions upon millions of dollars due from the Southerners to the merchants and mechanics of this city alone, the payment of which would be jeopardized by a rupture between the North and the South.

To this merchant, the conclusion was obvious:

We cannot afford, sir, to let you and your associates succeed in your endeavor to overthrow slavery. It is not a matter of principle with us. It is a matter of business necessity. We cannot afford to let you succeed. And I have called you out to let you know, and to let your fellow laborers know, that we do not mean to let you succeed. We mean, sir, to put you Abolitionists down—by fair means, if we can, by foul means, if we must.[4]

It was not only the southern slaveholder, then, who was aware that the philosophy of Abolitionism—its egalitarianism and, especially, its subordination of property rights to human rights—represented a basic threat to a social order based upon the latter.

When the institution of slavery was questioned following the slave uprising led by Nat Turner in Virginia in 1831, a Virginian minced no words in his reply:

This one thing we wish to be understood and remembered—that the Constitution of this State, has made Tom, Dick, and Harry, *property*—it has made Polly, Nancy, and Molly, *property* and be that property an evil, a curse, or what not, we intend to hold it. Property, which is considered the most valuable by the owners of it, is a nice thing; and for the right thereto, to be called in question by an unphilosophic set of political mountebanks, under the influence of supernatural agency or deceit, is insufferable.[5]

Somewhat later John W. Underwood, a major slaveholder and politician from Georgia, warned, as had Calhoun, that the "same torch" which, wielded by Abolitionists, threatened to consume the fabric of the slave South would one day "also cause the northeastern horizon to coruscate with the flames of northern palaces."[6] The essence of the matter was put even more dramatically by the ecclesiastical and educational leader of South Carolina Dr. James H. Thornwell in 1850: "The parties in this conflict are not merely Abolitionists and slaveholders—they are atheists, socialists, communists, red republicans, Jacobins on the one side, and the friends of order and regulated freedom on the other. In one word, the world is the battleground—Christianity and atheism the combatants; and the progress of humanity the stake."[7]

It was in the final decade of slavery's existence that Marxism made its appearance in the United States, and this by no means excluded the South. There were small organized Marxist groups not only in New York, Pennsylvania, and New England but also in Maryland, Virginia, Kentucky, Missouri, Louisiana, and Texas. In the latter state, serving twenty thousand refugees from the 1848 revolution in Germany, was Adolph Douai's *San Antonio Zeitung,* which described itself as a social-democratic newspaper. Within one year of its existence, the *Austin State Times* (19 May 1854) was suggesting: "The contiguity of the San Antonio River to the *Zeitung* office, we think suggests the suppression of that paper; pitch in." A year later, the paper closed and Douai fled for his life to Philadelphia.[8]

German working-class organizations, heavily influenced by Marxism, existed in St. Louis, Baltimore, and Louisville by 1850, and in 1851 a German Social-Democratic Association appeared in Richmond. It was denounced intermittently for the next few years by the local respectable press. A distinctly radical paper, *Der Wecker* (The Awakener), was established in Baltimore by Carl Heinrich Schnauffer, poet and refugee from the 1848 revolution. This paper, like social-democratic colleagues and groups in other southern areas, not only denounced slavery and urged its abolition; it also called for the formation of trade unions, an eight-hour day, and universal suffrage. After Schnauffer's death in 1854, the paper was edited by his widow for three years and then until April 1861 by Wilhelm Rapp, another revolution refugee and president of Baltimore's *Turnerbund.* A mob drove Rapp from the city that spring.

A newspaper of similar character was founded by still another refugee in Louisville in 1854. The *Herold des Westens,* edited by Karl Heinzen (an early associate of Karl Marx who later turned against Marxism), denounced slavery, called for "the protection of the laboring classes from the capitalists," and advocated universal suffrage, including the enfranchisement of women. It demanded the enactment of minimum-wage and maximum-hour laws, and the granting, without charge, of public lands to bona fide settlers. A similarly inclined newspaper, the *Deutsche Zeitung,* appeared about this time in New Orleans; in 1856 it boldly supported the Republican candidate, John C. Fremont, for president and advocated his party's slogan: "Free Soil, Free Speech, Free Men."[9]

The program of the Richmond Social-Democratic Association, as put forth in 1854, epitomized the program of the Marxist and near-Marxist southern groups prior to the Civil War. Here again the first demand was that of the Abolitionist—the immediate emancipation of the slaves—thus suggesting to the ideologists of the slaveholding classes the identity between Abolitionism and what they called, as we have seen, levelism, agrarianism, socialism, and communism. The association called not only for slavery's termination but also for the nationalization of railroads, better conditions for the working class with an eight-hour day for adults and a five-hour day for children, the development of trade unions, a mechanics' lien law, free public education, abolition of imprisonment for debt, and a revision of the system of taxation so that it would be based on the capacity to pay. It advocated the popular election of all officeholders by universal suffrage, with the power of recall vested in the electorate. This program was published (and so preserved) as an exhibition of horrors and the logical tendency of Abolitionism in a speech by Rep. W. R. Smith of Alabama made in the House on 15 January 1855.[10]

The appearance of Marxian and social-democratic associations, programs, and organs in the South in the last fifteen years of slavery's existence represented the left wing of a widespread class consciousness which characterized internal southern politics during that period.[11] It produced a mounting uneasiness on the part of slave owners as to the trustworthiness of southern white laborers, mechanics, and small farmers; it contributed to the appearance in these years of the conviction that slavery was the proper condition for the laboring population without regard to complexion. Indeed, it was insisted by some influential ideologues of the slaveholding South that—whatever its name—slavery, in fact, was the condition of laboring people everywhere. Well publicized by Abolitionists and Republicans alike, this argument was consequential in deepening the opposition of organized labor and the working class to slavery and to continued political domination by slaveholding interests. Intertwined was a growing awareness on the part of Abolitionists of the appalling conditions faced by nonslave working people in Europe and the United States.

Wendell Phillips addressed himself to this question a generation after the Civil War. He wrote to his black friend and comrade Robert Purvis on 4 December 1883: "Let it not be said that the old Abolitionist stopped with the Negro and was never able to see that the same principle he had advocated at such cost claimed his utmost attention to protect all labor, white and black, and to further the discussion of every claim of downtrodden humanity."

Phillips's recent biographer, James B. Stewart, states that this picture is "inaccurate for the anti-slavery movement as a whole."[12] Stewart's opinion may be widely held, but Phillips's view may be closer to the truth than most historians think. The contemporary evidence does show that some Abolitionists, like Phillips and Garrison, were impatient with those who would equate the conditions—hard as they were—of wage laborers with that of workers who, with their children, were the actual property of their boss. These Abolitionists feared, especially early in the movement's existence, that competing calls, such as those of wage workers, might detract from the energy and effectiveness of the antislavery movement. At the same time, there existed, among some labor leaders and organizations, not only racism but a certain resentment of those who could loudly lament sufferings hundreds of miles away and turn a blind eye to terrible conditions afflicting both adults and children within walking distance of their homes.

Yet Abolitionism was afire with egalitarianism, democratic fervor, and hatred of injustice; working people in facing their own problems did come to see the mutuality of the fight against chattel slavery and against the untrammeled exploitation of the wage worker that characterized capitalism in the nineteenth century. The great body of adherents of the antislavery movement were black and white folk with working-class ties; nor were the Abolitionist rural workers part of the affluent landed and farming interests. The most avid opponents of Abolitionism were the rich— the slaveowners and their lackeys, the merchants and their servitors, the dominant figures in politics, the press, the churches, and the schools.

Theodore M. Hammett has examined the occupational breakdown of 1,155 signers of an anti-Abolitonist petition in Boston in August 1835. He found that merchants, manufacturers, bankers, government officials, and professionals made up 74.5 percent of the total with the first group alone accounting for almost 54 percent. He quoted the *Boston Advocate* of 23 October 1835: "When the mob burnt down the convent, all the Boston papers raved a month about it; the aristocracy were in favor of the convent. When a mob attacks the female members of the Anti-Slavery Society, the same papers say it is a fine affair, a gentlemanly mob. The aristocracy are opposed to the anti-slavery women."[13]

The observations of Abolitionist leaders, in fact, are filled with condemnation of the frightful conditions existing among working people both in the United States and in Europe. As early as September 1832, Garrison wrote from Providence, Rhode Island (published in the *Liberator,* 13 October 1832), that he was pleased to see the great productive power of the impressive factories in that city. But, he added, his pleasure was "mingled with pain—for I fear it will be found in almost every instance, that an exorbitant exaction of labor and time is required of the operatives; that the education of the children is neglected; and that unnecessarily severe regulations are made for the government of the factories." Garrison added that he favored the efforts being made to reduce working hours; he thought anything in excess of the ten-hour day then being demanded "is, I conceive, a pitiful fraud and wretched economy. Ample respite is needed to restore the wasted energies of the body and the buoyancy of the spirit, and to cultivate the mind." He concluded: "Let our rich capitalists beware how they grind the face of the poor; for oppression injures the value of labor, begets resentment, produces tumults, and is hateful in the sight of God."

To his staunchest supporter, his wife, Helen Benson Garrison, he wrote from New York City on 20 May 1840:

Here Mammon rules in filthy splendor, and Humanity finds none to sympathize with it. All is heartless, selfish, exclusive. I am writing in Wall Street, where the money-changers congregate, and where affluence and beggary are seen side by side, but acknowledging no relationship by creation, and at mutual enmity with each other. It is rightly named *Wall*-street, for those who habitually occupy it in quest of riches at the expense of mankind, are *walled* in from the sympathies of human nature, and their hearts are as fleshless and hard as the paving-stones on which they tread, or the granite and marble buildings which they have erected and dedicated to their idol Gain.[14]

Garrison's visits to Great Britain intensified his class consciousness. After the second of these visits, he wrote to Samuel J. May from Boston on 6 September 1840: "I could not enjoy the beautiful landscapes of England, because of the suffering and want staring me in the face, on the one hand, and the opulence and splendor dazzling my vision, on the other. . . . nine-tenths of mankind are living in squalid poverty and abject servitude in order to sustain in idleness and profligacy the one-tenth."[15]

In a similar vein, he wrote his English friend, Elizabeth Pease, from Boston on 28 February 1843:

The present condition of England strikes me not only as extremely melancholy, but as absolutely frightful. What a spectacle, in a country famous for its industry and fertility, to see vast multitudes of the people famishing for bread! What is to be the end of all this? Of all your reform parties, not one goes far enough—not one is based on the broad, immovable foundation of human rights—not one raises the standard of Christian revolt against the powers of darkness.

The repeal of the Corn Laws may do something for the relief of the people— the extension of the right of suffrage may ultimately do more; but these measures are not radical, only palliative . . . but there is nothing so good as a blow aimed at the right source. The people are crushed beneath an overgrown monarchy and a bloated aristocracy, and are the victims of an atrocious alliance between Church and State. Why not then boldly aim for these?[16]

R. J. M. Blackett has shown, also, that British workers were especially attracted to the arguments of visiting Abolitionists from the United

States. He emphasized, in this regard, the great impact made by the numerous black Americans who lectured to tens of thousands in Britain. For British workers, Blackett reported, these Afro-Americans "symbolized successful resistance to oppression" and inspired their struggles against what they called their own "enslavement". Not only did these workers crowd the lecture halls presenting visiting American Abolitionists—particularly blacks—but the narratives of fugitive slaves were "best sellers" among them. [17]

Frederick Douglass spoke to an audience of workers when he delivered his speech on "The 1848 Revolution in France," in Rochester, 27 April 1848. He hailed the overthrow, the preceding February, of Louis Philippe's monarchy and the provisional government's decree, the next month, of measures for the termination of slavery in France's colonies. Having in mind plans announced by the new government for "national workshops," for the "right to work," and even for a "worker's parliament," Douglass observed that in his audience "in all sides" are the working men and mechanics "of the city." They are excited, said Douglass, "because they sense in the French events more than the mere establishment of a Republic"; they feel that France "is aiming not only to establish a government of equality for herself, but takes into view the rights of laboring men, as well as those of other men." [18]

The universality of Garrison's concern is indicated in a letter to Levi Woodbury (former governor of New Hampshire and secretary of the treasury) on 14 March 1845, which he wrote to protest the annexation of Texas. He included a condemnation of "our horrid cruelties" toward Native American peoples: "spilling their blood, and conspiring for their extermination." [19]

Once again in London, Garrison expressed in his correspondence his fervent partisanship for the Chartist movement as one favoring the cause of working people—for instance, in a letter to his wife on 3 September 1846. [20] Garrison was also acutely aware, of course, of the slaveholders' developing propaganda to the effect that slavery was, in fact, "the normal condition of the laboring classes without regard to race or complexion," as he wrote to the Vermont minister Nathan B. Johnston on 25 January 1858; it showed the democratic universality of the movement to end chattel slavery. [21] And Abby Kelley, one of the most militant of Abolitionists, wrote in 1843, in identical terms with Garrison, of "those terrible manufactories where the operatives starve, or suffer, while the manufacturer rolls in luxury." [22]

Even prior to an organized national movement against slavery, trade

unions of Massachusetts had submitted, in 1830, to that state's legislature what was called the "Workingman's Prayer." It included this sentence: "May the foul stain of slavery be blotted out of our fair
escutcheon; and our fellow men, not only declared to be free and equal,
but actually enjoy that freedom and equality to which they are entitled by
nature."[23]

Moreover, the organized Abolitionist movement was aware of the
close relationship between its effort and that of the working-class movement, the latter still in its infancy. The Middlesex County Anti-Slavery
Society, meeting in 1846 in what was then the heart of the factory system, Lowell, Massachusetts, urged support of "the workingmen and mechanics" since "they themselves are the victims of oppression and are
therefor specially called upon to remember that those that are in bonds
are bound with them; because it is impossible for them to obtain their
just rights so long as the vast body of southern laborers are held and
driven as beasts of burden; because there must be chains for all or liberty
for all" (*Liberator,* 8 May 1846).[24]

And the Massachusetts Anti-Slavery Society, early in 1849, adopted
the following resolution:

Whereas the rights of the laborer at the North are identical with those of the
Southern slave, and cannot be obtained as long as chattel slavery rears its hydra
head in our land; and whereas, the same arguments which apply to the situation
of the crushed slave, are also in force in reference to the condition of the Northern laborer—although in a less degree; therefore, Resolved, That it is equally
incumbent upon the working men of the North to espouse the cause of the emancipation of the slave and upon Abolitionists to advocate the claims of the free
laborer.[25]

There is evidence, too, of this kind of understanding among working-
class people. Thus, for example, in 1836, the Working Men's Association
of England asked workers in the United States: "Why, when she [the
United States] has afforded a home and an asylum for the destitute and
oppressed among all nations, should oppression in her own land be le-
galized and bondage tolerated?" Lewis Gunn, an outstanding labor leader
in Pennsylvania, when transmitting this to the United States through the
pages of a Philadelphia working-class newspaper, the *National Leader*
(13 September 1836), wrote: "Our voice should *thunder* from Maine to
Georgia, and from the Atlantic to the Mississippi—the voice of a nation
of *Republicans* and *Christians* demanding with all the power of moral
authority, *demanding* the immediate liberation of the bondsmen."

Nor did one have to be formally part of the Abolitionist movement to see a connection between upholding slavery and demeaning working people in general. Walt Whitman, for example, penned these lines in an editorial in the *Brooklyn* (New York) *Eagle,* 12 September 1847: "Slavery is a good thing (viewed partially) to the rich—the one out of thousands; but it is destructive to the dignity and independence of all who work, and to labor itself."[26]

Louis Filler, in his helpful study of Abolitionism published in 1960, wrote that "it would misconstrue" that movement "not to appreciate its roots in ordinary people." Several participants in their reminiscences made the same point.[27]

Thomas Wentworth Higginson, a militant and effective Abolitionist, in his memoirs published in 1898 remarked: "The anti-slavery movement was not strongest in the educated classes, but was primarily a people's movement, based in the simplest human instincts and far stronger for a time in the factories and shoe-shops than in the pulpits and colleges." This observation flowed from Higginson's considerable personal experience, including his dismissal in 1849 as minister of the Newburyport (Mass.) Unitarian Church because of his vigorous antislavery views. He wrote: "Not a dozen are really opposed to me, but they have all the *wealth.* Oh Christian Church!" Higginson noted, too, that hostility to Abolitionism in Boston, especially prior to the 1850s, was very great—its conscience was paralyzed, he believed, because its bankers and merchants felt themselves tied to slavery economically. Worcester, on the other hand, Massachusetts's second city, had a general sympathy for Abolitionism because it served as a trading center for many of the state's smaller farmers and because in its recently established factories many of its "workers took turns reading Abolitionist tracts during working hours."

Higginson's encounter with the wealthy members of his congregation reflected the typical response of that class. Other antislavery divines suffered similar class persecution, including the Reverend Asa Bronson, pastor of the First Baptist Church in Fall River, Massachusetts, vice president of the Bristol County Anti-Slavery Society, and a supporter of labor's demand for a shorter workday. He was dismissed from his pastorate in 1844 by "a few of our aristocratic manufacturers, who love wealth more than justice."[28]

The late Edward Magdol's last work was a valuable study of the social composition of signers of antislavery petitions in Fall River, Lynn, Springfield, and Worcester, Massachusetts, and Rome, Schenectady, and Utica, New York. Although he found a considerable participation by what he called middle-class folk and a relatively small percentage of the so-called elite, he identified a "preponderance of artisans and working-class petitioners"; indeed, "the bulk of the petitioners held no assessable real estate." In one detailed study, Magdol found that 60 percent of signers of antislavery petitions in the 1830s "were propertyless" and of those who did own property, the vast majority had "very modest holdings"—in the range of under five-hundred dollars. As a body—referring to anti-slavery *men*—the signers "owned less than their fellow citizens." And a great many women signers, as in Lowell and Lynn, were "weavers, spinners, and machine tenders." Leaders in the Lynn Female Society and the Saugus Female Society—workers' organizations—simultaneously were leaders in their respective towns' women's antislavery societies, as in the cases of Miriam B. Johnson of Lynn and Martha B. C. Hawks of Saugus.[29] Similarly, Eric Foner has noted that "in New York City the largest number of signers of Abolitionist petitions in the 1830s were the city's artisans."[30]

The evidence confirms the views of Wendell Phillips and Thomas Wentworth Higginson—despite dissenting opinion from a considerable number of historians—that the propertyless, the workers, artisans, and poorer farmers formed the vast majority of the mass following without which Abolitionism would have been inconsequential.

Conversely, the propertied in the North—especially until the mid and late 1840s when socioeconomic and demographic developments altered alignments—formed the main bulwark of anti-Abolitionist strength. These included leading figures in education, religion, politics, the press, and the economy. They were the main supporters of the slave owners and the major organizers of anti-Abolitionist and racist propaganda and assaults in the North. They acted, as we have seen, quite consciously out of class and business motivations. Much of their activity was collectively organized, deliberately financed, and maliciously conceived, and included palpably criminal behavior, sometimes even murder—and in the case of pogroms, mass murder. In opposing the revolutionary movement of Abolitionism, the propertied leaders not only showed contempt for life and limb but also manifested their scorn for elementary democratic precepts, such as freedom of speech, petition, and assembly, and for the legal and constitutional conduct of government.

Lydia Maria Child wrote in a letter to her brother, Convers Francis, on 25 September 1835, "We should be little troubled with mobs if people called respectable did not give them their sanction."[31] Later Theodore

Weld wrote to his wife, Angelina Grimké Weld, on 15 January 1842, "The city authorities themselves, the bankers and brokers, were the leaders of the mob against the abolitionists."[32] The postmaster general of the United States defended the mob-looting of the mail in Charleston in 1835 and the burning of Abolitionist literature, and President Jackson himself, in an address of 4 March 1837 (drafted by his attorney general, Roger B. Taney), denounced Abolitionists in the most provocative terms and defended those who, in the name of the sanctity of property, slandered the Abolitionists.

The mob that attacked Lovejoy's newspaper in 1837 in Alton, Illinois, consisted of the respectable leaders of the town as well as lumpen figures encouraged by them.[33] That mob and their violence were compared favorably to the leaders of the revolution in Massachusetts by that state's attorney general at a public meeting in Faneuil Hall. It was that slander that provoked Wendell Phillips's great counterspeech and helped commence his invaluable participation in the crusade.

Mob assaults against Abolitionists and black people in general were orchestrated in such cities as New York City in July 1834, Philadelphia in August 1834, Utica, New York, in October 1835, Boston during the same month, St. Louis in May 1836, and Cincinnati in July 1836. As Leonard L. Richards has shown, similar racist mobs wreaked havoc at least 7 times between 1812 and 1819 and 21 times between 1820 and 1829.[34] The high point, however, came in the 1830s when, according to press reports, at least 115 mob assaults occurred nationwide. These tapered off, as the movement against slavery matured and the conditions in the North altered; even so, from 1840 to 1849 another 64 such outrages were reported.

Typically, Richards wrote, "crowds gathered to hear mayors and aldermen, bankers and lawyers, ministers and priests denounce the Abolitionists as amalgamationists, dupes, fanatics, foreign agents, and incendiaries." He said that "In nine cases out of ten the mobs involved explicit planning and organization." Participants always included "many prominent and articulate men—doctors and lawyers, merchants and bankers, judges and Congressmen." The murderous outbreaks were defended in terms reminiscent of those employed by equally eminent figures who, in later generations, defended lynching. For example, the owner of the *New York Herald*, James Gordon Bennett, denounced on 1 September 1835 the "few thousand crazy-headed blockheads"—Abolitionists—who frightened the millions of decent folk until the latter acted: "the ordinary operation of laws against evil-doers are thrown aside as too slow."

There are many examples of what Richards described. An assault upon Abolitionists who planned to meet at Clinton Hall in New York City, 2 October 1833, was carefully orchestrated the day before in the office of James Watson Webb's influential paper, the *New York Courier and Enquirer,* with leading citizens participating. Posters plastered about the city hours before the meeting and Webb's newspaper that morning called for protesters to gather. A mob of fifteen hundred made the Clinton Hall meeting impossible; when the Abolitionists tried to assemble elsewhere, rejection from Tammany Hall hangers-on, plus prominent political figures, stopped them. Richards reports that this was characteristic: a "substantial amount of prior coordination and design," and participation by "many leading citizens" seeking "to preserve the status quo and their own supremacy" was normal.

The very destructive mob attack against Abolitionists in Utica, New York, in October 1835 was provoked by calls for lynch mobs by leading newspapers. Heading the assaulters was Samuel Beardsley, then a member of Congress, and soon to be New York's attorney general and later chief justice of the state's Supreme Court. The action itself was publicly defended by the powerful Silas Wright, U.S. senator from New York. This was, writes Richards, the "basic model" for the fierce Ohio mob of July 1836 who destroyed James G. Birney's newspaper, the *Philanthropist;* again, actually participating were the mayor, a bank president, and a former U.S. senator. Here the Cincinnati ghetto itself was assaulted. The same pattern marked the 1837 attack in Alton and the martyrdom of Elijah Lovejoy. Summing up, Richards says, "the typical anti-Abolitionist mob should be regarded as an attempt by an aggrieved class to protect its social dominance and to reinforce its traditional values."

Bennett's *New York Herald* maintained its vigilante advocacy for decades, even after the mob assaults of the 1830s. This was his advice to readers concerning the sixteenth annual meeting of the American Anti-Slavery Society to be held 7–10 May 1850 in New York City:

The merchants, men of business, and men of property, in this city, should frown down the meetings of these mad people, if they would save themselves. What right have all the religious lunatics of the free states to gather in this commercial city for the purposes which, if carried into effect, would ruin and destroy its prosperity? Will the men of sense allow meetings to be held in this city, which are calculated to make our country the arena of blood and murder, and render our city an object of horror to the whole South? We hope not. Public opinion should be regulated. These abolitionists should not be allowed to misrepresent

New York. . . . All who are opposed to having our city disgraced should go there, speak their views, and prevent it. [35]

The times were not then propitious for Bennett's call to violence, but just prior to the Civil War, in the winter of 1860–61, the mobbing of Abolitionist meetings did recur. These outbreaks were also planned events, inflamed by leading newspapers and personally led by outstanding lawyers, merchants, and politicians. Such assaults, taking place in Chicago, New York, and Boston as well as in Ohio and Michigan, were encouraged by editorials like this one in the *Chicago Times* of 7 December 1860: "Evil, and nothing but evil, has ever flowed in the track of this hideous monster, Abolition. . . . Let the South have her negroes to her heart's content, and in her own way—and let us get on getting rich and powerful by feeding and clothing them. . . . Abolition is disunion. It is the Alpha and Omega of our National woes—STRANGLE IT."

The Boston anti-Abolition mob of early December 1860 was led by merchants and attorneys, "nearly all of whom," according to the *New York Tribune* (6 December) "have uncollected debts [in the South] and many of them mortgages on slaves." In Boston, mobs were then led by leading lawyers like Richard Fay and such distinguished personages as Rufus Choate, Jr. One of the mobs at this time in up-state New York was led by Horatio Seymour, a governor in the 1850s and again during the Civil War. [36]

In general, then, the leadership of anti-Abolitionism came from the respectable. William Goodell wrote truly when—having in mind the entire phenomenon of extralegal assaults upon the antislavery effort—he penned these lines in a work published in 1852:

One uniform feature of these lawless proceedings has been that they have been either countenanced, instigated, or palliated by that description of citizens who complacently consider themselves and are commonly denominated "*the higher class of society*"—the men of wealth, of office, of literature, of elegant leisure, including politicians, and that portion of the clergy who naturally associate with the class just described, or are dependent upon them. [37]

Chapter Five

Organization of the Abolitionist Movement

A collective effort to change the state and society, Abolitionism was a social movement. Dissatisfaction with a social order based on the enslavement of one race by another gave rise to the movement. A group consciousness, both revolutionary and class-oriented, developed among those opposed to slavery. To disseminate their central ideology, Abolitionists organized with strategies and tactics, leaders and followers. Their work required careful organization: tasks had to be assigned, collective decisions made, and accomplishments assessed. This required knowledge and dedication on the part of all the participants.

An example of their tactics was the use of petitions. They provided the opportunity to publicize specific efforts, to reach wide areas of the public, and to develop the awareness and articulateness of the membership. This meant discussion not only of the form of the petition but also of its objective and then its wording. Should the petition demand simply an end to slavery? This had the virtue of directness, but was its practicality persuasive? Would the petition meet with more success if it were directed against the interstate slave trade? Against the slave trade in the District of Columbia? Against slavery in that district? Against allowing slavery into territory acquired as a result of the war against Mexico? Each had special virtues and particular limitations, which had to be debated before a collective decision could be made. When agreement was reached, specific assignments were handed out, followed by their accomplishment. Then the effort was assessed and—what should be done next?

To maintain the organization required agreed-upon rules (a constitution); a leadership (elected and subject to recall); propaganda means—newspapers, leaflets, pamphlets, agents, books; meetings (each requiring personnel); and the raising of funds through bazaars, raffles, literature sales, solicitation. Required, too, were cadre-training schools.

Of course, participation in the movement was voluntary, but it was also onerous; hence enthusiasm and dedication were needed. Agreement, too, was essential; without it, dissenting members breaking away was better than a divided organization. Perhaps the ultimate goal could be reached via several different routes: moral suasion only; or immediatism; or no compensation for slave owners; or political activity of a given kind; or nonresistance to the violence of slave owners and their abettors (perhaps nonviolent resistance by slaves too); or active resistance to the violence implicit—and explicit—in slavery and among those who supported it.

Debate over the ideology of the movement led to other issues. A bulwark of slavery was the idea of the black person's inferiority. If the promise of the Declaration of Independence meant, as its words stated, "*all* men," must not racism be cut out of the minds and practices of members? And must not the members combat racism in the larger society? Was not antiracism a necessary and logical component of antislavery? Clearly it intensified the revolutionary nature of the movement.

Was the nation's social order democratic? Could it be democratic if slavery was present? Did the enslavement of blacks make for the freedom of whites, as slave owners insisted? Or was the truth otherwise: did the continued enslavement of blacks restrict all peoples' freedom?

The Declaration of Independence, written in the eighteenth century, said, "all *men* are created equal." Did that mean, for those living in the nineteenth century, that women were inferior to men? They were certainly subordinate to men, but was that right? Blacks were subordinate to whites and the movement aimed at ending that. Should the movement exclude the equal, full participation of women? Would not such an exclusion be wrong, and would it not be harmful to the effort to end slavery? Or was one effort enough and more than one too many? Did Abolitionist men not face sufficient difficulty fighting racism and slavery? Should they fight for women's equality, too? Would this hurt or help? What of the strength and breadth women's participation could bring?

Then there was the matter of tactics. Would moral suasion be effective? Could one persuade slave owners to give up their slaves on the ground that ownership was sinful? If that didn't work, what then? Political action? Would that not be corrupting? Could the political power that buttressed slaveholding be overcome? How? By working to change the major parties, by creating separate parties, by running for office? Perhaps every possible force and every possible method should be employed: moral suasion, political action, militant resistance, black and white together as equals, directly confronting racism, men and women together as equals, directly confronting sexism.

What of the sanctity of contract, due process of law, sacredness of private property, constitutional limitations? Might freedom become license, democracy become anarchy? Was slavery a matter of debate? Did slave owners have rights?

What of patriotism? Should they attack "the country," "the Constitution"? Was Abolitionism an international movement? Did that movement weaken the nation or strengthen it?

A host of difficult questions—difficult on both the abstract and practical levels—confronted the Abolitionist movement.

Because the movement did not have one center, or one fount of wisdom, or one leader, it functioned as an organized movement comprising several leaders and a variety of viewpoints. Thus, after a particular year-long petition campaign in 1837–38, the chief responsibility for which fell upon Henry B. Stanton, John Greenleaf Whittier, and Theodore D. Weld, the American Anti-Slavery Society was able to announce that 414,471 men and women had petitioned Congress to terminate slavery and the slave trade in the District of Columbia. Clearly this accomplishment required careful preparation, dedicated personnel, effective argumentation, and courage. Only a well-organized movement could do this.

The Boston Female Anti-Slavery Society was formed in October 1833. Its leadership and assorted members met every week and undertook as central tasks specific agreed-upon assignments: getting subscriptions for the *Liberator,* helping distribute the paper, drawing up and soliciting signatures for the kind of petition described above.[1]

William Lloyd Garrison wrote his father-in-law (and comrade) Henry G. Benson, on 4 November 1836 from Boston that the board of the city's anti-slavery society had just met. The purpose of this meeting was "to see what should be done with our city, respecting the District of Columbia [that is, the petition campaign for ending slavery and the slave trade there]. Mr. [Ellis] Loring has agreed to take the 12th Ward, and all South Boston, under his supervision, Mr. [Francis] Jackson will take Ward 11;

I shall take Ward 10; Mr. [Joseph] Southwick Ward 9; Mr. [Samuel E.] Sewall Ward 8; Mr. [Isaac] Knapp Ward 7; Mr. [John S.] Kimball Ward 6; Mr. [John E.] Fuller Ward 4—etc. If we get one thousand names altogether, we shall do pretty well."[2]

Meeting after meeting brought debate and discussion, assignment of tasks, their carrying out—and one thousand signatures had been obtained. Then the process was repeated until finally over 400,000 signatures had been gathered to send to the Congress. No matter how indifferent and how hostile, a representative body of politicians could not help being impressed by that number of petitioners. No doubt many who were asked to sign refused to do so—perhaps even most. Still, as Mary Grew, from 1836 to 1870 the corresponding secretary of the Philadelphia Female Anti-Slavery Society, said in its Fourth Annual Report:

We do not regard those visits as lost labor, where our request is denied, or that time wasted which is spent in unsuccessful effort to convince persons of their duty to comply with it. . . . the seed then laboriously sown, falls into good ground [often], and after a little season springs up, bringing forth fruit, some thirty, some sixty, some an hundred fold.[3]

This, plus mass meetings and public lectures by the leadership of the Abolitionist movement, made up the heart of its activity. The leaders were constantly on call, and whenever asked, if they were physically able (and sometimes barely able), they traveled long distances, often under miserable conditions, staying with comrades wherever possible. Their efforts not infrequently entailed some danger, and veterans of the movement—men and women, black and white—suffered assaults, sometimes to the point of broken limbs. Usually, too, their labors were marked by emotional and psychological tensions, from time to time producing illness as in the cases of Maria Weston Chapman and Garrison himself.

The attention to preparation is shown in the movement's schools for its agitators. By November 1836, for example, Theodore D. Weld had recruited about fifty people prepared to devote themselves to spreading the movement's message. Most of them attended what might well be called, in modern terms, a cadre-training school in New York City. From 15 November through 2 December, these volunteer-students heard the questions most commonly asked of Abolitionists; suggesting appropriate answers were experts Theodore Weld, the Grimké sisters—Angelina and Sarah—William Lloyd Garrison, James G. Birney, and others. The group met from 9:00 in the morning to 1:00 in the afternoon, from 3:00 to 5:00 P.M. and from 7:00 to 9:00 P.M.[4]

Certainly, participation had its own rewards. For some—many, the data show—participating in the struggle against slavery was serving God; for those who recognized no God, it was sufficient to serve human beings and simultaneously help cleanse one's nation. Always there was the sense of solidarity much like that among combat veterans, and this was (and is) an exhilarating and precious feeling. Also present for many of the white participants—as Wendell Phillips and Abby Kelley Foster, for example, affirmed—was the sense of self-liberation and growth they achieved through fighting for the liberation of others. One senses, too, a special experience of deep kinship among the women Abolitionists as they realized the special horror of enslavement for women and discovered their own immense power. The "raising of consciousness" was an accompaniment of immersing oneself in an effort for human liberation and discovering a revitalizing sense of self. Moreover, the dedicated struggle helped create strength for other egalitarian and democratic movements—not least, the movement to unbind women themselves.

Helpful in comprehending the power of Abolitionism is knowledge of its actual body—the machinery that gave it energy whence came its power to influence a nation. That body consisted of numerous organizations; these had written constitutions, elected officers, regular meeting times, full-time agents, and periodicals and newspapers. There was a national organization, the American Anti-Slavery Society (split for a relatively short time so that an American and Foreign Anti-Slavery Society appeared); regional groups such as the New England Anti-Slavery Society; statewide organizations such as the Massachusetts, the Rhode Island, the New York, the Ohio, and the Pennsylvania Anti-Slavery societies; citywide groups like those in Boston, New York City, Providence, Philadelphia, Rochester, and Cincinnati; gender societies such as the Boston and the Philadelphia Female Anti-Slavery societies; youth anti-slavery societies; and societies in colleges, such as those at Amherst and Oberlin. In addition to these which were black-white groups, there were organizations of black people alone, secular and religious.

All these groups had their own publications, usually leaflets, pamphlets, sometimes books, and, most important, newspapers. Among the most significant of the newspapers was Garrison's *Liberator* issued in Boston from January 1831 to December 1865. This paper was always desperately short of funds and was frequently rescued by appeals to its

readers and occasional substantial contributions from men like Edmund
Quincy, Nathaniel Paul, Robert Purvis, Henry George Benson (Garrison's father-in-law), and George W. Benson (Garrison's brother-in-law).
Presenting a weekly barrage of argumentation and agitation, the paper
was provocative and its prose, exciting. For contemporaries it was riv-
eting; it makes stimulating reading even now as the twentieth century
recedes.

The *Liberator* was by no means alone. Among other movement papers
were the *Philanthropist* in Cincinnati, the *Anti-Slavery Standard* in New
York City, the *Anti-Slavery Bugle* in Salem, Ohio, and the *National Era*
in Washington in which, beginning in 1852, appeared serially *Uncle Tom's
Cabin*. These had circulations from about 2,500 shortly after the *Liberator* started to about 25,000 for the *National Era* twenty years later.
The papers were read by at least five people for every subscriber, however, and items and editorials in them were widely reprinted in newspapers throughout the nation.[5]

Other forms of printed matter excoriating slavery flooded the nation
(surreptitiously in the South) in the pre–Civil War generation. Pamphlets
such as those by Angelina Grimké Weld, Theodore Weld, Lydia Maria
Child, and Wendell Phillips sold by the hundreds of thousands; books by
Frederick Douglass, William Wells Brown, and Richard Hildreth sold tens
of thousands of copies, not to speak of Harriet Beecher Stowe's classic
which was bought by millions in the United States and, translated into
dozens of languages, was devoured by tens of millions in Latin America
and Europe. Her story was also seen, in dramatized form, on stages
throughout the North by hundreds of thousands of people.

By the 1830s, Garrison would regularly fill lecture halls; typically, he
wrote his devoted colaborer Samuel J. May on 14 March 1837 that two
thousand people had jammed a meeting place in Lynn, Massachusetts,
and that "a multitude were excluded for want of room."[6] When he spoke
to a larger throng in New York City, seventeen years later, the *New York
Times* printed the entire text of his remarks the next day (14 February
1854), using four full columns of small print.

By the time of the Civil War, the public's appetite for the Abolitionists'
message was insatiable—four thousand people filled Boston's Music Hall
to the rafters to hear Phillips's great speech, "War and Abolition" in April
1861 and two hundred thousand copies were sold within a week. Indeed,
the *New York Tribune* (4 April 1862) "estimated," wrote Prof. James B.
McPherson, "that during the winter and spring of 1862 no less than five
million people heard or read Phillips' anti-slavery discourses." By 1862,

the managing editor of the *Tribune* (then the newspaper with the largest circulation in the nation) was the Abolitionist Sidney Howard Gay, and the editor of the *Independent* (one of the country's most influential weeklies) was Theodore Tilton, also an Abolitionist.[7]

Abolitionist societies laced the nonslaveholding states. Estimates of their numbers vary. Merton Dillon thinks there were 200 in May 1835 and well over 500 a year later. Garrison, writing to his English friend Elizabeth Pease from Boston on 6 November 1837, declared "there are now not less than twelve hundred anti-slavery societies in existence." James G. Birney's figures were comparable; he estimated 225 societies in 1835, 527 in 1836, 1,006 in 1837, and 1,346 in 1838—with, he thought, about 120,000 members altogether.[8] The late Louis Ruchames, who devoted a fruitful life to the subject, estimated that in Massachusetts alone there were 145 local societies, in New York, 274, and in Ohio, 213—all this in 1838. In that latter year, the American Anti-Slavery Society in its official report stated that 1,350 societies existed locally with "perhaps 250,000 members."[9]

Although the Garrisonian wing of the Abolitionist movement disapproved of political activity—such as voting and seeking office—other Abolitionists thought differently. By 1840, the political Abolitionists managed to field the Liberty party whose candidate James G. Birney received 7,000 votes; four years later the same candidate received over 62,000 votes. The larger coalition, the Free Soil party, four years later had a former president, Martin Van Buren, as its candidate, and he received over 300,000 votes, or about 10 percent of the total. Of course, in 1856 the Republican party—with considerable Abolitionist input and support—nearly won the election and in 1860 it did win nationally.

One of the secrets of the great organizational power of the Abolitionist movement was its employment of scores of agents who devoted much of their lives to scouring the towns and villages of the North incessantly—often defiantly—bringing their transforming message of human emancipation and equality to millions of their compatriots. John L. Myers, in particular, has made a study of what he called the agency system of the antislavery movement in its first five years of existence. Among the earliest of these agents—who were usually paid traveling expenses, plus eight or ten dollars a week—was the Quaker Arnold Buffum, acting at the request of the New England Anti-Slavery Society. He began his arduous and dangerous work in 1832 and continued, with some interruptions, for five years, lecturing particularly in New York, Massachusetts, and Rhode Island.

Beginning in 1833, the American Anti-Slavery Society established a Standing Committee on Agencies. That year the committee hired eleven agents, nine of them ministers. Among them was Beriah Green, then president of Oneida Institute in New York, an appointment he had accepted after being dismissed from the faculty of Western Reserve College because of his Abolitionism. Others included people who, beginning as hired agents, would go on to become national leaders of the movement, like Theodore Weld, Charles Stuart, an immigrant from England, the lawyer William Goodell, and the Yale graduate and Congregational minister Amos A. Phelps.

These men and others regularly endured not only vicious abuse but frequently physical assaults. Most of them persevered, and their work was consequential in persuading many of the contradiction present in a Republic dedicated in theory to free human beings but actually based to a substantial degree upon the enslavement of millions of men, women, and children.

In New York State, for example, Myers demonstrated that by 1837, antislavery agents "had been eminently successful." This was shown by the appearance of numerous local antislavery societies, the recruiting of many people to the cause, and "the willingness of [numerous] political and religious bodies to oppose slavery or the annexation of slave territory and support the right of petition or of reform speakers to be heard." All this "affirmed that anti-slavery sentiment in the state had become an impressive determinant of history."[10]

Chapter Six

Abolitionism, Racism, and the Afro-American People

For the black vanguard and membership of the movement, Abolitionism had, of course, a special significance. Abolitionism meant emancipating their own people, themselves and their families, all their loved ones. This special significance made blacks the pioneers of Abolitionism, in many respects the most effective and clearheaded of Abolitionists and among the most steadfast in the difficult and prolonged revolutionary struggle.

David Brion Davis has written, "The frequency of insurrection has commonly been taken as a reassuring index of slave discontent, as if no more subtle evidence were available, and as if the main result of such occurrences was not always an increase in mass execution of blacks."[1] One is uncertain as to who was reassured or required reassurance, and certainly, as a few have shown in great detail, there were many other manifestations of slave discontent—most not especially subtle. Nor was the main result always increased execution of blacks; sometimes a result was the creation of a nation, or the shaking of the foundations of the slave owners' confidence or even their state, or the passage of ameliorative laws, or the holding of prolonged and troubled debate about the wisdom of slavery itself.

True, the suppression of slave unrest—especially of insurrection, the highest form of unrest—was merciless, including awful torture and the bodies or parts of the bodies of the rebels hung about for weeks as objects of intimidation.

One wonders, however, if slave unrest was not the main source of Abolitionism, despite the fact that this observation seems missing in Abolition's vast literature. Suppose the slave owners, and certain historians from U. B. Phillips to Stanley Elkins, were correct. Suppose that slavery *did* produce "Sambo," with only an occasional aberration—a "mad Negro" (as Nat Turner was dismissed by Phillips and others) to be sent to his reward in a hurry. Suppose all those worthies had been correct and that slavery *was* the proper condition for the African-derived person, so that his or her subordination was in no way onerous but "natural," inevitable, necessary. Suppose, in other words, that the "peculiar institution" *had* been peculiar—better, unique—and those subjugated thrived in the condition, relished it. Naturally, then, one would require no machinery of control—as there was none in Phillips's "slavery." One then would have a placid civilization, if only "outside agitators," characterized by the "mere rant and rhapsody of meddling fanatics," would not interfere in matters they did not comprehend (as the prominent Federalist, Rep. William L. Smith of South Carolina complained in Congress way back in 1792).[2]

If the slaves had embraced their "natural" status, there would have been no Abolitionist movement. Slavery induced slave unrest, and slave unrest induced Abolitionism. The thirst for emancipation arose, first and last, among the slaves and their own people, and then among those who felt compassion, who loved mercy, who were moved by pain, who valued humanity and its dignity, who were horrified at the enslavement of women, who found intolerable the sale of children, who took seriously the teachings of the Prophets and of Christ, who believed the inspired writing of the deist who put the best of his era into the Declaration of Independence, who abhorred and feared violence, who smelled the branded flesh, who, like Whitman finding the fugitive slave, busied themselves "putting plasters on the galls of his neck and ankles . . . had him sit next me at table, my fire-lock lean'd in the corner."[3]

Here are some "premature Abolitionists" in action and the words of their masters advertising for their absconding property:

Joshua Eden of Charles Town, South Carolina, reported the flight on 4 November 1775 of a slave man named Limus. Dismemberment being allowed by law for slippery or uppity property, this Limus, said Eden, might be identified by the fact that he had "the ends of three of his fingers cut off his left hand." Limus was especially "saucy" and Eden stated that he would be "much obliged to any Person to flog him," but, the property owner added, "so as not to take his life." And here was the "Abolitionist" speaking, as transcribed by his distraught owner: "Though he is my

Property, he has the audacity to tell me, he will be free, that he will serve no Man, and that he will be conquered or governed by no Man."

In May 1790 six adults, four men and two women, fled the plantation of Benjamin Wilson of Savannah, Georgia. One, named Sue, who was thirty-five years old, said the owner, "is now and has been for a long time lame with the rheumatism, even to her finger ends." Nevertheless, this Sue, so afflicted, had "carried her three children with her, viz. Juno, a girl of 10 years; Sarah, 7 years; and Dolly, 3½ years old."

Finally, moving to the very top of slave Virginia's society we come to the family of Robert Carter, called "King" by his familiars. This title reflected the fact that he and only he possessed, in the late eighteenth century, over one thousand slaves and 300,000 acres of land. King Carter had two sons. One was named Landon. He married into the Custis family (as did George Washington) and in this way and others accumulated property rivaling his father's.

Landon Carter placed the following ad in the *Virginia Gazette or American Advertiser* on 18 December 1784—a year after Great Britain had signed the peace treaty admitting the success of the revolution:

RAN AWAY

From my house in the county of King George, on the 24th ult. a negro man named GENERAL; he is a tailor by trade, very remarkable as a runaway having lost both his legs, cut off near his knees, which being defended by leather, serve him instead of feet. He is thick and square made in the body and arms, speaks readily, and without restraint, seeming to aim at a stile above that used generally by slaves, though something corrupt. I don't know his age, nor can guess at it, as he looks very much younger than he affects to be; his face is round, plump, and free from wrinkles. . . . I will give FIVE DOLLARS reward, beside what the law allows, provided the taker up do chastise him before he brings him home; and his ingratitude, and want of pretence to leave me, forces me to enjoin severity in the chastisement.[4]

This ungrateful General No-Legs also was an early Abolitionist.

Only one who experienced enslavement could fully comprehend its horror; to convey the experience to others was essential if the system was to be effectively challenged. And to have this depiction done by the person who was or had been *property,* by the human whose humanity was denied, by one allegedly incapable of feeling the indignity and enormity of slavery—this, a fundamental defense of the entire system—was to be especially and uniquely effective.

In the antislavery literature there is frequent reference to and at times even some description of slave auctions; these appear in the accounts of visitors and travelers. But to read of such an auction in a work by a black man who had been kidnapped and enslaved for twelve years before making good his escape was especially moving. This account, by Solomon Northup, was published in Buffalo and London in 1853; it was widely read and deeply influential. Among the slaves being sold by Theophilus Freeman in New Orleans in 1841 was a woman known as Eliza and her two children, Randall and Emily. A customer was interested in purchasing Randall; the mother "besought the man not to buy him, unless he also bought herself and Emily." The customer replied this was beyond his means. The mother "burst into a paroxysm of grief. . . . Freeman turned round to her savagely with his whip in his uplifted hand, ordering her to stop her noise, or he would flog her." She would not be quieted; but the customer bought only Randall. "Eliza ran to him; embraced him passionately; kissed him again and again; told him to remember her." Freeman "damned her, calling her a blubbering, bawling wench." The boy called after her, "Don't cry, mama, I will be a good boy. Don't cry." Northup closes: "I would have cried myself if I had dared."[5]

Frederick Douglass, as he wrote in his best-selling autobiography first published in 1845, was sent to a professional slave-breaker, a Mr. Covey, in the 1830s when it had become clear that he showed too much spirit to make a "good" slave. He was worked by Covey for six months and beaten by him more or less regularly, until one memorable day he decided to resist though it might cost him his life. But before that turning point: "I was made to drink the bitterest dregs of slavery." There was work and work again, to exhaustion on Maryland's eastern shore: "We worked all weathers. It was never too hot, or too cold; it could never rain, blow, snow, or hail too hard for us to work in the field. Work, work, work . . . The longest days were too short for him. . . . Mr. Covey succeeded in *breaking* me—in body, soul and spirit."

Although Douglass finally resisted, and resisted successfully, passing through the fire and emerging as one of the foremost figures of his century, even he felt for a time overcome:

I suffered bodily as well as mentally. I had neither sufficient time in which to eat, or to sleep, except on Sundays. The overwork, and the brutal chastisements of which I was the victim, combined with the ever-gnawing and soul-devouring thought—"*I am a slave—and a slave for life—a slave with no rational ground to hope for freedom*" rendered me a living embodiment of mental and physical wretchedness.[6]

It was possible, under some circumstances, for a slave to purchase freedom and, with less difficulty, for free people (especially free black people) to purchase the freedom of relatives.[7] Among the many hundreds who bought their freedom, for example, was Richard Allen, founder of the African Methodist Episcopal Church, and, Denmark Vesey, leader of the widespread slave conspiracy in South Carolina in 1822.

From time to time notices of appreciation to those who had contributed to buying a person's freedom appeared in the black and general Abolitionist press. For example, the following appeared in the *Liberator* on 2 January 1837. It was dated Portland, Maine, 16 December 1836:

George Potter and Rosella, his wife, would take this opportunity to express their gratitude to God, and under him, to the benevolent individuals, who generously contributed to aiding them to redeem their two children from Slavery. They have the unspeakable happiness of informing the generous donors that, on the 12th inst. they received their children, aged eleven and seven years, raised from the degradation of Slavery to the rank of Freemen.

As this paragraph indicates, appeals for funds to purchase relatives were publicly made and were a significant part of the work of the Abolitionist movement.

Levi Coffin, originally from North Carolina and later a chief conductor of the Underground Railroad, remarked that in the face of such appeals, "it was hard to refuse, almost impossible if one brought the case home to himself." And James Russell Lowell wrote his friend Sidney H. Gay in 1849 that, although he was short of funds and was in principle opposed to compensated emancipation, still "if a man comes and asks us to help him buy a wife or child, what are we to do?" Lowell said he could not refuse "such an appeal." In 1852 Harriet Beecher Stowe organized a tour for Milly Edmundson of churches in Portland, Boston, Brooklyn, New York, and New Haven, which resulted in funds sufficient to free Edmundson's two children. Among those contributing in this instance was the world-famous singer Jenny Lind.[8]

Many blacks participated full time in the onerous day-to-day work of Abolitionism. One of the most effective was Charles Lenox Remond, an agent of the American Anti-Slavery Society, whose work took him abroad as well as throughout the nonslave states. A letter written by Remond to a fellow black abolitionist, Thomas Cole of Massachusetts, conveys something of what being an agent entailed. Remond wrote on 3 July 1838 from Winthrop, Maine:

I met my friend Mr. Codding, at Brunswick, at which place, on the following Sunday afternoon, I addressed the friends a short time and was well received. On Tuesday following, left Brunswick for Alfred, to attend the formation of a County Anti-Slavery Society. . . . On the following evening I was invited to address a meeting and complied. On the next day, I was invited to go into the country a short distance. . . . Received requests to lecture in four different places on four successive evenings. I consented, and spoke in each place an hour and a half; and although my audiences were generally dark on the subject of prejudice and slavery, I received on every occasion the most marked attention. . . . At one place, they resolved at the close of the lecture, to form a society and lend their assistance in the great work.

Remond continued on to Saco and attended "the conference meeting of the Congregational denomination" where much was discussed, "save the cause of the poor slave." That was on Wednesday; on Thursday, he had a better response "in the Baptist meetinghouse." Present were many ministers and "a good number of interesting and intelligent ladies." Here the decision was made to form "a male and female [anti-slavery] society." On Sunday, Remond spoke at Bowdoin. On this occasion he was much encouraged; he wrote his friend that "slavery is trembling." Remond thought even prejudice was falling and that over its grave might soon be written: "Prejudice, the mother of abominations, the liar, the coward, the tyrant, the waster of the poor, the brand of the white man, the bane of the black man, is fallen, is fallen!" Overly optimistic, no doubt; but pessimism incapacitates a revolutionary combatant. In any case, soon or late, such an epitaph *will* be written; going into the writing were the efforts of the Charles Lenox Remonds of every generation.

The "partial speaking itinerary" of Frederick Douglass in the single month of January 1855 (in no way extraordinary) included at least twenty-one addresses given in various cities in Maine, Massachusetts, New York, and Pennsylvania. In fact, as the editor's introduction to one of the volumes of the Douglass papers states, from 1855 through 1863, he "delivered over five hundred known speeches in the United States, Great Britain, and Canada."[10]

Such onerous schedules were by no means confined to black Abolitionists; on the contrary all—black and white, men and women—subjected themselves to grueling efforts. Thus, the Grimké sisters, especially Angelina, in their speaking tour from spring to early fall of 1837, despite official bans and uncomfortable means of travel, spoke before large audiences in Lowell, Groton, Brookline, Charlestown, Cambridgeport, Pepperell, Bolton, Leicester, Worcester, South Scituate,

Scituate, Duxbury, and Hanover, Massachusetts. The pace made Sarah ill and Angelina seriously sick with typhoid fever.[11]

Another key role in the struggle against racism was played by the black Abolitionists: their very appearance and participation argued against slavery's main rationalization. A typical account of the struggle against racism came in a letter from Thomas Van Renselaer, a leading black Abolitionist from New York City, to his white comrade Joshua Leavitt of Boston. In this letter, dated 26 October 1838, Van Renselaer told of a trip in the steamboat *J. W. Richmond* heading for Providence. He had understood this boat was one that did not discriminate; hence, when he purchased his passage and berth, he hoped for "a pleasant entertainment." The captain, however, refused to allow him anywhere but on deck and remonstrance did not move him. But around midnight "one of waiters" (complexion not specified) invited Van Renselaer "to occupy a bed which he had prepared." In fact three waiters and "some of the passengers," notably a Methodist minister, the Reverend Mr. Scudder, "gave me great consolation by identifying himself with me at the time."[12]

A few years later, Remond was able to address the legislative committee of the Massachusetts House of Representatives (the first black person to do so) in support of petitions by black and white men and women opposing discrimination in travel facilities. In February 1842, he told the legislators that "complexion can in no sense be construed into crime, much less be rightfully made the criterion of rights. . . . It is *justice* I stand here to claim, and not *favor* for either complexion."[13]

Petitions, argumentation, and speeches—even before legislative bodies—were not sufficient to terminate discriminatory practices in transportation, education, and such matters as whom one might marry. To succeed, in Massachusetts, required militant action (like physically resisting jim crow arrangements on railroads, for instance) and mass demonstrations in the streets (like heroic black and white men and women, together, demanding an end to so-called antimiscegenation laws). It was a combination of all forms of resistance, protest, and education that removed jim crow regulations in transportation and marriage regulations in the state and in the Boston public schools by the end of the 1840s.

In many ways the battle to end the law prohibiting intermarriage of black and white people faced the most formidable—and disgusting—obstacles. But the battle was successful; playing decisive roles were not only black men and women but also white men and women, particularly the latter. The commitment of white Abolitionists to this effort testifies to their antiracism; as a group, and in their actions , they showed themselves generations ahead of their contemporaries.[14] Yet there was racism among some white members of the Abolitionist movement, and one of the notable contributions of the Black members was their role in combating it. I wrote back in 1950 that "there developed within the movement an attitude of toleration, an air of patronage, a feeling of condescension" among some white Abolitionists. It may be added that outright and gross chauvinism at times stained the correspondence of a few among them—Edmund Quincy is an illustration. [15]

The first editorial of the earliest black newspaper (*Freedom's Journal*, New York City, 16 March 1827) rather gently, but still firmly, remarked that "our friends . . . seem to have fallen into the current of popular feeling and are imperceptibly floating in the stream—actually living in the practice of prejudice, while they adjure it in theory. . . . Is it not very desirable that such should know more of our actual condition; and of our efforts and feelings, that in forming plans for our amelioration, they may do it more understandingly?"

Stronger and coming later, when a national, black-white, male-female Abolitionist movement was in existence, were the impassioned remarks of the influential black Abolitionist, the Reverend Theodore S. Wright, before the 1837 convention of the New York Anti-Slavery Society. There, insisting upon the falseness of the idea of white superiority and its existence even among some within the Abolitionist movement, Wright emphasized the burden to the movement such bias represented. This unpleasant fact, he said, "must be brought out to view." Denouncing slavery is not so very difficult, he went on, "but to call the dark man a brother . . . to treat the man of color in all circumstances as a man and a brother—that is the test." He concluded: "What can the friends of emancipation effect while the spirit of slavery is so fearfully prevalent? Let every man take his stand, burn out this prejudice, live it down." Were that done, Wright was sure, "the death-blow to slavery will be struck."[16]

Unlike the gross manifestations of racism that permeated much of northern society, among the white Abolitionists its form usually was paternalism. At the 1843 Negro National Convention held in Buffalo, for example, a leading Abolitionist, the Reverend Henry Highland Garnet, proposed that the convention urge the slaves to go on a general strike demanding freedom, and that when, as expected, the demand was rejected and the masters resorted to violence to break the strike, the response of the slaves be insurrection. After prolonged debate, the convention rejected this proposal by one vote, a fact reflecting the more widespread militancy among black than white Abolitionists—certainly at that point in the movement. [17]

Garnet was not surprised, therefore, that most of the opinion expressed in the antislavery press was adverse to his proposal, but when in the rejection a note of scorn appeared, that was something else again. Thus, when Maria Weston Chapman, a leading Garrisonian and frequent acting editor of the *Liberator,* rejected Garnet's position and added her fears that he had "received bad counsel," she was favored with a scorching reply. Garnet, himself an escaped slave, reminded Chapman that no one knew slavery so well as the slave and that those who escaped from it came "to tell you, and others, what the monster had done and is doing." Moreover, he went on, "You say that I 'have received bad counsel.' You are not the only person who told your humble servant that his humble productions have been produced by the 'counsel' of some Anglo-Saxon. I have expected no more from ignorant slaveholders and their apologists, but I really looked for better things from Mrs. Maria W. Chapman." For Chapman it is to be noted that Garnet's letter was published promptly and in full in the *Liberator.*

Frederick Douglass was arguing against this paternalism—if not worse—when he explained in the first issue of his Rochester-based newspaper, the *North Star* (3 December 1847), that it was begun not from a feeling of "distrust or ungrateful want of appreciation of the zeal, integrity or ability of the noble band of white laborers in this department of our cause." No, he had taken this step because "the man who has *suffered the wrong* is the man to *demand redress*—that the man *struck* is the man to *cry out*—and that he who has *endured the cruel pangs of slavery* is the man to *advocate liberty.*" Douglass insisted that black people "must be our own representatives and advocates, not exclusively, but peculiarly; not distinct from, but in connection with our white friends." And, most particularly, he concluded, "in the grand struggle for liberty and equality now waging it is meet, right and essential that there should arise in our ranks authors and editors, as well as orators, for it is in the former capacities that the most permanent good can be rendered our cause."[18]

To anticipate our story, when slavery's end had come, the failure to appreciate the weight of racism that still prevailed and its consequence in vitiating the social order helps explain the decision of the majority of the American Anti-Slavery Society in 1870 to disband. The black delegates to that meeting, like Douglass and Robert Purvis, opposed dissolution, as did a minority of the whites, like Wendell Phillips and Stephen S. Foster. They pointed out that the constitution of the society included the elimination of racism among its specific aims and that real freedom for black people was far from complete in the North and in the South. Until, said Douglass, the black person everywhere had full political, economic, and social equality, the national society that had pledged itself to fight for this should hold together and persevere. "Our oppression," he said, "has been called by a great many names, and it will cast itself by yet another name, and you and I and all of us had better wait and see what new form this old monster will assume, in what new skin this old snake will come forth." With this tragic disbandment, it was to be another forty years—marked by oceans of suffering—before a national organization of black and white men and women was to appear and undertake the vital, but enormous, mission.

While observing the existence of racist motives among some white Abolitionists, it is to be emphasized that they, as a group, were conscious of this poison and aware of the mortal threat it represented to the movement as a whole. Leading Abolitionists like Lydia Maria Child, the Grimké sisters, Theodore D. Weld, Abby Kelley Foster, William Lloyd Garrison, Samuel J. May, Stephen S. Foster, and, above all, John Brown (and Mary Brown and their sons) had quite consciously overcome this prejudice and consistently combated it in their writings, speeches, and, in particular, the conduct of their lives.

Garrison moved from advocacy of colonization to Abolitionism on the basis of observing and absorbing the argumentation of black people against the former. His *Liberator* was able to appear because of money raised by blacks and the subscribers to the paper, in its crucial early years, were overwhelmingly blacks. Garrison's first trip to England in 1832–33—so important to his development and to establishing vital ties between the more advanced antislavery movement in Great Britain and the fledgling in the States—was made possible by funds supplied by the black Abolitionist Nathaniel Paul. He regularly attended meetings and conventions of black people and habitually associated with them, *as a friend,* in social circumstances, and they with him and his family. He found among them "all that makes the human character worthy of admiration and praise," as he wrote to Ebenezer Dole on 29 June 1832.[19] In July 1835, commenting on the translation into English of Gustave de Beaumont's *Marie, or Slavery in the United States,* he was especially pleased, for "it is admirably suited to dissipate the degrading prejudice against race, which is at once the cause and effect of slavery, and which forms the basis of all the obstacles we have to encounter."[20]

Merton Dillon has pointed out that Abolitionists were keenly aware of the insidiousness of racism but "denied its inevitability." On the contrary, he notes, Henry B. Stanton of the American Anti-Slavery Society insisted in 1834 "that this prejudice was vincible," and in 1837 the agents of the society were directed "to wage the same warfare against prejudice which they do against slavery, and if possible to kill them both at one blow."[21]

White women in the movement often were notable in their war against racism. For example, Theodore Weld commented in 1844 that Phebe Matthews Weed of Cincinnati "perfectly identified herself with the scorned and persecuted class. . . . She lived in their families, made them her companions, linked herself to their lot, shared with them their burdens and their bonds."[22]

George Bourne, the English-born clergyman, migrated to the United States and became pastor of a Presbyterian church in Virginia in 1814. Slavery affronted him; in 1816 his very influential work *The Book and Slavery Irreconcilable* was published in Philadelphia. It was a pioneer advocate of immediate abolition of slavery; the volume was read by Garrison and deeply influenced him. The theme of the book was an insistence that Christianity's essential teaching was that *"God made of one flesh, all nations of men"* and that denying this equality was blasphemous; thus enslaving a human was a sin that could not be justified.

An essential feature of Lydia Maria Child's *An Appeal in Favor of that Class of Americans Called Africans* (Boston, 1833) was a denial of the inferiority of Blacks. A section devoted to this effort begins by quoting Montesquieu: "We must not allow Negroes to be *men*, lest we ourselves should be suspected of not being *Christians.*" Their tyrants, she wrote, "have been their historians"; naturally their "history" has served to justify their tyranny. The former was as fake as the latter was unjust.

Theodore D. Weld, writing to Lewis Tappan on 9 March 1836, remarked that he had been threatened with expulsion from Lane Seminary in 1834 because he had insisted that color was not to determine treatment, and, he said, "I acted out this principle from day to day in my intercourse with the Colored people." Indeed, given the persecution of the black person, Weld followed this principle: "Take *more* pains to treat with attention, courtesy and cordiality a colored person than a white."[23]

Angelina Grimké, in her response to the bias manifested in Catharine Beecher's *Essay on Slavery and Abolitionism* (1837) entitled *Letters to Catharine E. Beecher* (Boston, 1838) asked: "What is more ridiculous than American prejudice; to proscribe and persecute men and women, because their *complexions* are of a darker hue than our own? Why," she declared, "it is an outrage upon common sense." Grimké added—since Catharine Beecher insisted upon her own "pity" for the black given his unfortunate situation—that this "pity" appeared because of a sense of superiority. Not pity, but outrage was called for. Abolitionists, said Grimké, were acting on "the principle of *equal rights* irrespective of color or condition, instead of on the mere principle of 'pity and generosity.'"

Ralph Waldo Emerson, although never formally a member of an Abolitionist society, did speak at antislavery meetings and oppose racism. He, for example, spoke at a meeting sponsored by the Massachusetts Anti-Slavery Society on 1 August 1844, celebrating the tenth anniversary of the emancipation of slaves in the West Indies. Here he hailed Abolitionism as furthering "the annihilation of the old indecent nonsense about the nature of the Tiger. This assisted the very elevated consideration . . . that the ability of no race can be perfect whilst another race is degraded." Indeed, said Emerson, "it is a doctrine alike of the oldest and of the newest philosophy, that man is one and that you cannot injure any member, without a sympathetic injury to all the members."[24]

Acting on the principle of opposition to discrimination was characteristic of participants in the antislavery movement. Illustrative is the refusal of Charles Sumner, when he was still a young attorney in his mid-thirties, to address the Lyceum of New Bedford, Massachusetts. In his letter to its chairman, 29 November 1845, he observed that the Lyceum permitted black people only in a balcony set aside for them. This was in violation of decency because, wrote Sumner, "one of the cardinal truths of religion and freedom is the *Equality and Brotherhood of Man*. In the sight of God and of all just institutions the white man can claim no precedence or exclusive privilege from his color."[25] The evidence establishes that the Abolitionists, black and white, not only consistently fought for an end to slavery but also bore witness, in theory and in practice, to their detestation of racism. There were exceptions, but to smear the movement as a whole because of these exceptions is to pervert the truth.

It should also be noted that, as the late Gilbert Osofsky showed, the Abolitionist movement rejected know-nothingism and national chauvinism, in general.[26] Further, Louis Ruchames demonstrated that the charge, occasionally made, of significant anti-Semitism among Abolitionists is false. Indeed he concluded, persuasively, that they "understood, more than did others, the suffering of the Jew through the ages."[27]

It was mentioned earlier that the buying of freedom by black people was a significant component of the antislavery movement. But of even greater consequence was the flight by slaves. Such efforts to overcome enslavement—undertaken individually and collectively—was a continuous and decisive feature of the slavery years. Its impact in developing a sense of insecurity among the slave owners and in adding to the free black population of the North and of Canada, including many among its leading Abolitionists, was an additional fundamental component of the effort to destroy the slave system. It was also a notable illustration of the militant, the revolutionary commitment of Abolitionism.

These flights were facilitated by the Underground Railroad, a network that laced the United States, commencing with the greatest secrecy in the South and extending through scores of towns and cities and hundreds of homes to the border of Canada. It may properly be called *legendary*— as one historian has done—but the word in this case should not be confused with *mythical,* as some have done; rather, it was *legendary* in the sense of *extraordinary,* reflecting the nearly incredible.[28]

It is likely that many more slaves attempted flight than succeeded; nevertheless, tens of thousands did succeed, often with the assistance in the South of other slaves, of free blacks, and even of some sympathetic whites. The passengers on the line were all blacks and most of the conductors, too. The Quaker Levi Coffin, whose splendid service in assisting fugitives earned him the title of "President of the Underground Railroad," testified that when he left North Carolina and settled in Newport, Indiana, in 1826, he observed that "fugitives often passed through that place and generally stopped among the colored people." His offer to assist was accepted, and thus he began his remarkable career. As late as 1837, James G. Birney made a similar observation while in Cincinnati. He learned, he then wrote, that two fugitive slaves, a man and wife, had recently passed through the city and that they had been cared for by black people. This, he remarked, was typical, since "such matters are almost uniformly managed by the colored people. I know nothing of them generally till they are past."[29]

Most of the people in charge of the railroad, in the later years of the movement, were black. They included William Still in Philadelphia; David Ruggles in New York City; Stephen Myers in Albany; Frederick Douglass in Rochester; Lewis Hayden in Boston; J. W. Loguen in Syracuse; Martin R. Delany in Pittsburgh; George De Baptist in Madison, Indiana; John Hatfield in Cincinnati; William Goodrich in York, Pennsylvania; Stephen Smith, William Whipper, and Thomas Bessick in Columbia, Pennsylvania; David Ross and John Augusta in Norristown, Pennsylvania; Samuel Bond in Baltimore; Sam Nixon in Norfolk, Virginia. Others remained anonymous: "William Penn," "Ham and Eggs," "A ferryman on the Susquehanna," "an old seamstress in Baltimore."[30] Two free blacks, Leonard Grimes in Richmond, Virginia, and Samuel D. Burris in Wilmington, North Carolina, were imprisoned for their work.[31] Further, out of eighty-one free black people in the Richmond penitentiary in 1848, ten were serving sentences for the crime of aiding or abetting slaves to escape from their masters.[32]

In the South, of course, the strictest means were taken to prevent successful flight. Punitive measures were, however, nationwide and appear in the original Constitution as well as statutes enacted in 1793 and, the most notorious one, in 1850. Some black people apprehended in the North were actual fugitives, but others, such as Peter Still and Solomon Northup, were simply kidnapped free blacks, worth hundreds of dollars in the southern market.[33]

An instance of what appears to be of the latter category was detailed in a letter from David Ruggles of New York City, dated 23 July 1836 and published in the *New York Sun;* it was widely reprinted, especially in the antislavery press (like the *Liberator,* 6 August 1836). Here was told the story of the apprehension by police officers of George Jones, originally on the pretext of his having "committed assault and battery." This was a device by which to press the charge by "several notorious kidnappers" that he was a runaway slave. No one was present to plead his cause and Jones was pronounced, by the recorder, a slave. "In less than three hours after his arrest, he was bound in chains, dragged through the streets, like a beast to the shambles." Black people, said Ruggles, could depend only on themselves; "where such outrages are committed, peace and justice cannot dwell." Ruggles called for a meeting to suggest remedies; passiveness would not do.

It was from such cases that vigilance committees appeared wherever a sizable black community existed outside the South. These kept informed of fugitives and of hunters; they functioned both to spirit away the former and, where necessary, to resist the latter. They were vehicles of revolutionary struggle.

The flight of slaves did more than deal a direct blow at the slaveocratic structure and more than help induce antislavery activity. It also put fresh vigor and determination into the hearts of Abolitionists, for, as William Still wrote, "the pulse of the four million slaves and their desire for freedom were brought home to them by the steady flow of new arrivals."[34] This, too, as perhaps the most consistent manifestation of slave unrest and ingenuity, gave the lie to the slaveholders' essential propaganda— that the Afro-American relished slavery and was destined by nature to be a slave.

An entry in Bronson Alcott's journal is indicative of how the act of flight confirmed Abolitionist sentiment. Early in 1847 a Maryland fugitive arrived at Alcott's home in Concord, Massachusetts. He wrote on 9 February:

Our friend the fugitive, who has shared now a week's hospitality with us, sawing and piling my wood, feels this new taste of freedom yet unsafe here in New England, and so has left us for Canada. We supplied him with the means of journeying, and bade him a good godspeed to a freer land. He is scarce thirty years of age, athletic, dextrous, sagacious, self-relying. He has many of the elements of the hero. *His stay with us has given image and a name to the dire entity of slavery* and was an impressive lesson to my children, bringing before them the wrong of the black man and his tale of woes. (italics added)[35]

Repeatedly, spectacular escapes of slaves, or attempts to rescue apprehended fugitives, or legal battles waged by antislavery groups to prevent the return of black people did for the nation as a whole what the individual visit did for the Alcott family:

In 1842 a slave, Nelson Hackett, escaped from Arkansas and made his way to Canada. The governor of the state started extradition proceedings on the ground of burglary, since, of course, Hackett did not own the clothes on his back. The governor-general of Canada actually ordered Hackett's return, but he escaped again and was again captured. A third time this redoubtable black escaped from slavery; this time he was not retaken.[36]

In 1843, seven slaves in a small boat set sail for freedom from Florida. For seven weeks they sailed the Atlantic. Finally, a British vessel picked them up and deposited them in the Bahamas, exhausted, but free.

Two slaves out of Georgia, a man and a woman—the latter almost white in appearance—escaped by traveling as master and slave, the woman disguised as a sickly young man and the man as "his" faithful attendant. Thus, in 1849, William Craft and Ellen Craft appeared before the astonished eyes of the North to tell their story. In October 1850, two slave catchers appeared to claim the Crafts as fugitives. William threatened to resist recapture to the death. They were hidden in the homes of both black and white Abolitionists—Ellis Gray Loring, Lewis Hayden, and the Reverend Theodore Parker. The latter legally married the two runaways and on 11 November 1850 they were spirited aboard a ship for England. There both spoke before tens of thousands concerning the realities of slavery in the United States and recounting their exploits in reaching freedom. William Craft also rejected the idea of the innate inferiority of peoples of African origin and argued against this poison before large audiences.[37]

In 1848 peculiar freight had been hauled from Richmond to Philadelphia (a twenty-six-hour trip) by the Adams Express Company. In a trunk three feet long, two feet wide, and less than three feet deep, crouched a man with biscuits and water. That trunk had been forwarded—it was revealed years later—by a white man, a shoe dealer named Samuel A. Smith, to the offices of William Still in Philadelphia. There Henry ("Box") Brown emerged. Tremendous numbers of people gathered in many northern cities to hear him explain why he preferred a long journey in a coffin to remaining contented as a slave. Never before, wrote Garrison to his English friend and coworker Elizabeth Pease on 20 June 1849, have we "had so many runaway slaves on our platform." He continued, "The remarkable case of the one who escaped in a box from Virginia, excited the deepest interest, and created a powerful sensation."[38]

Rescue attempts by organized groups of militant blacks attracted attention as far back as the 1790s. Thus in 1793, just after passage of the Fugitive Slave Law, a black man was seized in Massachusetts by one claiming to be his master. Defending the black was the very young Josiah Quincy, son of the Revolutionary patriot of the same name. As Quincy was about to present his argument, a group of black people entered the court, and then Quincy "heard a noise, and turning around he saw the constable lying on the floor, and a passage opening through the crowd, through which the fugitive was taking his departure without stopping to hear the opinion of the court."[40]

Indeed, five years prior to this forcible rescue, free blacks in Massachusetts had presented on 27 February 1788 a petition bearing many signatures to Governor John Hancock. They appealed to him to intervene with the governor of the French Caribbean island of Martinique on behalf of three kidnapped free black seamen who had been sold there into slavery. Hancock did so, and that summer the three victims were returned to Boston amid widespread celebrations. The same petition, backed by some white people, also protested against the African slave trade. At the end of March 1788, Massachusetts enacted a strict anti–slave trade law with provision, also, for the recovery of damages by any victim of a kidnapping.[41]

By 1826, newspapers were reporting a number of such rescue efforts by black groups. Benjamin Quarles has observed that forcible rescue efforts freed two defendants in Detroit in 1833, two in Boston in 1836, two in Chicago in 1846 and two in Pittsburgh the next year.[42] In the

Boston case the press reported that the rescuing blacks were composed mostly of women. In this instance, the sheriff was Charles Sumner's father. It was observed that his efforts to prevent the rescue seemed halfhearted.

In the first three decades of the nineteenth century, agitation against slavery in Great Britain and the United States took on a depth and breadth in content and organizational dimension that were markedly different from the preceding generation. It is not that the earlier era—marked by the American, French, and Haitian revolutions with their immense impact upon world history—did not witness in both Great Britain and the fledgling United States a rising concern with the slave trade and slavery itself. On the contrary, the era from the 1770s to the nineteenth century had been marked by increasing challenges to the slave trade and to slavery—many hoping that curbing the former would undo the latter. The American Revolution itself, and especially its thundering manifesto affirming the rights of individuals to equality, liberty, and the pursuit of happiness on earth, had seemed aimed at the elimination of slavery, clearly the most direct denial of all three conditions. Indeed some contemporaries in England assumed the declaration was also an emancipation proclamation; and until the Civil War there were foes of slavery in the United States who insisted that the declaration and the Constitution's preamble *did* terminate slavery or, at least, were intended to.[43]

Decisive in the development of antislavery feeling in Great Britain, which had its greatest impact upon the slave trade and the institution itself in the West Indies, were several factors as argued by four scholars. The late Eric Williams, in *Capitalism and Slavery,* suggested that the rise of industrial capitalism in Great Britain reduced the significance of West Indies crops and of the trade consequent upon their production and that it intensified interest in Africa and the colonies generally as markets; it also brought in its train the rising influence of manufacturers in Great Britain's politics. This, plus the possibilities offered in the development of India and Asia generally led to a receptivity to anti–slave trade pleadings and to antislavery itself.[44]

Some commentators have found this argument not fully persuasive. David Brion Davis, especially, observed that there was a steep decline early in the nineteenth century in the relative weight of the West Indian contribution to the British economy. From 1812 to 1822, both British West Indian imports and exports fell, and subsequently, the West Indian share of total British trade, by value, declined almost 21 percent from 1828 to 1832.[45]

Thomas L. Haskell pointed to what he called "the most important contribution of Marxian historiography," namely, "that the humanitarian impulse emerged when and where it did because of its kinship with those social and economic changes that we customarily denominated as 'the rise of capitalism.'" His emphasis here was on "the rise"—the early period of capitalism—not the later period when monopolization helped induce opposite tendencies.[46] Certainly, the rejection of feudalism's postulates—ordained graduations in society, stability in preference to mobility, innate sinfulness as the source and justification of human woes—by the Enlightenment associated with capitalism's ascendancy offered fertile soil for the questioning of enslavement.

Seymour Drescher, in his *Econocide: British Slavery in the Era of Abolition,* added that one "must imaginatively allow for the possibility" that in addition to these economic developments and changes there might also have been "produced a new balance of social power sufficient, for the first time, to redefine a thriving trade as man stealing, and then to destroy that trade, regardless of either its economic value or its stage of development."[47]

I suggest that all these explanations are valid and interrelated. It would be well to consider, too, the ethical-ideological impact of the antislavery argument, which accompanied, grew out of, and reinforced the economic-political forces described by the above authors. As Betty Fladeland pointed out, "The struggles in Great Britain and the United States against slavery and the slave trade were so closely connected that they deserve to be studied together"—which she then proceeded to do in a persuasive volume.[48]

To the forces mentioned above, however, must be added the impact of the slaves themselves and of free people of African derivation. Du Bois, in his *The World and Africa* first published in 1947, suggested that slave uprisings in the New World (especially but not exclusively in Haiti) were consequential in pushing forward the bourgeois-democratic revolutionary development of the era. And both David B. Davis and Eugene D. Genovese have also commented upon this.[49] In my *American Negro Slave Revolts* (1943) one of the themes was the interconnection between antislavery agitation and slave unrest and violence—each influenced the other. In general, when considering the history of antislavery, primary weight should always be given to the activities of black people, slave and free, for they were the catalysts and indispensable components of the movement to end slavery. Indeed, although Engels declared that "circumstances make man," he added (though others occasionally forget this) that "man makes circumstances." The interplay is of the essence of history's dialectic. It should be added that an essential part of the "circumstances" are precisely the activities of human beings, constituting the "fire bell in the night," to use Jefferson's characterization of the arguments about slavery in 1820. He believed that human beings clang those bells and that the receptiveness of other humans to a particular clanging depends both on "circumstances" and on "man."

Specifically, when considering the growth of antislavery feeling in the United States and Great Britain, one should not neglect the impact of slave unrest in the West Indies. This involved not only the maroon phenomenon characteristic of those islands but also repeated slave uprisings in the 1820s in Martinique, Puerto Rico, Cuba, Antigua, Tortola, Demerara, Barbados, St. Lucia, Grenada, Dominica, Trinidad, and Jamaica.[50] Reports of these events reached the southern press. Declining production and falling profits were bad enough; but threats to one's continuing existence were of quite a different urgency.

Chapter Seven

Women and Abolitionism

A hallmark of the revolutionary character of the Abolitionist movement was the indispensable role played by women. It was the first great social movement in U.S. history in which women fully participated in every capacity: as organizers, propagandists, petitioners, lecturers, authors, editors, executives, and especially rank-and-filers. Every revolutionary movement needs—and produces—participants who cannot be dissuaded, who overcome not only persecution and prosecution but also vilification and ostracism, who finally remain firm, devoted, and active despite all odds, and who are willing literally to give their lives to its vision.

Odious conditions, grievances, and the development of an ideology lay the foundation for a social movement, but for the movement to actually mobilize, the human players must act. This vital human participation and interacting societal developments together forge the movement's nature and its dynamic. In this case, the prevailing conditions of women as a whole, and of distinct classes of women and of black women as differentiated from white women—which necessarily encompassed dominant male attitudes—were fundamental components of Abolitionism.

The dialectics of the women's movement and the Abolitionist movement has been well expressed by Bettina Aptheker:

The intersection of Abolitionism and woman's rights in organization and personnel confirmed the revolutionary impulse of the anti-slavery cause. A mutually compelling dialectical arrangement sustained the two movements, so that each reinforced the radicalism of the other. The female presence helped to shape the revolutionary character of abolitionism, and practical engagement in the struggle against slavery impelled a consciousness of a distinctly feminist vision.[1]

Here is suggested a complex feature of Abolitionism and women's participation, namely, not only the connection between that relationship and the development of the effort for the civil rights of women, but also the connection between both, participation in both, and the development of a movement for women's emancipation—for her reemergence into personhood. Precisely the same triad appears in the history of blacks in the United States: (1) a termination of slavery; (2) the achievement of civil rights (full citizenship); and (3) the achievement of liberation—autonomy, full equality, but not equality in which one's freedom annihilates one's particularity. On the contrary, freedom *is* the fullest affirmation of that particularity. By achieving real equality and retaining themselves, black people do not simply join U.S. society; they transform it. Better, by joining it as equals they therefore simultaneously transform it from a racist society into an egalitarian one. By achieving equality, women too transform society.

The Abolitionist movement had this ultimate achievement in its logic; that is, it required an assault upon racism to undercut a basic socio-ideological bulwark of the slave system. Black Abolitionists especially understood this and incessantly spoke of it. It was this vision—and the differences in perceiving it—that helped abort Reconstruction and, as early as 1870, produced the liquidation of the Abolitionist movement.

Participants in Abolitionism sensed this logic in the case of women as well as of black people. More was involved than deprivation of civil and property rights—horrendous as these were for many to contemplate. Personal and sexual relations were involved. Gerda Lerner, having in mind the predominantly upper-class character of the women's suffrage movement, has remarked that its leadership "never departed from a strictly mainstream, Christian, Victorian approach toward marriage and morality."[2] But in the Abolitionist movement even such sacred precincts were attacked. Those in the left wing of the movement, for example, in a convention held in Vermont in 1858 heard a woman—unidentified in the proceedings—insist that societal tyranny had deeper roots than any had enunciated even there among anarchists and atheists: "I go a step further back," she announced, "and say it is the marriage institution that keeps woman degraded in mental and moral slavery."

Another woman at the same convention, Julia Branch, also denounced the institution of marriage, as then constituted. Further, she said that a woman should assert and maintain "her right to bear children when she will and by whom she will." Otherwise, women were little better than slaves—objects for a marketplace. Several men assented. Henry Clapp said it certainly was a fact that coercion was involved in the marriage relationship, and Stephen S. Foster announced his agreement. William Lloyd Garrison affirmed general sympathy with the remarks of both women, although he added that perhaps Branch had gone too far in her ideas about bearing children.[3]

It must be noted, however, that the redoubtable Frances Wright, although never a part of the Abolitionist movement itself, not only pioneered as a woman in public lecturing in the early and mid-1820s but also attacked slavery as such and advocated full equality for women. In regard to the latter, Frances Wright specifically called for birth control, the equal right of women to divorce, and the propriety of women remaining in possession of their own property after marriage.[4]

Prior to the public enunciation of these concerns about sexual conduct and the marriage relationship in 1858, some women active in antislavery and the woman's movement brought these questions up in private correspondence. At a temperance convention in 1853, Lucy Stone had suggested that women ought to have the right to withdraw "from all unholy alliances." Two years later, Stone and Antoinette Brown, Susan B. Anthony, Elizabeth Cady Stanton, and Paulina Davis discussed the question in their correspondence.[5] Davis had wanted to bring the matter of marital relations up publicly, and Stone commented it was "clear" to her "that question underlies the whole movement." She added: "Has woman a right to herself? It is very little to me to have the right to vote, to own property, etc., if I may not keep my body, and its uses in my absolute right." And she pointed out that "not one in a thousand can do that now." Nevertheless, she considered that publicly airing the issue was "untimely."

Following the 1858 conference in Vermont, the question of marital relations was raised publicly again at the 1860 National Woman's Convention. Here Elizabeth Cady Stanton, supported by Ernestine Rose and a handful "of the bolder women," introduced a resolution affirming that divorce represented greater morality than continued marriage when the latter was characterized by the "violence, debauchery and excess" that sometimes appeared—especially if drunkenness was present. Some men participated in this convention; they and some of the women opposed the Stanton-Rose resolution. Wendell Phillips thought it was out of order since the convention's essential purpose was "to discuss the laws which rest unequally upon women"—not a good argument, for such laws favored men. At any rate, he added, the question of divorce applied to men as well as women and therefore was out of order. The resolution was allowed to stand, but it was not formally adopted. The question would wait two generations before it would again be seriously discussed in public.

Stanton, however, publicly lamented the position of Wendell Phillips on this matter, writing in a letter published in the *Liberator* (1 June 1860) that the objection against man holding man as property—the heart of Abolitionism—applied to the marriage relationship wherein women were the property of men. This tendency to equate the subordinate position of women to men with the actualities of chattel slavery troubled some Abolitionists, especially the blacks among them, like Frederick Douglass.

Some marriages between Abolitionist men and women reflected the impact of antislavery upon women's consciousness and militancy. For example, when Lucy Stone and Henry Blackwell were married (with Thomas Wentworth Higginson officiating) in May 1855, the bride promised to "love and honor" her husband—and no more—while the groom read a joint statement pledging recognition of the wife as "an independent, rational being" and promised not to obey any laws that might "confer upon the husband an injurious and unnatural superiority."[6]

Expressions of explicit attacks upon the sexual subordination of women and of women's right to control the uses of their own bodies are rare, however, in the literature of antislavery movement. The concept nevertheless was at least implicit in the rejection of the most notorious of Biblical male-supremacist injunctions as that in Genesis 3:16, "he shall rule over thee," and Paul's admonition in Ephesians 2:22–24, "Wives, submit yourselves unto your husbands, as unto the Lord." It was present, too, in somewhat sublimated form when white women Abolitionists passionately attacked the sexual domination and abuse of black women and the breeding and selling of black children that were integral parts of chattel slavery. Black women, however, who were the object of this sexual domination, expressed their outrage directly not only in words but through their actions. Black men, too, faced with the reality of the institutionalization of the sexual violation of black women, were frequently moved by this circumstance to the point of assaulting slave owners and overseers.

That the sexual aspect of Afro-American enslavement was at the foundation of the undercurrent of hostility to the institution among southern

Frederick Douglass
Courtesy of the Historical Society of Pennsylvania

Sojourner Truth
"Entered according to Act of Congress, in the year 1864, by S.T., in the clerk's office of the U.S. District, for Eastern District of Michigan."
Courtesy of the Sophia Smith Collection, Smith College

John Brown
Courtesy of the Massachusetts Historical Society

John Copeland
Courtesy of the Library of Congress

Harriet Tubman
Courtesy of the Library of Congress

Ellen Craft
Courtesy of Harvard College Library

William Lloyd Garrison
From a daguerreotype by T. B. Shew, P. S. Duval Lith., Philadelphia., On stone by Albert Newsam.
Courtesy of the Sophia Smith Collection, Smith College

upper- and middle-class white women has been asserted by Anne F. Scott. One such woman noted, in a letter to another, that Harriet Beecher Stowe, in making Simon Legree a bachelor, had ignored one of the most festering sores of slavery.[7]

Differing attitudes among male and female Abolitionists toward the rights of women were strikingly displayed in a case involving a Mrs. Phelps of Massachusetts. Beaten and divorced by her husband, a member of the State Senate, and stripped of her children, Mrs. Phelps early in 1860 managed to flee with one daughter and ended up at the home of a Quaker woman, Lydia Mott in Albany, New York. It happened that Susan B. Anthony was visiting Mott; the two women promptly offered refuge to Phelps and her daughter. Anthony took the two fugitives in disguise to the New York City house of another Quaker, Abby Hopper Gibbons, where they eluded capture for almost a year. Detectives hired by the husband found them and returned them to him, as the law provided. Mr. Phelps had, meanwhile, appealed to Garrison and Phillips to help regain the fugitives; it appears that both men, accepting the law, urged Susan Anthony to yield. She saw the case as not unlike that of a fugitive slave—where the law also favored the master—and refused to give up the fugitives willingly.[8]

Women in the United States, both black and white, had founded their own organizations prior to the appearance of women's anti-slavery organizations. These had come into existence as social, insurance, and benevolent efforts.[9] They provided the women with experience for later antislavery organizations, which in turn led to organizations devoted to the women's rights movement itself. Women had also been active in various philanthropic and religious societies.

Early in 1830 William Lloyd Garrison was surprised when he learned of a petition to Congress opposing cruel practices against American Indians signed by seven hundred women in Pittsburgh, Pennsylvania. Garrison, then editing the *Genius of Universal Emancipation,* wrote on 12 February 1830 that "this was an uncalled for interference, though made with holiest intentions." He continued: "We should be sorry to have this practice become general. There would then be no question agitated in Congress without eliciting the informal and contrarient opinions of the softer sex." When, some decades later, Abby Kelley Foster laughingly called this to Garrison's attention, he replied. "Whereas I was blind, now I see."[10]

By the 1820s, women in Great Britain had become active in antislavery efforts—some, like Hannah More, Amelia Oppie and Elizabeth Heyrick, especially prominent. By 1825 a Women's Anti-Slavery Society was functioning in Birmingham, England. In the previous year Heyrick's significant and militant pamphlet *Immediate, Not Gradual Abolition* had been published in London. Two years later it was issued in pamphlet form in New York and was reprinted in serial form in Benjamin Lundy's pioneering *Genius of Universal Emancipation,* beginning in November 1825.

In Lundy's paper, contributions regularly appeared from Elizabeth Chandler, beginning in 1826 when she was nineteen years old; three years later she edited a "Ladies Repository" section in the paper. She was also among the earliest contributors to Garrison's *Liberator.* Her contributions were in the form of poems as well as prose and focused on moral-religious objections to slavery. Chandler died at the age of twenty-seven in 1834, but she had lived long enough to be part of the first Abolitionist organizations of the thirties. Although in her time she was a legendary figure in the Abolitionist effort, her pioneering role was all but forgotten by the 1850s.[11]

In 1833 the best-selling author Lydia Maria Child issued in Boston her *Appeal in Favor of That Class of Americans Called Africans,* which from its title to its concluding line was unequivocal and militant, so much so that publishers banned her work and the Boston Atheneum withdrew her reading privileges. Here Child, like Heyrick, demanded an immediate termination of the sin and outrage of slavery, denounced colonization as a racist plan whose actual purpose was to make slavery more secure, and pointedly rejected compensation for slave owners (Heyrick had suggested the propriety of compensating the slaves rather than their owners). Child's effort was particularly powerful in denouncing racist practices in the North and in the South and argued in favor of the essential equality of human beings, rejecting concepts of innate racial inferiority as blasphemous and unscientific. Like most of the antislavery work coming from women, it was notable for its assault upon racist conduct and its fierce denunciation not only of slavery in general but of the enslavement of women in particular. In pioneering quality, scope, and fierceness, Child's pamphlet of 1833 is comparable to David Walker's extraordinary 1829 *Appeal,* which it is likely she had read.

Women's work as authors, from Child to Angelina Grimké, and Sarah Grimké to Harriet Beecher Stowe, was of decisive significance in the development of Abolitionist sentiment. Their work as editors, from Lydia Maria Child to Maria Weston Chapman to Jane E. Hitchcock Jones, of papers like the *Liberator,* the *Anti-Slavery Standard,* and the *Anti-Slavery Bugle* also was indispensable. As lecturers and organizers for Abolitionism their roles again were extraordinary; from the Grimké sisters to Abby Kelley, and Susan B. Anthony to the very young Anna Dickenson working just before and during the Civil War, women had few equals.

By 1833 women's antislavery organizations (generally with black and white members and leaders, and also some with black women alone) had made their appearance. They proliferated within a few years throughout the northern Atlantic states and into the Midwest, Ohio, Illinois, and Michigan particularly. Black women pioneered and participated in these groups, creating their own societies as well as forming part of the original women's societies. One of the first women's antislavery societies in the United States, in fact, was founded by black women in Salem, Massachusetts, in February 1832; its existence was commented upon in the *Liberator* later that year (17 November). Black women served as petitioners, lecturers, authors, and agitators, for, like black men, they could make sharp impressions upon a northern population suspicious of Abolitionism and particularly prone to racism. In this connection such figures as Sojourner Truth, Ellen Craft, Harriet Purvis, Charlotte Forten and the Forten sisters (Marguerite, Harriet, and Sarah) were important. As activist and Underground Railroad conductor, no one surpassed (perhaps none equaled) Harriet Tubman.

Historical sources suggest that although antiracism was a salient feature of Abolitionism in general, it was especially true of the women in the movement. In the struggle against antimiscegenation laws, all Abolitionists faced fierce opposition and vulgar abuse, but black people and particularly black women met affront and insult of a kind unusual even for them. And in fighting against jim crow transportation aboard coaches, ships, and trains, Abolitionists did valiant service, and the black women among them, including Sojourner Truth and Mary Green of Lynn, Massachusetts were outstanding.

Women as teachers among black people played a special role, including not only the renowned Prudence Crandall but others like Phebe Mathews Weed, Lucy Wright, Eveline Bishop, Elizabeth Chandler, and Laura Haviland. Weed, one of the "Cincinnati Sisters" who worked devotedly for emancipation, was eulogized, early in 1844 by Theodore Weld as having devoted herself especially "to the lowest class of the colored people. . . . She lived in their families, made them her companions, linked herself to their lot, shared with them their burdens and their bonds, and meekly bowed her head with theirs to the storm that swept over them."[12]

But by no means were the Abolitionist women always meek. Their courage was unbounded, for example, in preventing the lynching of Garrison in Boston in 1836, in defying a mob in Philadelphia in 1837, and in facing the taunts of fanatically prejudiced men, some holding high office. Sojourner Truth, with her six-foot-tall figure, dark face, and large, expressive eyes, repeatedly bested her hecklers. Immortal is her Akron, Ohio, speech of 1851 demanding both freedom for her people and equality for her gender with its repeated refrain in reply to a loud-mouthed doubter, "And ain't I a woman?"

Parker Pillsbury has left a description of Sojourner Truth at an 1855 antislavery convention in Ohio where one of those who had come to bait—a young attorney—said Afro-Americans were "but the connecting link between man and animals." For nearly an hour he spewed forth his bile, deliberately seeking to provoke and disrupt. Finally, spent, he fell silent. Truth responded. She began: "When I was a slave away down there in New York, and there was some particularly bad work to be done, some colored woman was sure to be called upon to do it. And when I heard that man talking away there as he did almost a whole hour, I said to myself here's one spot of work sure that's fit for colored folks to clean up after." Pillsbury said that Truth "spoke but a few minutes . . . not loud nor in rage . . . singularly calm, subdued and serene." Even the loquacious young man seems to have been abashed. Pillsbury concluded that "the convention was a success" with "that scene alone"—the black woman "dressed in dark green, a white handkerchief crossed over her breast, a white turban on her head"—cleaning up the mess left by a moral idiot.[13]

Reflective of the concentration upon the evil of racism in particular was the resolution proposed by Sarah Grimké and adopted at the 1838 Antislavery Convention of American Women: "It is the duty of Abolitionists to identify themselves with these oppressed Americans, by sitting with them in places of worship, by appearing with them in our streets, by giving them our countenance in steamboats and stages, by visiting with them in their homes, and encouraging them to visit us, receiving them as we do our fellow citizens."[14]

Abolitionists, black and white, men and women, conducted sit-ins at racist hotels (as in Cleveland in 1857), frequently on boats and stages and railroads, from time to time ending up bloody but unbowed as in the repeated case of Frederick Douglass and of Mary Green, the black woman who was secretary of the Lynn Anti-Slavery Society.

Demonstrating the work of women in the theoretical assault upon racism is the extraordinary book published anonymously by Mary Putnam, elder sister of James Russell Lowell.[15] Issued in Boston in 1861, *Record of an Obscure Man* brought together the findings of Africanists like Dixon Denham and Mungo Park and Hugh Clapperton to demonstrate that the idea equating "Africa" with barbarism was the construct of rationalizing European exploiters. The book received high praise from the general Abolitionist press, like the *Liberator* (20 November 1861), and from the black publication, the *Anglo-African* (15 February 1862).

The participation of women in the Abolitionist movement was opposed on several grounds. The most widely cited was simply male supremacy: women's place is in the home; women naturally are dependent; the Scriptures teach male domination; women's participation in political agitation is unseemly and denigrating—it is destructive of their special function and unique quality.

There were other arguments, especially that women's insistence upon participation would weaken the Abolitionist movement for it would affront many who might otherwise participate; or that women's activity within Abolitionism brought forward the idea of women's rights as a whole and that was a different crusade—pushing it would weaken the antislavery effort. Slavery, it was insisted, was the central canker in the Republic's body; nothing should detract from its excision.

The responses came mostly from women, who were joined by some men—Wendell Phillips, William Lloyd Garrison, Theodore Dwight Weld, and Frederick Douglass. Except for Phillips, however, even they had some objections to full and equal participation of women. Garrison, as mentioned earlier, blanched at exposing sexual domination and the inequality of the marriage relationship. Weld argued with the Grimké sisters (until more or less won over by them) that perhaps they should curb or moderate their assaults upon slavery, especially in mixed (male and female) gatherings. Douglass suggested that it would be preferable if women (he had in mind especially Abby Kelley) did not accept officer posts in Abolitionist organizations.

It was necessary in counterargument to point out that human liberation required universal application; that the idea of the inferiority of women had no more validity than that of the inferiority of black people; that inhibiting the role of women violated the Bill of Rights as surely as inhibiting the role of men; that half the slaves were women and their enslavement was especially horrendous—to keep women from participating in the effort to emancipate their sisters was wrong.

One argument applied to the issue of women's participation in Abolitionism was analogous to the antiracist argument stressing the humanity

of blacks. The Anti-Slavery Society's constitution invited all persons who
favored its goals to join, and, it was pointed out, women were persons.
Garrison added, accurately, that in insisting upon the right of women to
participate fully and equally in the Abolitionist effort, the movement's
constitution was not taking a stand as to the civil rights of women. Although in his language Garrison spoke as though Abolitionism was and
should be a male enterprise, this reflected a limitation of the language of
the time, not his *advocacy* of such a limitation. It hints at what women
faced at this time.

The linguistic problem is striking in a passage from a public letter
written by Garrison on 17 July 1839. As secretary of the Massachusetts
Anti-Slavery Society, he responded to the creation of the schismatic
Massachusetts Abolition Society. The latter group had split off because
of differences over the role of women in the antislavery movement, as
well as over questions of political activity, pacifism, and Sabbath observ-
ance. Garrison wrote:

The anti-slavery enterprise claims of every abolitionist that he shall remember
those who are in bonds as bound with them, that he shall act consistently and
conscientiously, according to his anti-slavery professions, and that he shall not
sacrifice the cause of bleeding humanity to any sectarian or party object whatever. Occupying, therefore, this extensive field, it has ever welcomed to its
ranks every human being who is willing to recognize the poor despised Negro as
"a man and a brother."

Continuing, Garrison noted that seceders had insisted that women must
be excluded and silenced or the efforts of Abolitionists would be divided.
Such efforts, they said, are "important and onerous enough to demand
all our efforts—our *undivided* efforts." But, said Garrison, that is "the
very reason why the aid of women is deemed to be indispensable by
abolitionists!"[16]

Some men made powerful—even unequivocal—speeches in defense
of the rights of women to participate in the antislavery struggle. Thus,
James Forten, Jr., son of the widely known black Philadelphia leader,
speaking on 14 April 1836 before the Ladies Anti-Slavery Society of that
city, pointed out:

It has often been said by anti-Abolitionists that the females have no right to
interfere with the question of slavery or petition for its overthrow; that they had
better be at home attending to their domestic affairs, etc. What a gross error—

what an anti-Christian spirit this bespeaks! Were not the holy commands: "Remember them that are in bonds, as bound with them," and "Do unto others as ye would they should do unto you," intended for women to obey as well as men? Most assuredly they were.[17]

Douglass, as is well known, attended the Seneca Falls Convention in 1848 and supported women in their ensuing campaign to achieve civil rights. Indeed, speaking at the National Women's Rights Convention of 1850 held in Worcester, Massachusetts, in October, Douglass urged: "Let woman *take* her rights, and then she shall be free."[18]

Nevertheless even Douglass drew the line at women accepting leadership responsibilities in general Abolitionist societies. Speaking in Rochester on 19 May 1855, he recalled that at the national convention of the American Anti-Slavery Society held in May 1840, Abby Kelley's appointment to its business committee was upheld by a vote of 557 to 451. On this occasion Amos Phelps, Lewis Tappan, and some other male members of the committee resigned and soon thereafter established the short-lived American and Foreign Anti-Slavery Society. That society's constitution provided for the separate organization of women's anti-slavery affiliates, and these were to be represented by male delegates at national conventions.

Douglass, with this turn of events in mind, declared, "Thus was a grand philanthropic movement rent asunder by a side issue, having nothing whatever to do with the great object which the American Anti-Slavery Society was organized to carry forward." Upon whom did Douglass place the onus for this unhappy result? He continued:

Before I would have stood in such an attitude, and taken the responsibility of dividing the ranks of freedom's army, I would have suffered my right arm to be taken off. How beautiful it would have been for that woman, how nobly would her name have come down to us in history, had she said: "All things are lawful for me, but all things are not expedient! While I see no objection to my occupying a place on your committee, I can for the slave's sake forego that privilege." The battle for Woman's Rights should be fought on its own ground; as it is, the slave's cause, already too heavy laden, had to bear up under this new addition; but, I will not go further on that subject, except to characterize it as a mistake.[19]

Wendell Phillips, in Worcester on 16 October 1851, when speaking on "Woman's Rights" urged that women should "TAKE your rights" and by the latter he made clear he had in mind full equality. He said, "We do not seek to protect woman, but rather to place her in a position to defend herself." She had, he continued, all the duties of a citizen; hence, she should have all the rights of a citizen. Further, said Phillips, "Leave it to woman to choose for herself her professions, her education, her sphere"—this after declaring that "the proper sphere for all human beings is the largest and highest to which they are able to attain." He demanded that all positions and professions be open to women and that equal pay for equal work be applied to women as well as to men. "It is competition in too narrow lists," he declared, "that starves women in our cities; and those lists are drawn narrow by superstition and prejudice." The movement for women's freedom, said Phillips "is a great social protest against the very fabric of society"; indeed, he thought it "the great question of the age." He said this while devoting his life to eliminating *the* most awful scourge of his time. [20]

The leading women Abolitionists saw nothing contradictory in their devotion both to antislavery and to the full freedom of their gender; on the contrary they saw the complementary, interlocking character of the two.

Lucretia Mott, for example, chairing the May 1837 Anti-Slavery Convention of American Women emphasized that "by the concentration of our efforts in this way, we not only advance the emancipation of the slave, but . . . the fettered mind of women is fast releasing itself from the thralldom in which long existing custom has bound it and by the exercise of her talents in the cause of the oppressed—her intelligence as well as moral being is rising into new life."

Angelina Grimké, in a private letter of 25 July 1837, noted that "our *womanhood* is as great an offense to some as our Abolitionism." Vast, she said, was the "discussion in the *province* of women and I am glad of it." She and sister Sarah, she continued, were "willing to bear the brunt of the storm, if we can only be the means of making a breach in that wall of public opinion which lies right in the way of woman's true dignity, honor and usefulness."

They spoke publicly only on slavery, Angelina Grimké wrote in another letter on 10 August 1837, but in doing so they would not accept the advice of those who urged that they bar men from attending. No, they would not do that, she said in a profoundly radical paragraph: "In doing so we should surrender a fundamental principle, believing as we did that as *moral* beings it is our duty to appeal to all *moral* beings on this subject without any distinction of sex." She concluded this letter: "This will soon be an absorbing topic, it must be discussed whether women are moral and responsible beings, and whether there is such a thing as *male* and *female* duties, etc. My opinion is that there *are none* and that this false idea had driven the plowshare of ruin over the whole field of morality."

Angelina Grimké aimed another letter, 2 September 1837, at the Reverend Amos A. Phelps, a Congregational minister and then general agent of the Massachusetts Anti-Slavery Society who shortly was to lead the secessionist movement from that society precisely on the grounds of the role of women. She felt it helpful to point out to the minister that "woman has been used as a drudge and caressed like a spoiled child, and man inflicted no less an injury on himself in thus degrading *us,* for some of the noblest virtues are too generally deemed unmanly."

Sarah Grimké, a month earlier, had already written to Phelps that if pleading the cause of the slave had involved them in controversy over the rights of women, then "the consequence we must leave to Him who has pointed out this path for us to walk in. . . . God has unexpectedly placed us in the forefront of the battle which is to be waged against the rights and duties and responsibilities of woman; it would ill become us to shrink from such a contest."[21]

These letters to Phelps were preparatory to two publications by the Grimké sisters to appear in 1838 both in serialized newspaper form and as separate and widely read publications. Angelina's work was a response to an essay by Catharine E. Beecher, eldest daughter of the Reverend Lyman Beecher and sister of Harriet Beecher Stowe and the Reverend Henry Ward Beecher. Catharine Beecher, though herself a woman of great independence and founder and director of several outstanding schools for women, was of a socially conservative outlook and specifically opposed both Abolitionism and the enhancement of women's civil rights. Arguing both positions, she published early in 1837 *An Essay on Slavery and Abolitionism with Reference to the Duty of American Females.* Addressed specifically to Angelina Grimké, this essay argued in favor of colonizationism and in opposition to political activity—even petitioning— by women.

Beginning later in May, Angelina replied to Catharine Beecher in letters published in the *Emancipator* and the *Liberator* (and in 1838 as a book), arguing both the propriety and duty of immediate emancipation and the necessity of agitation, including political struggle, to achieve this vital goal. In the latter effort the strength of all was required, and this meant the full participation of women and men in the effort. In developing this theme, Angelina Grimké affirmed that she believed "it is woman's right to have a voice in all the laws and regulations by which she is *gov-*

erned, whether in Church or State, and that the present arrangements of society, on these points, are *a violation of human rights, a rank usurpation of power."* This led her to the transforming conclusion that "woman has . . . just as much right to sit upon the throne of England, or in the Presidential chair of the United States."

Explicitly joining the Abolitionist and women's rights efforts, and the necessity of civil liberties—anathema to the slaveholders—she wrote: "The discussion of the rights of the slave has opened the way for the discussion of other rights, and the ultimate result will most certainly be the breaking of *every* yoke, the letting the oppressed of every grade and description go free—an emancipation far more glorious than any the world has yet seen."

At about the same time, Mary Parker, then president of the Boston Female Anti-Slavery Society, suggested to Sarah Grimké that she put on paper her ideas on the equality of the sexes and especially on religious equality. The result was the appearance of fifteen letters published in the *New England Spectator* and the *Liberator,* which appeared in book form as *Letters on the Equality of the Sexes and the Condition of women* . . . (Boston, 1838).

Responding to public attacks from various clergymen and their organizations directed against both the alleged vituperation and impetuosity of the Abolitionists and, especially, the unseemly departure from proper female conduct by agents of and lecturers for the impractical agitators (meaning the Grimké sisters), Sarah Grimké rejected the male supremacist reading of the Bible. God, she held, had produced both the male and the female in his image and no inequality of either existed. Let men "take their feet from off our necks" so that "we might stand upright on that ground which God designed us to occupy." The injunction that women had to be instructed by men, including reverend gentlemen, she dismissed; and the suggestion that women should heed their advice as to whom they listened to—that "I utterly defy."

Sarah Grimké here denounced what she called men's corrupt "passion for supremacy." After summarizing the grossly unequal condition of women in Europe and the United States, she especially denounced the inferior education they were offered and the domesticity emphasized as their proper—indeed, sole—function. She particularly condemned the economic subordination of women, as basic to their general dependence. With indignation she dwelled upon woman's low wages and even here— in 1838—demanded equal pay for equal work. She appealed to women directly to combat their sense of inferiority and to realize that "woman must feel that she is the equal, and is designed to be the fellow laborer of her brother."

Having seen slavery firsthand, she passionately denounced it and especially lambasted the barbaric treatment of women slaves. She called on women to activate themselves in every sphere of civilization; it was their obligation and they were fully capable of performing all tasks at least as well as men. As for the latter, the equality of women would redound to *their* benefit, for women possessing full equality would be "unspeakably more valuable than woman as their inferior."[22]

By 1840 women in the United States were integrated within the mainstream of the Abolitionist movement and separate conventions of antislavery women were a thing of the past. But when several black and white women were elected as delegates to the first World Anti-Slavery Convention, held in London that year, they were met with the refusal of the English majority to seat them as delegates. After a spirited debate, the women adjourned to the balcony as spectators, there to be joined by some of the U.S. male delegation, including Wendell Phillips and William Lloyd Garrison.

This international convention was predecessor to many such historic gatherings that have since occurred. It forwarded antislavery feeling and organization (notably in Ireland) and stimulated, in particular, an effort to cleanse U.S. church establishments of their support of slavery. It was also at this 1840 convention that two of the banned women—Lucretia Mott and Elizabeth Cady Stanton—decided to press forward the organized movement of women, particularly for civil rights, thus sowing the seeds for the historic Seneca Falls meeting of 1848.[23]

Although women Abolitionists participated in every aspect of the movement, their role in petitioning campaigns and in antislavery bazaars was especially outstanding. The latter seem to have been almost entirely initiated and conducted by women. These bazaars, or fairs, lasted for several days and featured exhibits and stalls where artifacts of various kinds and books, annuals, and periodicals were sold, many with antislavery themes. Not atypical was the twenty-third annual National Anti-Slavery Bazaar, held in 1856–57, at which $5,250 was raised to help sustain the *National Anti-Slavery Standard,* then edited by Lydia Maria Child. Maria Weston Chapman played a key role in initiating and directing this important form of propaganda and money-raising.[24]

Campaigns to collect signatures to petitions seeking an end to the domestic slave trade or slavery in the District of Columbia or in the federal territories marked the entire life of the antislavery struggle. Men and women participated in this effort, which helped bring Abolitionism to the consciousness of hundreds of thousands in every corner of the nonslave-holding areas. The struggle involved not only gathering signatures but also campaigning to get the petitions considered by Congress, which raised the issues of freedom of speech and petition.[25]

Women also took leading positions in statewide petition campaigns. Outstanding were the efforts in Massachusetts to eliminate jim crow schools and to terminate the laws prohibiting miscegenation. Both succeeded and in both, petitioning, especially by women, was a notable form of the political pressure.[26]

Numbers of signatures ran into the hundreds of thousands. In 1838 petitions presented to Congress urging the prohibition of slavery in the District of Columbia carried over 400,000 signatures about equally distributed between men and women. Gerda Lerner has made a careful study of the gender of signers of petitions. Some were circulated by men and those contained about 3.3 male signatures to 1 female; in those circulated by women the figures were almost reversed: 3.5 females to 1 male. Totals for antislavery petitions sent to the twenty-fifth Congress (1837–38) were about 67,000 signatures in all, of which 22,000 were male and 45,000 female. Other studies cited by Lerner support this proportion of signatures for other periods. Lerner concluded: "The petitioning activities of anti-slavery women in the 1830s and 1840s were of far greater significance to the building of the anti-slavery movement than has been previously recognized." And she added, "Moreover, these activities contributed directly to the development of a contingent of local and regional women leaders, many of whom were to transfer their political concerns to feminist activities after 1848."[27]

The petition campaigns by women assumed decisive significance again during the Civil War itself. In the spring of 1863 a petition campaign to enact what became two years later the thirteenth Amendment—the abolition of slavery—was launched under the auspices of the Women's Loyal National League. This effort, led by Elizabeth Cady Stanton and Susan B. Anthony, resulted in the gathering of 400,000 signatures. (One of those especially active in this signature-gathering campaign was William Andrew Jackson, the escaped former slave-coachman of Jefferson Davis.)[28]

There is some evidence that women's organizations took the lead in efforts to overcome the disunity and factionalism that hurt the movement. Individuals like Lydia Maria Child, for example, played a part in this. A group of women, led by Susan F. Porter and Julia Griffiths, who formed the Rochester Ladies' Anti-Slavery Sewing Society in 1851 (as distinct from the Sewing Circle formed in that city in 1835), explicitly declared its desire to "cooperate with all those whose love for the antislavery cause rises superior to their connection with any particular party or sect of abolitionists." The Cincinnati Ladies Anti-Slavery Sewing Circle, which sponsored annual conventions in that city 1851–55, "attempted," wrote John Blassingame, "to bring together the broadest possible range of opponents of slavery." Frederick Douglass, speaking at its 1854 convention, alluded to his pleasure that the circle had succeeded into shaming "into silence" "all the bitter strifes of new and old organization, of moral suasionists, and of legal suasionists." This unity, he said, had flowed from the "overshadowing influence of a common desire to regenerate the moral sentiment of the country and to emancipate the slave." Soon even Garrison and Douglass buried their deep political and personal differences of the late 1840s and early 1850s and appeared together.[29]

The contemporaneous antislavery sources are sprinkled with evidence of the special fervor of women participants. Garrison, for example, in a letter of 28 September 1836, wrote that women were the "life of the cause" and in another, dated 6 November 1837, he affirmed that their overall influence was greater than men's. In this letter, Garrison told Elizabeth Pease that "in their petitions to Congress, they outnumbered us at least three, perhaps five to one." He added that the Grimké sisters, in particular, were "exerting an almost angelic influence," speaking to throngs of people "of both sexes" with remarkably positive results. Again, writing to his father-in-law from Boston on 28 September 1836, Garrison noted that "the abolition men in this city are somewhat drowsy, but the women are, as usual, wide awake, and the life of the cause."[30]

Women who were black had reason enough to be especially dedicated to Abolitionism; but white women, too, had a special motivation insofar as their own oppression as women strengthened their passionate adherence to the cause of ending chattel enslavement—of men and women. The clear relationship between emancipation of chattel slaves and elimination of male supremacy was a decisive part of the revolutionary quality of Abolitionism. The striking similarity in the content of racism and of male chauvinism further strengthened women's participation in the struggle against the former as it strengthened their own consciousness of their oppression. This, too, speaks of Abolitionism's revolutionary essence.

Chapter Eight

Political Prisoners and Martyrs

A hallmark of a revolutionary movement is its crop of victims and martyrs. Maria Weston Chapman, in drafting the *Report of the Boston Female Anti-Slavery Society* for 1835, remarked that the struggle had "occasioned our sons to be expelled from colleges and theological seminaries—our friends from professorships—ourselves from literary and social privileges." Among those so victimized she named Dr. Henry J. Bowditch, Theodore Parker, Adin Ballou, Charles Follen, William Jay, Joshua Coffin, James Russell Lowell, John G. Fee, and Henry B. Stanton.[1]

Chapman had in mind mostly professional and occupational punishments suffered by Abolitionists. Certainly all "reputable" institutions carefully screened those whose views might be unsound on the question of slavery. Not only, for example, did Lane Theological Seminary forbade debate on the inflammable question and dismiss students and faculty who refused to "behave." Institutions like Yale, Harvard, Andover, Amherst, not to speak of southern colleges, similarly forbade discussion of slavery and dismissed or refused to hire those who did not act "responsibly." Dismissed from their positions were the Reverend D. D. Whedon, from the University of Michigan in 1851 by the Board of Regents; Professor Benjamin Hedrick, from the University of North Carolina in 1856 for indicating a preference for John C. Fremont; Elizur Wright, Jr., from Yale University in 1833 for Abolitionist activities; and Charles Follen, from Harvard for the same offense.[2]

These cases for the individuals involved were serious tragedies, but they were minor inconveniences compared to the experiences of the scores of men and women who suffered imprisonment, physical assault, even death. Many of these were whites, but the greatest number, by far, of those politically victimized, jailed, deported, lashed, lynched, executed, were black men and women, mostly slaves or fugitive slaves, but also a significant number of free blacks. It is not customary in the literature to consider these people political prisoners or refugees or martyrs, but that is what they were. They were protesting against dominant social and political arrangements and seeking their transformation. For this they suffered; they were political victims.

Since the institution of slavery long antedated the appearance of a national, organized movement for the immediate uncompensated emancipation of the slaves (starting in the late 1820s and full-blown by the next decade), the existence of political prisoners, martyrs, and victims also long antedated the movement. Indeed, with the introduction of slavery in America came the people battling it—to the point of facing jail, torture, death. That is, with the institution of slavery appeared its combatants.

Prior to the Abolitionist movement, hundreds of blacks were executed, banished, branded, tortured—imprisonment was the least of it.[3] It is noteworthy that in this earlier period expressions of sympathy from and even joint participation by whites and free blacks were far from uncommon. They supported or led insurrections, assisted fugitives, and openly expressed their hostility to slavery. Whites were accused of sympathy with slave rebels in 1741 both in New York and in South Carolina; a free black man, Charles Deslondes, was a leader of rebellion in Louisiana in 1811; Joseph Wood, a white man, was executed for this crime in the same state the next year; George Boxley was convicted and sentenced to hang for such complicity in Virginia in 1816 (although he escaped). There are still other examples in the early period. Four white men, residents of Charleston, were convicted for the crime of encouraging the widespread slave conspiracy, centering in that city in 1822 and led by Denmark Vesey, himself then a free black; they were Andrew Rhodes, William Allen, Jacob Danders, and John Igneshias. Only the motives of Allen were suspect, since a free black man charged that he expected to reap financial gain from successful rebels. The others, however, simply hated slavery and let the blacks know their feelings. As Danders was alleged to have said, the black people "had as much right to fight for their liberty as the white people." All were fined from one hundred to one thousand dollars and sentenced to jail terms ranging from three months to one year.

In the general slave unrest in Louisiana in the 1790s, three white

men—Joseph Rayado, George Rockenburg, and John Sarge—were convicted as accomplices and sentenced to jail for seven years. In 1802 a
white man named James Hall Mumford was forced to leave Virginia for
allegedly encouraging slave rebellion. And early in 1804, a judge of the
eastern district of Georgia, Jabez Brown, Jr., created a sensation by his
"inflammatory" charge to a grand jury in Chatham. The jury refused to
permit the publication of the charge and bitterly denounced the judge.
Other evidence establishes that Judge Brown had criticized slavery in the
severest terms, even stating that he thought rebellion by the slaves fully
justifiable. This remarkable Georgia official was briefly jailed for "inciting
insurrection"; upon his release he was remanded out of the state and
seems to have settled in Rhode Island.

In August 1818, a Methodist camp meeting held on the plantation of
Jonas Hogsmire of Washington County, Maryland, was attended by several thousand white people (estimates ranged from two to four thousand)
and as many as four hundred black people, apparently mostly slaves. For
reasons not made clear the designated preacher for the occasion was
unable to speak. His place was taken by the presiding elder of the district, the Reverend Jacob Gruber from Pennsylvania. His sermon was
delivered in the evening "without the least premeditation or concert with
any individual, black or white"; its theme was "Righteousness exalteth a
nation, but sin is a reproach to any people." The particular sin emphasized by the Reverend Mr. Gruber was that of slavery, and charges were
brought against him for inciting slaves to rebellion.

The Reverend David Martin, a colleague of Gruber's, in his preface to
a small book detailing the subsequent trial and the arguments of opposing
counsel, stated that the accused had "discussed the subject of negro slavery . . . as a national sin, detrimental to the true interest of the nation
and individuals, and awfully offensive in the sight of almighty God." The
main direction of the sermon "was a call to repent and seek the pardon
of their sins": this was clearly addressed to the whites for only they could
be guilty of slaveholding. Moreover, the preface continues, "to prevent
all possible misunderstanding among the whites, as to [Gruber's] motives, and to suppress the least thought of insubordination among the
blacks," he directed the closing section of his sermon to them. Here he
"enforced the necessity of obedience to their masters, resignation to
their condition, of conversion, of religion, of joining their pious masters
in prayer, that by getting an interest in the merits of the Redeemer they
would be happy in this world and happy in that day when the Lord should
judge the quick and the dead." Nevertheless, a grand jury saw fit to "put
the preacher upon his trial for the monstrous offense of maliciously and

wickedly endeavoring to incite the slaves of Maryland to insurrection and rebellion."

Gruber was released on bail of one hundred dollars (plus four hundred dollars for "security"), and his case was transferred from Washington to Frederick County. He surrendered for trial on 1 March 1819. Some who testified against him insisted that his sermon had not only condemned slavery but logically (some even said explicitly) seemed to justify actual rather than merely spiritual resistance. Witnesses for the defense testified otherwise; Gruber, they said, had carefully refrained from such advocacy. On the contrary, he had urged resignation, passivity, and obedience, with final trust in a just and rewarding Lord.

Chief attorney for the defendant was none other than Roger B. Taney, a future chief justice of the U.S. Supreme Court. He said the case was unprecedented in Maryland law, that to affirm slavery as evil was no more than a commonplace and that the writings of Thomas Jefferson himself abounded in such descriptions. But his client had not advocated conspiracy or sedition; he had not delivered his sermon as part of a criminal plot and therefore had no criminal intent. The essence of Taney's defense was a substantive one, not a technical one; he at the time clearly agreed with Gruber's evaluation of slavery, although precisely how to eliminate the sin he did not know. Indeed, Taney said, as the law now stood, "Any man has a right to publish his opinions on that subject whenever he pleases." Furthermore, he added, "we are prepared to maintain the same principles, and to use, if necessary, the same language here in the temple of justice, and in the presence of those who are the ministers of the law."

The prosecution, in closing comments to the jury, admitted that it believed "from the evidence, there was no crime committed"; Roger Taney offered some concluding remarks—only briefly summarized—and the jury returned a verdict of not guilty.

In a later biographical sketch, Gruber quoted passages from the Bible that he believed clearly condemned slavery; he concluded therefrom that "traffic in slaves is totally irreconcilable with the principles of justice and humanity—not to say Christianity." He affirmed that he had preached no sedition, although he added, "I have heard of Republican slave-holders, but I understand no more what it means than Sober Drunkards." Gruber concluded, "Some have been in hopes that I had learned a useful lesson in my trial." He had not yet learned, however, "to call *good evil,* or *evil good.*" "While I keep my senses," he said, "I shall consider *involuntary perpetual slavery* miserable injustice; a system of *robbery and theft.*"[4]

Similarly, the same year of Gruber's trial, a grand jury in Howard

County, Missouri, indicted a white man named Humphrey Smith. The charge again was verbally inciting slave rebellion, but the outcome of this case is not known.[5]

In the late 1820s, the encouragement of slave rebels by the antislavery effort became more highly organized, urgent, and national in scope. Free black people in the North led this effort, developing a newspaper, a Colored Association, and an anticolonization movement, and issuing the extraordinary *Appeal to the Colored Citizens of the World* (Boston, 1829) by David Walker. During these years, also, Benjamin Lundy undertook his important work and influenced Garrison, who by 1829 was concentrating on Abolitionism.

Walker's pamphlet, which contains every significant argument and feature of Abolitionism (even its culmination—the advocacy of militant resistance), was widely distributed, although few copies survived the systematic destruction of the dangerous work on the part of the authorities. Walker, living in the port of Boston, personally helped disperse the pamphlet. Precisely how many copies were made is not known, but since it went through three printings, the total must have been several hundreds and possibly a few thousands. Its distribution throughout the South caused consternation. It was also the subject of nationwide discussion, and, indeed, it had a lasting impact to the Civil War.[6] Within the slave states, its possession and/or distribution was a serious criminal offense.

Governor John Forsyth of Georgia informed the state legislature in December 1829 that the pamphlet had reached free blacks and slaves in that state. He accompanied this news with a reminder to the legislators of the "late fires in Augusta and Savannah" and a slave conspiracy in Georgetown, South Carolina. Governor Forsyth added that the mayor of Savannah had informed him that the city's police had recently seized sixty copies of the inflammatory *Appeal.* He, the governor, said that he had been told the pamphlets had been brought by the steward of a vessel— a white man—and by him turned over "to a negro preacher for distribution." It is likely that arrests occurred as a result of these events, although confirmation has not been found. The Savannah mayor wrote to Harrison Gray Otis, mayor of Boston, asking that the latter prohibit Walker's activity. Otis in turn had an emissary get the facts from Walker; he was told that Walker had indeed sent the pamphlets and that he intended to continue to do so. Boston law being what it was, Otis could do no more than warn ships' captains sailing out of the port to be alert to seditious cargo; he so informed the Georgia official.

A white printer in Milledgeville, Georgia, was accused in February 1830 of introducing the pamphlet into the state; this was Elijah H. Burritt, brother of the famous Elihu Burritt, linguist and pacifist. According to Merle Curti, Elihu Burritt's biographer, Elijah "was finally forced to flee for his life in the middle of the night when a hostile mob attacked his dwelling." That he safely reached the North is certain, since in July 1832 a subscription to the *Liberator* in his name was entered; the later career of this political refugee is not known.

The mayor of Richmond, Virginia, reported in January 1830 the finding of the pamphlet in the home of a recently deceased free black. In the same year and city, Thomas Lewis, another free black person, was found to possess thirty copies of the bombshell. Lewis's fate is not on record; it could not have been pleasant. William H. Pease and Jane H. Pease have published evidence of the discovery of the pamphlet in Charleston, South Carolina, in March 1830. In this case a culprit was discovered— Edward Smith, a white man who served as steward on the *Columbo* out of Boston. He confessed his action and on 11 May a grand jury indicted him. On 17 May he was tried, found guilty of "seditious libel," and, five days later, sentenced to a year in jail and a fine of one thousand dollars. The later life of Smith is also unknown.[7]

A similar incident occurred in New Orleans in 1830. In May, one James Smith was convicted of circulating the *Appeal.* He was sentenced to one year in prison; the relatively light sentence indicates he was probably not black. In his memoirs, the eminent Abolitionist the Reverend Samuel J. May declared that two missionaries to the Cherokee Indians in Georgia— named Worcester and Butler—"were maltreated and imprisoned in 1829 or 1830, for having one of Walker's pamphlets, as well as for admitting some colored children into their Indian school."[8]

Walker's pamphlet was discovered repeatedly in his native state and at a time when evidences of a slave disaffection were especially marked. Copies were uncovered, for instance, not only in his home city of Wilmington but also in Fayetteville, Chapel Hill, Newborough, and Hillsborough. A free black person in Wilmington brought the police, in August 1830, a copy of the *Appeal.* Apparently this led to the arrest of an unnamed slave suspected of being a distributor. Although the police interrogated him, he refused to implicate others.

Meanwhile, it became the turn of William Lloyd Garrison to taste prison. This resulted from Garrison's role as Lundy's junior editor of the *Genius of Universal Emancipation,* being published in Baltimore. Both Lundy and Garrison had ample opportunities, in their positions, to witness personally the cruelty of slavery and, in particular, of the auctions and coffles marking the slave trade—so important a part of the port's business.

Lundy, late in the 1820s, had denounced Baltimore's leading slave trader, Austin Woolfolk, for conducting the foul business; as a result Woolfolk attacked and severely beat him. Lundy sued for damages and was awarded one dollar—this munificent sum, said Judge Nicholas Brice, because Lundy's language had, quite understandably, provoked Woolfolk.

It was this judge who presided at the 1830 trial for libel brought by another, less notorious, slave trader named Frances Todd, who, as it happened, was a native of Garrison's hometown, Newburyport, Massachusetts. In the *Genius* for 13 November 1829, Garrison revealed that Todd's ship had transported seventy-five (actually eighty-three) slaves to the New Orleans market. The next week Garrison added further details and offered the opinion that Todd should be "*sentenced to solitary confinement for life*" for conducting such a business, that, in fact, at the proper time, Todd should "*occupy the lowest depths of perdition.*"

A libel suit was filed by Todd, and the trial commenced on 1 March. Garrison was defended with great vigor, and without charge, by an attorney named George Mitchell. The court pronounced Garrison guilty and sentenced him to pay a fine of fifty dollars plus costs (coming altogether to one hundred dollars). Of course, Garrison had no such sum and was sent to jail. While there he wrote poetry, many letters, and a brief pamphlet, and sent appropriate communications to the judge, the prosecuting attorney, Todd, and the press.

Notice was taken of his case by at least one hundred newspapers; Garrison in turn received many letters and was visited by slave traders (come to purchase incarcerated fugitive slaves) with whom fierce arguments developed. The pamphlet account of his trial was read by the New York reformer and philanthropist Arthur Tappan, who sent Lundy the required one hundred dollars which freed Garrison after forty-nine days in jail; thus began the two men's lifelong connection—also with Arthur's brother, Lewis—in the Abolitionist movement.

A civil suit entered by Todd against Garrison remained pending; Todd promised to drop the suit if Garrison apologized. He refused and chose instead to move to Boston, outside the jurisdiction of the honorable Judge Brice. Garrison did not return until April 1865 when, as the honored guest of a transformed U.S. government, he visited Baltimore—and found that the building that had served as his prison had been torn down. The Baltimore period, with its sights of slavery, its justice, and its jails, was an important component of Garrison's revolutionary education.[9]

Although the Garrison case is well known, another journalist, much more obscure, was suffering imprisonment also in 1830. Very little more than this is known, except that the locale was New Orleans, and the journalist-publisher was one Milo Mowrer whose paper was called the *Liberalist.* He was jailed for having circulated "a seditious and inflammatory handbill among the colored people"; there are no further details. [10]

Among the more notable struggles early in the history of Abolitionism was that revolving about Prudence Crandall of Canterbury, Connecticut, and her effort to maintain a school for black female youngsters. As a young woman of twenty-seven, a Quaker, and a graduate of the Friends' Boarding School in Providence, she began teaching in Plainfield in 1830. She then was invited by well-off women to open a school in Canterbury; moving to that town, she started a "select school" in a home purchased for that purpose in 1831.

According to a letter written by her on 7 May 1833 after her "celebrated case" had begun (and published in the *Liberator,* 25 May), at the time she opened her school, she had had no contact with Abolitionism. It happened, however, that she employed a black domestic helper known as Marcia. This young woman was engaged to a Charles Harris whose father, William Harris, served as one of the many black agents of Garrison's *Liberator.* Marcia brought that seditious sheet into Crandall's home. The latter, already convinced of the sinfulness of slavery, found Garrison's paper persuasive; it moved her to consider how she might contribute to the struggle.

A friend of Marcia's, named Sarah Harris, often visited the Crandall home; she was the daughter of William Harris and was at least as anxious as her father to advance the cause of equality. In September 1832, Sarah Harris asked Prudence Crandall to accept her as a pupil; the latter made no reply at first. After Harris repeated her request (more than once apparently and emphasizing her own desire, according to Crandall's letter to the *Liberator,* "to get a little learning, enough if possible to teach colored children"), Crandall decided to teach her. At the beginning of this extraordinary venture, there seems to have been no objection from the other students. But within a relatively short time, reverberations were heard from some of the parents; the wife of the Episcopal clergyman in the town "told me," Prudence Crandall wrote to Garrison, "that if I continue the colored girl in my school, it could not be sustained." Crandall announced to this lady her historic resolve: "I replied to her, *That it might sink, then, for I should not turn her out!*"

The children and their teacher persevered for weeks. Stores were closed to them, services (even medical) were denied them, and transportation withheld; rioters harassed them, the home-school was set afire, windows broken, and the well putrefied. A special law was passed prohibiting education of out-of-state black children. This finally succeeded: Crandall was tried, found guilty, spent a day and night in jail (in a cell recently occupied by a murderer), and was freed on a technicality.

Her work, however, seems to have terminated not because of this experience but because of her decision, in the summer of the same year, 1834, to marry a Baptist clergyman, the Reverend Calvin Philleo. A few days after their marriage in September 1834, the newlyweds' home was again severely damaged. The school was closed and the students sent home, and shortly thereafter Mr. and Mrs. Philleo went to his hometown of Ithaca, New York. They later moved to Illinois and then to Kansas. Prudence survived her husband by some sixteen years; she died in Elk Fall, Kansas, 28 January 1890. During her last four years she had the satisfaction of receiving an annual stipend of four hundred dollars by way of an apology from Connecticut. She remained—especially after Philleo's death—radically committed and quite articulate.

Her case attracted the ardent support of black and white Abolitionist activists, as well as international attention. Thus like all the excesses of reaction, the Prudence Crandall case boomeranged; it did not intimidate movement activists but rather helped unite and invigorate them.

The expulsion from the South of whites accused of antislavery views or actions continued. Often little more than a few bare facts are available, as in the cases of the Reverend Joel Parker, hanged in effigy in New Orleans and driven out in 1834, and the Unitarian minister George Frederick Simmons who was similarly dealt with in 1836 in Mobile, Alabama.[12] In 1835 two white men referred to simply as Fuller and Bridges, from Illinois, entered Missouri and helped several slaves escape. Posses pursued and caught them; all were returned to St. Louis. Some thought seems to have been given to hanging the white men at once, but this was reconsidered. Both were lashed and driven out of Missouri; the fate of the fugitive slaves was not recorded.[13]

A free black, Francis J. McIntosh, accused of killing a white man, was burned alive in St. Louis in April 1836, and threats were directed against Marion College in Palmyra, Missouri. The Reverend David Nelson, who was acting with Theodore D. Weld's guidance as an antislavery organizer, was driven from the state. The McIntosh lynching and the forced exile of Nelson were closely connected with the developing militancy of Elijah P. Lovejoy, whose martyrdom in 1837 we shall return to.

Numerous reports of slave unrest, outbreaks, and mass flights in much of the South marked the years 1835–36. In several cases whites as well as free blacks were implicated. Mississippi especially was the locale of mass executions of slaves, and whites, too, were lashed and hanged in this state. Others met similar fates in Virginia, Georgia, and South Carolina.

The mob scenes, particularly the events in Mississippi, the lynching of McIntosh in Missouri, and the martyrdom of Lovejoy in Illinois (the latter case was alluded to although the martyr's name was not mentioned), evoked a major address, "The Perpetuation of Our Political Institutions," delivered in Springfield, Illinois, on 27 January 1838 before a lyceum by Abraham Lincoln, then a member of the state legislature. The events in Mississippi and St. Louis, were, he said, "perhaps the most dangerous in example and revolting to humanity." After expanding on the Mississippi events, Lincoln devoted a paragraph to the killing of the free black man, McIntosh. Surely this is one of the earliest, if not the very first, public denunciation by a young American politician of the recurring violence. Lincoln invited his audience to turn its attention

to that horror-striking scene at St. Louis. A single victim was only sacrificed there. His story is very short; and is, perhaps, the most highly tragic, of anything of its length, that has ever been witnessed in real life. A mulatto man, by the name of McIntosh, was seized in the street, dragged to the suburbs of the city, chained to a tree, and actually burned to death; and all within a single hour from the time he had been a freeman, attending to his own business and at peace with the world.[14]

While such scandals recur, he said, throwing printing presses into rivers, shooting editors, and lynching people "at pleasure, and with impunity, this government cannot last." He continued by remarking that *no* provocation justified mob law and referred explicitly to the Abolitionist movement. If it is right, support it, he said, if it is wrong, prohibit it by law. But under no circumstances, said Lincoln—unlike President Andrew Jackson and Senator John C. Calhoun—must we excuse, palliate, let alone justify mob law, as when the mail was burned in Charleston in 1835.

Among the tribulations Abolitionists endured in the 1830s was the celebrated case of Amos Dresser. Dresser, a law student rebel who had served as a teacher among blacks in Cincinnati, went South with the purpose, apparently, of visiting a relative in Mississippi. His reputation having preceded him, he was apprehended by one of the ubiquitous vigilante committees—this one composed of sixty men in Nashville, Tennessee. Antislavery literature was said to be among his belongings; these were publicly burned. He was sentenced to twenty lashes which were administered in the public square by an employee of the city. Dresser was then tarred and feathered and driven out of the South. Pamphlets telling of this case were promptly printed in New York in 1836 and others were issued as late as 1849 in Oberlin, Ohio.

In June 1836 a student at the Princeton Theological Seminary, Aaron W. Kitchell, was seized by a mob in Hillsborough, Georgia, and accused of anti-slavery sympathies. He was also lashed and tarred and feathered and driven out.[15]

Another 1836 case, rivaling that of Dresser for notoriety, involved Reuben Crandall, brother of Prudence. This case actually began in August 1835 when Reuben was jailed in Washington, D.C., on the charge of "publishing seditious libel by circulating the publications of the American Anti-Slavery Society," to quote the title of the pamphlet (New York, 1836) detailing his trial. Reuben Crandall, a physician, was in the District of Columbia at the invitation of the Washington Medical College to lecture on botany. Although related to the notorious Prudence Crandall, the evidence is mixed as to whether or not he sympathized with her efforts. No proof was offered of his acting on behalf of any organized antislavery group. Apparently his name was enough to assure surveillance; the latter resulted in the discovery, it was alleged, of antislavery literature in his luggage, some of which was marked in an unknown hand, "Read and distribute."

This was sufficient to bring his indictment, and he was lodged in jail from August 1835 until mid-April 1836 when his trial commenced. The U.S. attorney for the district was Francis Scott Key—author of the national anthem and brother-in-law of Roger B. Taney. Key argued the criminality of Abolitionism as such and distinguished it from mere antislavery sentiment. The awful purpose of the former, said Key, was to actually *free* black people, to eliminate discrimination against them, indeed, he told the jury, "to associate, and amalgamate with the negro." Fatal, however, to Key's case was the fact that he could not show Crandall's *membership* in the Abolitionist movement nor his agency for it. The jury acquitted him, but within weeks the toll of his prolonged incarceration had resulted in his death.[16]

Abolitionism's revolutionary quality is demonstrated not only by the existence of mob and vigilante activities but also by the pleadings of learned counsel—such as the creator of the national anthem—seeking to suppress it as indeed revolutionary. Further, states enacted resolutions like that of South Carolina's on 16 December 1835, requesting nonslave-holding states to "promptly and effectually suppress all those associations within their respective limits, purporting to be abolition societies." North Carolina, Alabama, Virginia, and Georgia in the next months adopted similar resolutions; North Carolina on 19 December urged legislation making it a penal offense to print anything that "may have a tendency to make our slaves discontented." The intent was to make the nonslaveholding states as enthralled as was slave territory.[17] Congress did gag itself in this manner, of course, beginning in 1836, and it took a fierce struggle of seven years—led by a former president of the United States—to break the fetters.

The Reverend John B. Mahan, minister of the Methodist Episcopal church in Sardinia, Ohio, was arrested in September 1838 on the order of the governor because Kentucky's governor had requested this on suspicion that the minister had assisted fugitive slaves, although it was admitted that he had last been in Kentucky eighteen years before. Mahan was actually extradited and held in jail in Kentucky, but a jury acquitted him late in November 1838.[18]

Earlier, George Storrs, also a Methodist preacher, and an agent for the American Anti-Slavery Society, was forbidden by police authorities to speak in New Hampshire and was arrested while in the pulpit in Pittsfield in March 1836. He was tried and sentenced to three months' hard labor, although contemporary records do not confirm whether he actually served the sentence. There is also evidence that a George Rye, of Woodstock, Virginia, was convicted and fined for sedition—affirming antislavery views—in 1837.

The late Russell B. Nye, in his valuable study of the impact of slavery upon civil liberties first published in 1948, asked why it was that various pre–Civil War reform activities such as "prison reform, prohibition of alcoholic beverages, women's rights, or any other reform could be preached without meeting violent opposition, but that antislavery agitation was immediately to be put down?" The answer is that in their time the other efforts (including even "women's rights" as understood then) were not truly revolutionary as was the Abolitionist movement.[19] This can explain the martyrdom incurred by Abolitionists and the concerted mob activities, North and South, that always challenged the movement. Mob violence, carefully orchestrated by the "best" elements, as we have seen, came in tides—higher in the 1830s and 1850s, and lower at other intervals—but always a serious threat, albeit one that did not succeed.

Repeated assaults by organized mobs composed of community leaders resulted in the destruction of James G. Birney's *Philanthropist* in Cincinnati in 1836 and Elijah P. Lovejoy's *Observer* in Alton, Illinois, the next year. The former was destroyed, after several warnings and minor assaults, on 30 July 1836. The paper was reestablished under the able editorship of Gamaliel Bailey, but it was twice destroyed again. Finally, in 1847 Bailey went to Washington to edit the influential antislavery paper, the *National Era*. A result of the assaults upon the *Philanthropist* was to bring the then young attorney Salmon P. Chase—later governor of Ohio, member of Lincoln's cabinet, and chief justice of the U.S. Supreme Court—into the antislavery struggle.

Somewhat similar were the assaults upon the Reverend Lovejoy's *Observer,* first in St. Louis and then in Alton. His principled defense of freedom of the press was as magnificent and thorough as his excoriation of slavery and lynch law. Facing a "distinguished" mob and acting in defense of his press (twice before destroyed) with the blessing of the mayor, Lovejoy killed one of the mob before himself falling as a martyr. As the Birney case recruited Chase, so the Lovejoy case recruited Wendell Phillips—also then a young attorney—to the Abolitionist cause as well as John Brown. Thus was repeated the boomerang effect of reaction's barbarism, so vital an element in the final destruction of slavery.[20]

In June 1837, Marius R. Robinson, one of Weld's students at Lane, denounced slavery in a lecture at Berlin, Ohio. He was waylaid the next day, tarred and feathered, beaten, and dumped for dead several miles out of town. He never fully recovered his health, but his devotion and importance to the struggle remained undiminished. For several years, beginning in 1845, he was editor of the potent *Anti-Slavery Bugle,* published in Salem, Ohio.[21] In all these cases as well as in many others, no one was ever arrested, let alone convicted of any crime.

Two slave uprisings aboard ships produced crops of prisoners and significant political results. On board an international slave trader, the *Amistad,* operated illegally out of Cuba, the approximately 150 slaves, led by a man named Cinque, rebelled in 1839, took control of the ship after inflicting some casualties, and tried to sail for Africa. They failed, were seized off the Long Island coast, and spent long weeks in prison. The case reached the Supreme Court after Abolitionists took up the slaves' cause. The federal government sought the severest punishment, but the chief counsel for the defense, John Quincy Adams, was especially persuasive. In 1841, the rebels were declared free, having acted in defense of their liberty against illegal profiteers.

In the same year as this triumph, another successful slave uprising, led by a man named Madison Washington, rocked the nation. This occurred among some fifty slaves being transported in the domestic trader the *Creole,* traveling from Virginia to the New Orleans market. Here the slaves made it to the Bahamas—British territory where slavery had been abolished for several years. Again efforts by Washington to return the rebels to slavery failed, although Secretary of State Calhoun practically threatened England with war.[22]

These cases advanced concepts of the righteousness of militancy and resistance by the slaves. Joshua Giddings, representative from Ohio, insisted in Congress that rebelling slaves were doing no more than emulating Washington and Jefferson. John Quincy Adams suggested that in time of war between slaveholding and nonslaveholding states, the latter could well utilize liberation of slaves as a just war measure. Giddings was censured by the House and returned to his constituency, and then was triumphantly sent back to Congress. Adams's suggestion was explicitly noted during the Civil War and was a basis for the military order known as the Emancipation Proclamation.[23]

No doubt the most numerous political prisoners in the history of slavery were the many fugitives, or alleged fugitives, flung into jail in every slave state and the District of Columbia throughout the pre–Civil War era. One can hardly offer a guess of the numbers involved; certainly it reaches into the several thousands. Slaves who tried to flee commonly failed; they usually ended up in prison and, often after "correction," were returned to their masters. But also common, as in the case of Frederick Douglass, were repeated flight attempts followed finally by a successful escape. Southern papers, diaries, and plantation accounts are filled with reports of flight. Thus a study of fugitive slave advertisements in newspapers of the slave area from 1732 through 1790 disclosed a total of 7,846 men, women, and children so described; their incarceration was common.[24] The numbers did not decline as the decades went by. Thus, Representative Charles Miner of Pennsylvania, campaigning in Congress in the late 1820s to terminate slavery in the District of Columbia, affirmed on the basis of personal investigation that 290 alleged fugitives had been held in the district's public jail between 1824 and 1828. He declared he was convinced that many among them were actually free persons of color mistakenly or deceitfully imprisoned.

Ira Berlin has demonstrated the widespread incidence of arrest, imprisonment, and lashing of free black people throughout the slave South;

punishment often included sale into servitude for extended periods of time. He observes that, for example, in early 1842 the Baltimore Circuit Court "sold [an unspecified number of] free Negroes into servitude for up to five years for stealing shoes, a dress, a buggy harness, and a coffee pot." In 1860 the *Richmond Enquirer,* having in mind its local court, reported: "There was nothing of moment before His Honor yesterday. An average amount of niggerdom was ordered to be thrashed . . . for violations of the police regulations and city ordinance of so slight a character that it is hardly worthwhile publishing them in a newspaper." Berlin remarks that "most free Negroes dared not protest this harsh justice for fear of further antagonizing whites, but after being sentenced to death [in January 1861] one New Orleans free Negro blurted out what many felt, and boldly declared 'he was going to be hung because he was a negro.'"[25]

Arrests of persons seeking, or alleged to be seeking, to assist slaves to flee recurred regularly. In July 1841, for example, Alanson Work, a teacher at Mission Institute in Quincy, Illinois, and two students, James E. Burr and George Thompson, were arrested just across the border in Missouri for assisting slaves to flee. They were tried and convicted in September 1841. Sentenced to twelve-year jail terms to be served in Jefferson City, Missouri, they served several years until pardoned. Work was released in January 1845, Burr twelve months later, and Thompson in June 1846.[26]

One of the most extraordinary, and effective, among the antislavery prisoners was Calvin Fairbank (1816–98) born in New York and a student at Oberlin College in Ohio. At the age of twenty-one, Fairbank began his personal crusade by helping a slave flee from Virginia. Later he concentrated his efforts in Kentucky.

In Lexington, in 1844, he befriended Delia A. Webster, a Vermonter, who was then principal of a school for young women. Together they undertook in September to help liberate Lewis Hayden, Harriet Hayden, and their young son, in a coach driven by a black man known only as Isaac, apparently himself a slave. They made a two-day journey to Ripley, Ohio, where the Haydens were placed in the care of the well-known Abolitionist the Reverend John Rankin—himself originally from Tennessee.[27] While returning, Fairbank, Webster, and Isaac were caught. The driver was lashed and, under torture, confessed to their activities. They were tried separately and found guilty. Fairbank was sentenced to fifteen years, Delia Webster to two. She was released by the governor after serving six weeks and returned to Vermont. Fairbank, who was put to hard labor, became seriously ill. Governor John J. Crittenden pardoned him in August 1849, after he had served almost five years. Isaac's fate is not recorded.

Both Webster and Fairbank later returned to Kentucky separately, Webster in 1853. Using funds collectively raised for the purpose, she purchased a farm in Trimble County. Her declared intent was, by using only free labor, to demonstrate its superiority over slave labor. It was discovered, however, that significant numbers of slaves were disappearing from the area, and in 1854 she was placed in jail for refusing to pledge her departure. Released on a writ of habeas corpus, she was indicted as a slave stealer. Now Delia Webster took her permanent leave of Kentucky and continued speaking out against slavery from the soil of Indiana. Earlier—in November 1851—Fairbank was seized in Indiana by three Kentuckians and brought back to that state on the charge of slave stealing. Again he was sentenced to fifteen years imprisonment. His treatment in prison was very harsh; he suffered repeated whippings. He was finally pardoned—a mere skeleton—in 1864 through the intercession of President Lincoln.[28]

Lunsford Lane, a free black man of Raleigh, North Carolina, was accused by a vigilante mob in 1842 of antislavery sentiments. Although he was not murdered, he was beaten, tarred and feathered, and driven into exile.[29] Another free black man, Henry Boyer of New Bedford, Massachusetts, was sentenced in 1844 to four years in prison for being implicated in the effort of a fugitive slave, known as Rudder, to escape. This happened when the master, Gilbert Ricketson, of the schooner *Cornelia,* out of New Bedford, sailing north from Norfolk, Virginia, discovered the fugitive and returned him to Norfolk. Ricketson's steward, Henry Boyer, was arrested and convicted of assisting Rudder.[30]

An unusual case, also in 1844, attracted international attention and indignation. This involved a white man, John L. Brown, a native of Maine, who was arrested and at first sentenced to death for having assisted in the escape in South Carolina of a female slave—unnamed—who was reputedly his mistress. According to Betty Fladeland, this case and its sentence provoked mass protest meetings in several cities in England and Scotland and reached the floor of Parliament. She reports that Governor Hammond commuted Brown's sentence to thirty-nine lashes. But even this punishment seems not to have been inflicted, and Brown is said to have been released.[31]

The fate of Charles T. Torrey was much more somber than that of John L. Brown. Indeed his martyrdom evoked almost as much passion as did that of Lovejoy. Torrey, born in Massachusetts in 1813, studied at Yale and Andover Theological Seminary. In 1837 he served as pastor of a Congregational church in Providence, Rhode Island, but by 1839 he was a full-time antislavery lecturer. In 1842 he became editor of an antislavery paper, the Albany, New York, *Patriot.* While Torrey was in this post, a fugitive slave from Virginia prevailed upon him to assist in an effort to free his wife. The effort failed, but Torrey was not captured. This was the beginning of what became a full-time occupation; contemporaries credited him with assisting as many as four hundred slaves to flee.

Finally, in June 1844, Torrey was arrested in Baltimore; he failed in an effort to escape. In November he was tried for slave stealing and was sentenced to six years' hard labor. An offer of release was made if he would promise to abstain from assisting fugitives; he refused and began serving his sentence 30 December 1844. Sickly when he entered—this may have evoked the offer of release—he died of tuberculosis in the Baltimore prison on 9 May 1846. Torrey was refused funeral services in the Congregational church but was honored by black and white mourners in a public funeral held in Boston. His memory was evoked for years by comrades in the Abolitionist movement.

Torrey's life was of the stuff that results in legends, very much like Fairbank's. From the Baltimore jail on 9 July 1844, he wrote his wife: "Shall a man be put into the Penitentiary for doing good? That is the real question at issue, and it is one which will shake down the whole edifice of slavery, even if there were no other issue." His memoir illuminates the dire nature of imprisonment in the pre–Civil War South. He refers to about eighty fellow prisoners, the blacks among them "confined for loving freedom too well" and some other "free colored persons, shut up in prison to compel them to *prove* their legal title to be free." All such prisoners were political criminals; how many so suffered in the jails of slavery seems beyond count.[32]

A case involving two seamen, Captain Edward Sayres and his mate, Daniel Drayton, of the schooner *Pearl,* made headlines in the late 1840s. Both men regularly carried fugitive slaves as well as more legitimate cargo. Their most ambitious, and disastrous, journey began in April 1848 when they took aboard the *Pearl* over seventy fugitives—men, women, and children—coming from the region around the District of Columbia. So great a loss was keenly felt by the property owners; chase was undertaken and the schooner was captured on the Potomac on 18 April. The fugitives wanted to resist by force but were ordered by Sayres not to. After capture all narrowly escaped being lynched.

Sayres and Drayton were prosecuted by Francis Scott Key and convicted. The apprehended slaves had been jailed at once; their fate is not
clearly stated in contemporary sources. The defense of Sayres and Drayton was conducted—at Sen. Charles Sumner's urging—by Horace Mann.
Both men were heavily fined, but being unable to meet the levy, they
were jailed. A petition for their release with many signatures was turned
over to Sumner. The senator decided that a personal appeal to President
Fillmore would be more effective than bringing the matter to the Senate
floor. Fillmore yielded and pardoned them in August 1852 after both men
had been in prison for four years. Senator Sumner engaged a coach and
had them driven to Baltimore and then transported by train to safety in
the North. Drayton died in 1857, in his fifty-fifth year; when Sayres
passed away is not known.

Thanks to Harriet Beecher Stowe's *Key to Uncle Tom's Cabin,* the
names of some of the slaves aboard the *Pearl* are preserved. These were
the few it was possible to ransom—that is, to purchase their freedom
from the owners. They included the Edmundson family—Richard and his
two sisters, Mary, aged sixteen, and Emily, aged fourteen. The Abolitionist community managed to raise many hundreds of dollars to rescue
others, but they seem to have been sold South. All this, of course,
heightened the impact of the case upon public opinion. [33]

In July 1844 a ship's carpenter, Jonathan Walker, was arrested at sea
off the Florida coast when his sloop was stopped by naval authorities and
several fugitive slaves were discovered aboard. Walker (born in Cape
Cod, Massachusetts in 1799) was influenced by Benjamin Lundy in the
1830s, and lived and worked in various parts of the South for several
years. His antislavery views intensified. When he was visiting Pensacola
in June 1844, three slaves asked him to assist a larger group in an effort
to reach the Bahamas and freedom. Seven fugitives came aboard the
sloop and on 22 June the voyage began. It was early in July when they
were captured.

All were jailed; the fate of one of the captured fugitives is known—he
committed suicide. Walker experienced various punishments after several trials. He was pilloried for one hour while citizens pelted him with
garbage. He was branded on his hand by a federal marshal (Florida being
then a federal territory) with the letters *S.S.* (for slave stealer), although
this would seem to have been "cruel and unusual punishment." Unable
to pay heavy fines and court costs (his possessions were appropriated
by the owner of the fugitives), he served a total of eleven months confinement, almost all of it in chains.

There was some objection among local residents to the severity of his punishment. Friends wrote letters to him; British Abolitionists wrote to Florida officials; the governor of Massachusetts communicated with Florida's governor. But Walker's release came only after the necessary funds were raised in the North to pay his fine and court costs.

Walker, in describing his experience in a brief book published in 1845 by the American Anti-Slavery Society (with a preface by Maria Weston Chapman), not only offered the details of his own experiences but also told of witnessing repeated lashings of slaves and the daily jailings of fugitives. The vindictiveness of Walker's punishment and especially the branding (inflicted by the federal government and not just the government of a slave state) served again to stoke the flames of Abolitionism.[34]

Two outstanding Underground Railroad conductors, John Hunn and Thomas Garrett, underwent civil suits in a federal court in New Castle, Delaware, in May 1848. Both were Quakers living in Wilmington. Neither man actively sought to help slaves flee, but both freely gave sustenance, haven, and transportation to hundreds of fugitives, who either came through the assistance of such deliverers as Harriet Tubman or somehow made it on their own, especially from Virginia and Maryland. There is good evidence that Garrett helped about three thousand fleeing men, women, and children. In this period prior to the passage of the barbarous Fugitive Slave Act of 1850, harborers of escaped slaves often faced civil suits for damages filed by the slave owners.

This is what occurred in 1848 when Hunn and Garrett were tried before Chief Justice Taney with James A. Bayard as prosecutor (Bayard was elected to the U.S. Senate three years later). Eight black people were involved—a family consisting of a free father, a slave mother and six children. The seven slaves were claimed by two owners, E. N. Turner and E. T. Glanding; the court found in their favor to the tune of fines of $2,500 to be paid to Turner and $1,000 to Glanding—the payment of which brought both defendants near impoverishment. Garrett, on hearing the verdict, defended his behavior before Taney in an hourlong speech, in which he argued that Christ's teaching took precedence over Taney's court. Garrett's home for many years thereafter was guarded by a committee of blacks. When he died in 1871 all the surviving Old Guard Abolitionists from Lucretia Mott to Garrison and Phillips and William Howard Day offered eulogies, and black men were his pallbearers.[35]

A serious fugitive attempt, rising to the point of insurrection, occurred in Fayette County, Kentucky, in August 1848. About seventy-five slaves, many armed with guns and crude weapons and led by Patrick

(Edward J.) Doyle, set out for the Ohio River and liberty. Doyle was a student at Centre College in Danville; little more is known of his early life. A reward of $5,000 was offered for their interception, and scores of armed whites set out in pursuit. When they caught up with the fugitives, a pitched battle ensued. One of the fugitives and one of the pursuers were killed, and another among the latter was wounded. The flight continued; reinforcements came to the pursuers and another battle followed. Apparently all, or nearly all, those fleeing, including Doyle, were captured. Three of the black leaders, identified as Shadrack, Harry, and Prestley, were hanged. Doyle was held in the Lexington jail, tried, convicted, and sentenced to twenty years at hard labor. No further information about this extraordinary man has been found.[36]

In the summer of 1849 the Reverend C. W. Robinson of Shelby, Kentucky, was accused by the town's trustees of allowing certain black people—apparently slave and free—to participate in receiving instruction at his Sunday school. For this threat to security, the Reverend Mr. Robinson was cowhided—on a Sunday, at his school, by the town's sheriff.[37]

That same year Henry Brown had himself shipped, in a box of his design, by Adam Express from Richmond, Virginia, to the company's Philadelphia office. The building and shipping of the box out of Richmond was done by a white man, Samuel A. Smith, who made his living by selling shoes. When the Brown effort succeeded, Smith undertook the same task for two other Virginia fugitives, but the scheme was discovered. The fugitives were returned to an unknown fate, and Smith was sentenced to eight years in the penitentiary and a heavy fine. Thus stripped of his property, Smith was kept in chains in a four-by-eight-foot cell for five months and then permitted to join other prisoners. His unselfish behavior won him the favor of his jailers, and they actually tried to get him pardoned. They failed, however, and Smith served his full time.

He was finally released in June 1856 and went on to Philadelphia, accepting the ministrations and hospitality of James and Lucretia Mott and also of William Still. A mass meeting to honor him and raise funds for his sustenance was held by the black population in Philadelphia on 30 June 1856. They welcomed him—as the meeting resolved—"as a martyr to the cause of freedom." Smith married in Philadelphia and moved to upstate New York.[38]

A few years prior to Brown's sensational flight from Richmond, Leonard A. Grimes (1815–73), free-born in Leesburg, Virginia, was arrested in Richmond for assisting, in 1843, a family of eight to escape slavery.

Grimes served a two-year term in the Richmond jail and then went North. From late in 1845 until his death, Grimes served as the minister of the Twelfth Baptist Church in Boston. He was very active and militant in the ensuing struggles there, most notably in the celebrated case of Anthony Burns, of which more later.[39]

There are several contemporaneous references to southern prisons during the Abolitionist period in addition to those in the Fairbank book, noted earlier, which are germane to this account. Lydia Maria Child, in a letter from Boston, 22 November 1833, to her brother Convers Francis, stated that she had met with William Crawford (1788–1847), an English prison reformer, then serving as a commissioner to the United States for the London Prison Discipline Society. She wrote: "He tells harrowing stories of what he has seen at the South during his inspection of prisons there. Slaves kept in readiness to join their coffle were shut up in places too loathsome and horrid for the worst of criminals. He says had anyone told him such things as he has seen, he should have considered it excessive exaggeration."[40]

The well-known Samuel Gridley Howe visited parts of the South in 1841 to 1842, and his firsthand observations helped turn him against slavery. He made a point of visiting prisons; those in New Orleans impressed him as awful—"There are abominations which should bring down the fate of Sodom upon the city." In letters to Sumner and to Mann he told of sections of the jail reserved for black people; he saw "much that made me blush that I was a white man." He remarked especially the merciless lashing of a slave girl at the master's order.[41]

A description of Kentucky jails in the 1850s was offered by Thomas Brown and his wife. They were milliners; she tended a shop whiie he traveled as a salesman. In 1850 the family moved from Indiana to Henderson, Kentucky, where they continued their occupation. Later the same year, Thomas Brown was arrested and charged with being implicated in "aiding the slaves, who, to a great number had recently escaped from the counties of Henderson, Union, Davies and Hopkins." Brown affirmed his detestation of slavery but neither admitted nor denied implication in the escapes.

He was arrested again early in 1854 on another charge of helping slaves escape. His wife and children returned to Indiana, where she successfully reestablished a shop. Meanwhile, Brown was held in a jail in Morganfield, Union County, Kentucky. Mrs. Brown visited him there several times. Its entrance was through a trap door; she found her husband in a room sixteen by eighteen feet, together with two black men, both of them chained. The food was poor, sanitation nonexistent. It was cold in the winter and very hot in the summer. One of the black men, confined for the crime of arson, was executed. The other was a fugitive slave who refused to tell the jailers the name or whereabouts of his owner, although he told Brown he was from Alabama.

Brown was finally tried in April 1855, found guilty, and sentenced to two years' imprisonment. In May 1855 he began serving his time in Frankfort. Brown stated that others were jailed with him for the same crime; one he identified as a Kentuckian, "a mechanic, charged with giving a runaway something to eat." This person is not otherwise identified. Another, "a colored man, of Evansville, Indiana, [was] accused likewise of furnishing a meal to a brother in distress." This unnamed individual "died in prison, some time after receiving a severe blow from one of the keepers."

With Brown in this jail were Doyle and Fairbank, mentioned earlier. Of the latter, Brown wrote that he had by then served five years of his twenty-year sentence and was brutally treated—once receiving over a hundred lashes. "Mr. Fairbank is charged with no crime," said Brown; "he is accused of succoring, in their great distress, some of the Ethiopian sons and daughters of chivalrous Kentuckians."[42]

The decade of the 1850s witnessed the deepening crisis of the Union, brought on by the intensified panic of the slaveholding class. The expansionism consequent upon the Mexican War did not quiet national turmoil; on the contrary, that policy and how to deal with the new areas precipitated further ferment. Efforts at compromise—the hallmark of statesmanship—did not succeed.[43] The 1850 Compromise unsettled national politics rather than the reverse. The Fugitive Slave Act of that year, with its violation of elementary rights to trial by jury, confrontation of witnesses, and assumption of innocence, made militant antislavery partisans of those who—like Ralph Waldo Emerson—had tried to remain detached. Emerson entered in his journal: "This filthy enactment was made in the 19th century by people who could read and write. I will not obey it by God."[44] Enforcement efforts of the act induced in every case, whether successful or not, reactions costly—sometimes very costly—to the interests of the slave owners.

Nationally, the result was the fragmentation of the political structure with clearer and clearer fissures appearing vis-à-vis slavery and its expansion. Just when the slave owners' interests demanded the nationalization of slavery and at least acquiescence in its rationalization, socioeconomic forces were dictating otherwise, and worldwide forces were inducing a view of slavery as increasingly anachronistic.

Within the South, the decade witnessed not only increased slave unrest but also intensified dissatisfaction on the part of nonslaveholding whites. As the slave system's oligarchic tendencies intensified, the latter increasingly combined into groupings and parties reflecting class consciousness and, therefore, opposition to the continued domination, within the South, of the slaveholding class.

As repression—ideological, political and physical—intensified, resistance widened and deepened. The 1850s saw within the Abolitionist movement increasing ascendancy of the propolitical and proresistance forces as opposed to the pacifistic and anarchistic approaches that had tended to dominate the outlook of that movement in the 1830s and even the 1840s. Confrontation grew, coming to boiling points in the election years of 1856 and 1860 when the question of slavery or freedom became the only significant political question. [45]

What the Abolitionists called a new reign of terror began in the South and was accompanied by the marked sharpening of dramatic confrontations between the two systems in Congress, in the streets, and finally in the colossal symbol of John Brown. Martyrdom culminated with the latter, but scores of bodies—mostly of black people—swung from gallows before that Old Man went to his immortality. The struggles of the past, the developments they reflected and influenced, and the impact of the earlier passions combined to make possible Brown's moment and the phenomenal impact his immolation had upon the nation—and the world. A major part of Brown's genius was his knowledge that the time was ripe for him, that his blow would be mighty in history's scale if not in battle casualties, and that, if Virginia dared hang him, the world would be appalled, as Victor Hugo said, at Washington killing Spartacus.

Victim was piled on victim in the South in the 1850s. Other sources have presented the reality; here may be offered merely samples of the crop of political prisoners, refugees, and martyrs the decade produced, culminating in the Brown phenomenon. The main locale was the South itself, although—as shall be noted—the North, too, was the setting for memorable confrontations.

The 1850s witnessed slave unrest in the forms of individual assaults, maroon activity, flight, arson, conspiracy to rebel, and actual uprisings that rivaled the most notable high points of the past. In impact upon the slaveholding class, *in its perception,* often its panic—sometimes exaggerating if not simply inventing the peril—the decade was without equal.

The turmoil formed a main backdrop for the drama of secession; one sometimes suspects it was exaggerated or promulgated by partisans of secession for the worst possible motives. Some of the cases within the South that resulted in political prisoners and exiles may be offered as illustrative of the general conditions.

Attracting considerable notice was the case of William L. Chaplin (1796–1871), an attorney and Harvard graduate. His antislavery feelings induced him to assist, in 1850, the escape of two slaves in the nation's capital. Arrested, Chaplin was jailed in Rockville, Maryland, in August and remained incarcerated until late December 1850. At that time he was released on heavy bail for future trial; the bail was provided by Gerrit Smith. Chaplin chose to leave the court's jurisdiction and never was retaken.[46]

In 1850–51 many arrests and vigilante assaults recurred; the Reverend Jesse McBride was jailed in North Carolina for antislavery expressions and expelled; Elijah Harris, a schoolteacher was tarred and feathered in Clinton, South Carolina; a physician, Dr. Larkin B. Coles, was imprisoned in Columbia, South Carolina; the Reverend Edward Mathans was beaten and expelled from Richmond, Kentucky. In Grayson County, Virginia, in the fall of 1851, a local farmer, John Cornutt, was accused of antislavery sympathies. A mob estimated at two hundred demanded he renounce "abolitionism." Refusing, Cornutt was stripped and lashed until he promised to leave Virginia. His effort to sue in court was rebuffed.[47] That same year, in Warren County, Georgia, Nathan Bird Watson, described as a white mechanic, was expelled by a vigilante committee; the charge was that he had been spreading Abolitionist ideas among the slaves.[48]

A Mrs. Douglas, a white woman, was sentenced in 1853 to one month in prison in Norfolk, Virginia, and was subjected to paying a fine and court costs for the crime of "assembling with negroes to instruct them to read and write, and for associating with them in an unlawful assembly."[49] Four years later, a black man, Samuel Green of Maryland, who had purchased his freedom, was suspected of assisting the flight of slaves. In consequence his home was searched and much subversive literature—including *Uncle Tom's Cabin*—was discovered. He was tried for sedition, found guilty, and in April 1857, sentenced to ten years' imprisonment. He remained in jail until freed during the Civil War.[50]

Many black people throughout the South were arrested for the crime of seeking literacy. Not atypical was the report in the Richmond, Virginia, *Daily Dispatch,* 21 August 1858, of recent arrests of ninety black persons for such activity. The paper urged severe punishment. "Scarcely a week passes," it said, "that instruments of writing, prepared by negroes, are not taken from servants [slaves] in the streets, by the police."

The 1850s were marked, also, by dramatic escapes or near-escapes, often accompanied by violence and attracting national attention. Thus, in 1853, an escaped slave known as William Thomas, was working as a waiter in Wilkes-Barre, Pennsylvania. Three U.S. deputy marshals tried to seize him, but Thomas broke away and, though wounded, pressed ahead and flung himself into the Susquehanna River. Summoned to surrender, he refused and stayed in the river perhaps an hour while the officers tried to kill him. Finally an enraged crowd—appalled at the cruelty—drove the officers away. With the aid of black friends, William Thomas made good his escape.[51]

In 1857 another dramatic, violent slave escape attracted national notice. This involved Addison White found hiding at the farm of Udney H. Hyde in Merchanicsburg, Ohio, by five pursuing Kentuckians assisted by two U.S. marshals. White, who was armed, resisted and wounded a marshal before fleeing. The white sympathizer, Hyde, was arrested and was charged with aiding a fugitive; Hyde countersued for invasion of his property. When citizens raised one thousand dollars to compensate Addison White's owners, the suits were dropped.[52]

In the North defiance of the Fugitive Slave Act took the form not only of reinforced state personal liberty laws but also of concerted mass action—black and white—of extraordinary militancy. Among the best known of these cases were those occurring in 1851, especially the case in Boston in April of Thomas Sims who, despite tremendous efforts, was returned to his owner in Georgia; the Christiana, Pennsylvania, slave rescue case, which involved a pitched battle, a trial for treason, and the acquittal of the defendants (with the young attorney Thaddeus Stevens being part of the defense team); and the successful Jerry rescue case in Syracuse in October.[53]

Thereafter not a year went by without some outstanding rescue case. Their impact brought to the movement as activists not only figures like Emerson and Henry David Thoreau but literally thousands of folks who had conscientiously tried to pursue their own lives without political "distractions." These cases—like those of Sims and Anthony Burns in 1854—also brought indictments against figures like Theodore Parker, Thomas Wentworth Higginson, and Wendell Phillips. Successful defenses in such cases—those mentioned never went to trial—reached tens of thousands through speeches, pamphlets, newspapers, and books.[54]

Their impact, too, was to intensify militancy in the Abolitionist ranks, so that by the 1850s a person like Douglass was openly advocating slave rebellion and Phillips was saying that a slave he pitied but a slave rebel he admired. Even a pacifist like Garrison, while retaining his principles, was pointedly referring to the hypocrisy of a nation that immortalized a militant revolutionary like Washington and denounced black rebels whose cause for rebellion was clearly greater than that which had moved the general.

In the Sims case and that of Anthony Burns, a determined federal government employed naval vessels, Marines, cannon, and artillery re-inforcements to ensure the return of fugitives to their owners, and chains were used to barricade the courthouse. All this served as dramatic illus-tration of "what the North had to do with slavery" and the direct involve-ment of the federal government in its maintenance. The impact of such cases upon public opinion was immense.

In addition to these cases, those of Passmore Williamson and Margaret Garner were perhaps of equal impact. In many respects the Williamson case, although less well known than some of the others, had greater theoretical significance. The case developed in 1855. Its principal was a black woman originally known only as Jane and later, after she gained freedom, as Jane Johnson. She was the slave of Col. John H. Wheeler of North Carolina, at the time U.S. minister to Nicaragua.

Colonel Wheeler, having been in New York, was on his way to Wash-ington prior to undertaking his diplomatic duties. For convenience, he took a domestic slave, Jane. She was accompanied by her two sons aged eleven and seven (a younger child considered an encumbrance by the colonel had been sold back in North Carolina). While in New York, Jane managed to whisper to a black woman and later a black man that she was a slave and desired freedom. Word of this was relayed to William Still, the black director of the Philadelphia office of the Underground Railroad.

Still informed Passmore Williamson, a white man and secretary of the Anti-Slavery Society office in Philadelphia. Williamson went to the ship docked in that city, which carried Jane, and the boys, and the colonel, and informed her that since the three of them had been brought volun-tarily onto the free soil of Pennsylvania, they were as free as he was. The colonel objected, expostulated with Jane, and sought to persuade her to stay. Several black deckhands and stevedores were attracted to the scene; the mother and her children disembarked. Waiting below was Still with horse and carriage, and the party left.

Passmore Williamson was arrested for violating the rights of Colonel

Wheeler and ordered in federal court by Judge John K. Kane (1795–1859)—notorious for his proslavery attitude—to bring forward Wheeler's property. Williamson, protesting truthfully that he did not possess the "property" and never had and had no knowledge of their whereabouts, did not obey Judge Kane. For this he was sentenced to jail for contempt of court. Williamson remained in prison for over one hundred days, while an outcry resounded in the nonslave states. Finally, in the face of this pressure and the reality of Williamson's inability to produce the "property," he was released.

Meanwhile, Still and five black men, who had seen to the "properties" disembarking, were tried separately for "assault and battery"; they had restrained Colonel Wheeler when he had tried to prevent his loss of the mother and children. The trial of the six men—Still, William Curtis, James P. Braddock, John Ballard, James Martin, and Isaiah Moore—was in a state court, and prosecutor and judge, Still stated in his account of the episode, sympathized with the defendants. Four were acquitted, and two, Ballard and Curtis, served one week in jail. Helping the defense was the sensational, and heroic, appearance as a witness of the mother, Jane Johnson, who came down from Massachusetts and was guarded by black and white sisters, including Lucretia Mott and Sarah Pugh.

Judge Kane, in justifying his imprisonment of Williamson, insisted that black people had, at best, only a defective kind of citizenship and added that property in slaves differed in no way from other property. Therefore its movement anywhere within the United States could not be inhibited constitutionally—anticipating by two years the Dred Scott decision. Kane remarked that he offered no opinion as to Williamson's motives—"I have nothing to do with them." They might, added the judge, "give him support and comfort before an infinitely higher tribunal," but this was irrelevant. Kane insisted it was wrong "to regard slave property as less effectively secured" by the Constitution than any other property. No one, therefore, could properly "single out this one sort of property from among all the rest and deny to it the right of passing over its soil." Furthermore, he agreed with the view that "if public opinion is suffered to prostrate the laws which protect one species of property, those who lead the crusade against slavery may at no distant day find a new one directed against their lands, their stores, and their debts."

Judge Kane warned of the "danger" of "the indulgence of the humane and benevolent feelings of our nature"; such "indulgence" lead some of us to "forget the first duty of citizens of a government of laws," namely, "obedience to its ordinances." How neatly put, again, was the revolutionary essence of Abolitionism.[55]

Equally dramatic and effective in swaying public opinion was the case revolving around Margaret Garner. In January 1856, seventeen slaves in Boone County, Kentucky, set out in an attempt at mass flight; some being armed, this amounted to an insurrectionary effort. Those fleeing consisted of Simon Garner, his wife, Mary Garner, and their son, Simon, Jr., the slaves of James Marshall. Simon, Jr.'s wife, Margaret Garner, and their four children were owned by Archibald K. Gaines of a nearby plantation. In the evening of Sunday, 27 January, the Garner group, plus nine other slaves from nearby plantations fled.

They made their way by horse-drawn sleigh along icy roads to the Ohio River, a distance of some sixteen miles. Here the sleigh was abandoned and all seventeen (including a pregnant Margaret Garner) walked across the frozen Ohio into Cincinnati. The group then separated, and nine made it safely to Canada. The Garners headed for a free black person, Elijah Kite, apparently a relative. Kite welcomed them and hurried on alone to the intrepid Levi Coffin for help. Coffin offered directions; Kite returned but almost at once a fugitive-hunting party had surrounded his house. Apparently someone had betrayed the fleeing group.

The hunters consisted of Gaines, accompanied by the son of James Marshall—the other slave owner involved—and several U.S. marshals. The slaves resisted, but the attacking force was too numerous and broke into the barricaded home. Simon Garner, Jr., continued fighting and wounded one of the marshals, but the cause was lost. Then it was that Margaret Garner killed one of her children, a girl, and wounded others, all the while calling on Mary to help kill the children. She could not; all were overpowered, Margaret Garner crying all the while that she wanted her children dead rather than returned to slavery. The description of Margaret Garner included mention of a scar running from her forehead to her cheekbone. When asked about its source, she replied, "White man struck me."

A legal battle royal then developed between Kentucky and Ohio with its personal liberty law and its Free-Soil governor, Salmon P. Chase, elected in 1855. The federal government, led personally by President Pierce, backed Kentucky and the Garners were returned to slavery, despite massive protests and demonstrations by black and white men and women, led in one case by Lucy Stone Blackwell. The federal government spent over $21,000 to return the Garners to slavery. As soon as

Gaines had them back in Kentucky, he sold them south, but the ship carrying them sank. Margaret Garner was rescued, but she managed first to drown one of her children. She was quoted in the contemporary press as rejoicing that still another of her children would not know slavery. She herself disappeared into continued bondage.

This case evoked the widest possible statewide and nationwide attention. Julius Yanuck, whose account of the Garner case is the best available, concluded by noting that after the death of the second child, "the angry state legislature enacted a law requiring state officers to take persons out of the possession of U.S. authorities upon the issuance of a state writ of habeas corpus." Further, the state legislature denounced the Fugitive Slave Law of 1850 as not only unconstitutional but as "repugnant to the plainest principles of justice and humanity."[56] Again, this case made Abolitionists of hitherto conscientious nonpartisans. Converted by its drama and horror, for example, was the Ohio attorney and future president Rutherford B. Hayes. "From this time forward," he vowed, "I will not only be a black Republican, but I will be a *damned Abolitionist.*"

Meanwhile one of the "damndest" of these, John Brown, had reached the conclusion that the time for talk had ended; action, the more dramatic the better, was now needed. Having gained experience in the Kansas civil war and having led out eleven slaves, successfully, in the dead of winter from Missouri to Canada, he began in 1857 to devote all his energies to the effort to "bring the war into Africa."

Chapter Nine

John Brown and Revolution

The apotheosis of revolutionary commitment, determining the basic nature of Abolitionism, was John Brown. Among white participants in the movement, Brown was extraordinary—perhaps unique—in the completeness with which he, his wife, Mary Brown, and their children shed concepts and feelings of white supremacy. This was the result of deliberate practice, so that, by word as well as by consistent deed, the Browns not only advocated but lived equality. The Browns, and especially John himself in his frequent travels, sought and earned the friendship of black people, meeting with them, praying with them, socializing with them, and jointly thinking out common problems.

Of modern historians—many of whom have hated Brown—the first to emphasize this feeling of identity that Brown achieved was W. E. B. Du Bois in his analytical biography published in 1909. There Du Bois observed: "John Brown worked not simply for the Black Man—he worked with them, and he was a companion of their daily life, knew their faults and virtues, and felt, as few white Americans have felt, the bitter tragedy of their lot."[1]

John Brown truly believed that all people were created in God's image and that black men and women were the brothers and sisters of those who were white. Brown actively sought out black people, lived among them, listened to them, learned from them. His friends and associates included Frederick Douglass, Harriet Tubman, Martin Delany, J. W. Loguen, Dr. and Mrs. J. M. Gloucester, Henry Highland Garnet, William Still, Harry Watson, and many others, as well as those who, at Harpers Ferry, pledged their lives to his leadership.

These black men and women manifested complete confidence in Brown; they believed him, accepted him, loved him as a brother. And Brown felt their enslavement as though it were his own; he frequently said this and often thought of what the enslavement of his wife and children would mean to him. He knew that what it would mean to him was what it really meant to black people. Thus, his hatred of slavery was fierce. He dedicated his life, from the 1840s, to its eradication. "I have only a short time to live—only one death to die," he wrote in his fifty-sixth year. "I will die fighting for the cause."

This was enough to earn the hatred of the ruling forces in the United States, as well as many of their later chroniclers. But, in addition, Brown grasped the connection between the fundamental character of black oppression and the nature of U.S. society. This was the source of his response, as he lay bleeding in the armory after Col. Robert E. Lee's Marines had smashed their way in, to the baiting reporter from the rabidly proslavery *New York Herald:* "You may dispose of me very easily; I am nearly disposed of now; but this question is still to be settled—this Negro question, I mean—the end of that is not yet." It explains, too, the last note he handed to a guard as he was led on 2 December 1859 to the gallows: "I John Brown am now quite *certain* that the crimes of this *guilty land will* never be purged *away,* but with Blood. I had *as I now think, vainly* flattered myself that without *very much* bloodshed it might be done."

Another central feature of John Brown's thinking was his militancy—his conception of slavery as a product of and exercise in violence on the part of the masters and his belief that therefore physical resistance by or on behalf of the slaves was not only just but necessary. Brown believed in the Declaration of Independence as completely as he believed in the Ten Commandments. To him, if the grievances of the colonists had justified armed resistance to the king's efforts at forcible suppression, then the slaves—with infinitely more awful grievances—were certainly justified in resorting to armed resistance.

To understand Brown and his impact upon his time, it is necessary not only to comprehend this militancy but also to understand that the concept of militancy—of the propriety and justice of armed resistance by the slaves—was widespread within the Abolitionist movement by the 1850s. Indeed, it had become a dominant view within the movement by the decade preceding the Civil War. This point is important in explaining the sensitivity of Brown: his conviction that the Harpers Ferry effort would electrify the country, would actually strengthen the foes of slavery, would gain the sympathy of major components of the American population—of course, among the black millions, but also among a significant proportion of the white multimillions.

Deep in the consciousness of those whites had always been the feeling that believing in the Declaration of Independence and abiding the existence of slavery was blatantly contradictory. The rationalization that made it possible to live with the contradiction was racism, the idea of the subhumanity of black people or, at least, their marked inferiority to white people. To justify slavery, it was necessary to develop the myth of the black peoples' docility, of their acceptance of slavery so that, uniquely, they embraced their servitude. John Brown, knowing black people and studying them, understood the myth was just that.

Although few, even among the white Abolitionists, had developed Brown's feeling of complete identity with the black people, many within the movement, including some on its fringes, by the late 1840s and 1850s had accepted if not embraced militant Abolitionism. For this reason, when Frederick Douglass had first met with Brown at his home in 1847, he was not startled when Brown placed the nub of his plan before him. Douglass stated that after a brief visit to Brown's business office, he returned home with him. Following dinner with the family, Douglass and Brown considered the latter's plan from eight in the evening to three the next morning.

The plan as then presented—and Brown said that developments in the country led him to believe that its time for implementation was not far off—was, Douglass felt, "very simple"; he thought it "had much to commend it." What was the plan? It was not, Douglass continued, one that "contemplate[d] a general rising among the slaves, and a general slaughter of the slave masters." He added in parentheses, "(an insurrection he thought would only defeat the object)."

Brown then called Douglass's attention "to a large map of the United States and pointed out to me the far-reaching Alleghenies, stretching away from the borders of New York into the Southern States." Brown believed they were placed there by God "to aid the emancipation of your race." In what way? Why, "they are full of natural forest, where one man for defense would be equal to a hundred for attack; they are also full of good hiding places where a large number of men could be concealed and baffle and elude pursuit for a long time." Brown, like Douglass, was familiar with the existence of maroons, that is, outlying pugnacious fugitive slaves who terrorized surrounding plantations. The hiding places in the mountains would be natural centers for bands of such resisters.

Brown told Douglass that he knew "these mountains well and could take a body of men into them and keep them there in spite of all the efforts of Virginia [note Brown's mention of the intended spot] to dislodge me." At first, he went on, he would pick "about twenty-five men and begin on a small scale, supply them arms and ammunition, post them in squads of five on a line of twenty-five miles." These groups would "busy themselves for a time in gathering recruits from the surrounding farms, seeking and selecting the most restless and daring."

Soon, he thought, he could gather a hundred stalwart men; properly trained, "they would begin work in earnest; they would run off the slaves in large numbers." The strong and brave among those would then enlarge the number of liberators and the area liberated; others would go North. In some cases slaveholders would face nightly visits, ordered to give up their slaves together with their best horses. If it then came to a fight, "he would of course do his best." Slavery, he reminded Douglass, in any case "was a state of war" and slaves had the right "to anything necessary" for their freedom. John Brown thought his scheme, when implemented "would weaken slavery in two ways"; it would make the "property" insecure and it would enliven antislavery agitation and lead to national measures to end it. Nat Turner, he pointed out, shook slavery in 1831; this plan could shatter it.

Douglass, in this discussion, did his part by "finding all the objections I could against it," but he does not specify any. He had already said, as has been noted, that the plan "had much to commend it." At any rate, from 1847 on, Douglass moved away not only from the pacifism of Garrison (he had already abandoned that) but also from a reliance upon political struggle (again contrary to Garrison) to an acceptance, and even an advocacy, of resistance by the slaves.[2]

John Brown had enunciated another important proposition when, early in 1851, he formed the League of Gileadites for the protection of fugitive slaves in Springfield, Massachusetts, then the hometown of the Browns. In what he called "Words of Advice," he penned these sentences which, in view of his own experience, have an extraordinary prophetic quality: "Nothing so charms the American people as personal bravery. . . . The trial for life of one bold and to some extent successful man, for defending his rights in good earnest, would arouse more sympathy throughout the nation than the accumulated sufferings of more than three millions of our submissive colored population."[3] Clearly, Brown's words of advice were not forgotten by him eight years later.

In his swing toward militant resistance, Douglass was typical of the

Abolitionist movement.[4] Ann Phillips, for example, militant wife of the radical Wendell Phillips, in a letter of 25 May 1854 to her friends, expressed a widely growing impatience: "We may as well disband at once if our meetings and papers are all talk and we never do anything *but talk.*"[5] Brown himself some years later left an antislavery meeting while it was still in session, complaining that it was nothing but talk, devoid of action.

Characteristic of the developments of the 1850s were these three statements:

- Frederick Douglass, speaking 11 May 1855 in New York City at a meeting of the National Council of the Colored People, said: "I would have you fight for your liberty when assailed by the slave hunter. This will gain you some respect. . . . Fear inculcates respect. *I would rather see insurrection for the next six months in the South than that slavery should exist there for [the] next six years.*"[6]

- Gerrit Smith, at a convention in Buffalo, 10 July 1856, assembled to consider the developments in Kansas, said: "There was a time when slavery could have been ended by political action. But that time has gone by—and, as I apprehend, forever. There was not virtue enough in the American people to bring slavery to a bloodless termination; and all that remains for them is to bring it to a bloody one."[7]

- Charles L. Remond spoke before a State convention of Massachusetts black people held in New Bedford in August 1858. He had been a devoted and effective Garrisonian for decades, which made more significant his remarks: "We must depend on our own self-reliance. If we recommend to the slaves in South Carolina to rise in rebellion, it would work greater things than we imagine. If some Black Archimedes does not soon arise with his lever, then there will spring up some Black William Wallace with his claymore, for the freedom of the black race." Remond then "moved that a committee of five be appointed to prepare an address suggesting to the slaves at the South to create an insurrection." This suggestion was rejected—as had been the similar suggestion, that Henry Highland Garnet had made fifteen years earlier—but it suggests the shift in Abolitionist feeling.[8]

Garrison himself observed this marked change in the Abolitionist movement. At the twenty-fifth anniversary meeting of the American Anti-Slavery Society in New York City in May 1858, he said, "A sad change has come over the spirit of anti-slavery men, generally speaking. We are growing more and more warlike, more and more disposed to repudiate the principles of peace."[9]

By this time, of course, John Brown's plans were well advanced, but their betrayal that year by his hired drillmaster, Hugh Forbes, forced the postponement of their implementation for one year. To keep his hand in, Brown, at the urging of a black fugitive, went into Missouri, freed eleven slaves, killed the master who resisted, and in the dead of winter escaped successfully to Canada with the eleven men and women. By the time they arrived in Canada, a twelfth "fugitive" was free—having been born on the journey. By this time also, others were projecting, even in letters and printed circulars, elaborate plans for inciting and assisting slave rebellions in the South. One such circular, from the attorney Lysander Spooner, was withdrawn when Brown himself learned of it and told Spooner its continued circulation would interfere with his own plan.[10]

This turn to militancy was a reflection of the intensification of crisis that enveloped the nation. Because the decade 1850–60 marked a high point in slave unrest, repression intensified in the South, especially of free black people. There was a rising class consciousness and political organization among the southern nonslaveholding population, and in Missouri, North Carolina, and parts of Tennessee and Virginia successful political challenges were mounted to Bourbon domination. One result of this, as noted earlier, was growing extremism on the part of proslavery theoreticians, culminating in the insistence that slavery was a natural and salutary condition for *all* working people.

The decade also witnessed the outbreak of veritable civil war in Kansas—where John Brown played a key role—as well as movements toward the nationalization of slavery as affirmed by the U.S. Supreme Court in the *Dred Scott* decision (1857) and the *Ableman* v. *Booth* decision (1859), again written by Chief Justice Taney. The 1859 decision reiterated the national scope of slavery and affirmed the constitutionality of the Fugitive Slave Act of 1850. It arose out of the militant action of Abolitionists in Wisconsin, led by Sherman M. Booth of Milwaukee, who forcibly freed a captured fugitive, Joshua Glover, in 1854.[11] A representative from South Carolina entered the Senate floor in 1856, walked to Sen. Charles Sumner's desk, and clubbed that stalwart antislavery statesman into insensitivity, very nearly killing him—to the fervent applause of the southern press.

John Brown and his sons fought in the Kansas civil war; it was there he first gained fame—or notoriety. The latter derived especially from the bloody Pottawatomie slaughter, or executions, on 25 May 1856. Garrison's sons, in their biography of their father, referred to "the midnight extirpation with the sword, in true Southern fashion—of a nest of Border

Ruffianism."[12] Slaughtered were five leaders of the proslavery forces in retaliation for the killing of six free-state men and the burning and looting of Lawrence, their headquarters. The slaughter put the fear of God in the ranks of the proslavery forces. It was followed in a few days by Brown's men defeating a party of proslavery partisans in the Battle of Black Jack Creek on 2 June 1856—"the first regular battle fought between free-State and pro-slavery men in Kansas."[13] Stephen B. Oates, in his recent biography of Brown, closes the account of "Bloody Pottawatomie" with this sentence: "The enemy had murdered six free-state men since the struggle had begun in Kansas. Now, in killing five slavery men, Brown and his Northern Army had about evened the score."[14]

John Brown was involved shortly before the Harpers Ferry attack in another case producing political prisoners. This was the Oberlin-Wellington rescue effort which began on 13 September 1858 when John Price, a fugitive slave living in the college town, was betrayed (for a payment of twenty dollars) into the hands of four slave catchers. The four forcibly carried Price from Oberlin to a hotel in Wellington from whence he was to be shipped back to slavery after the formality of a hearing had been completed.

News of this event reached the ears of the faculty and students at Oberlin College, a center of antislavery feeling. Quickly many of them, joined by some townspeople, thirty-seven in all, set out after the slave catchers, caught up with them in the Wellington hotel, and forcibly freed Price.

A grand jury—one of whose members was the father of the betrayer—promptly indicted all of them and all were deposited in jail. Two were tried immediately. One was Simon M. Bushnell who, when he refused the judge's suggestion that he show contrition, was sentenced to sixty days in jail, fined six hundred dollars, and charged with court costs.

Tried next was the black man, Charles H. Langston, who was recording secretary of the Ohio Anti-Slavery Society. After being convicted, Langston took advantage of the court's offer to hear him prior to sentencing. Langston delivered an eloquent speech denouncing slavery and racism and affirming his intention to continue fighting both, no matter the consequences.

He told the judge: "I know that the courts of this country, that the laws of this country, that the governmental machinery of this country, are so constituted as to oppress and outrage colored men, men of my complexion. I cannot then, of course, expect, judging from the past history of the country, any mercy from the laws, from the constitution, or from the courts of the country." He reiterated the details of Price's rescue, and described it as just and gallant. He said his participation in it was right and not really criminal. In any case, he added, he could not be fairly tried, for judge and jury were white and the prosecutor was white; colored people were "oppressed by certain universal and deeply fixed *prejudices.*" Langston concluded by saying that no matter what the court decided, he would, under similar circumstances, do again what he had done in the present case.

The judge seems to have been moved by Langston's address; he sentenced him to twenty days in jail, a fine of one hundred dollars, and court costs. Langston served his time and promptly returned to his antislavery office. Eleven other men who remained in jail for about forty-five days awaiting trial were shortly released without a trial. In the attack to free Price, black men had played a leading role; twelve of the thirty-seven were black and five of them were released, after forty-five days, with the others.[15]

This case created great excitement in Ohio and was prominently noticed throughout the nation. As it happened, John Brown and John Henry Kagi were both in Ohio throughout the trials and the furor. Both men visited the jailed rescuers, and Kagi wrote about the case for New York and Cleveland newspapers. Kagi also enlisted at this time two of the blacks prominent in the case, John A. Copeland, an Oberlin student, and Copeland's uncle, Lewis Sheridan Leary. Both men fought at Harpers Ferry; Copeland was hanged and Leary was killed. Brown—although there was a warrant outstanding for his arrest—walked the streets of Cleveland openly and spoke at meetings in defense of the rescuers. Learning at one point that President Buchanan had offered a $250 reward for his capture, Brown told reporters that he offered a reward of $2.50 to anyone who would bring the president to him!

With events of this nature convulsing the nation, John Brown's action at Harpers Ferry in 1859 seemed almost fated to many contemporaries. His act was not aberrational. If it had been out of step with the pace of the era, it would not have had the impact it did upon both the South and the North—and the world. By the time Brown acted, as has been shown, the Abolitionist movement itself had developed to the point where militant action was more common and more widely justified. John Brown knew this, of course. Hence, he was supremely confident that now was the time, that succeed or fail, the blow he contemplated would electrify an expectant nation and would have, therefore, an enormous historic impact. Brown was not eccentric—let alone mad; he was, rather, acutely sensitive, to the point, I think, of genius.[16]

John Brown also epitomized the revolutionary quality of Abolitionism inasmuch as he possessed an acute class consciousness. (This may well be an additional explanation for the passionate denunciation that befell him from conventional commentators.) His hatred of slavery reflected a rejection both of racism and of elitism. He repeatedly insisted that he was a partisan of the slave and of the poor. When he lay on the armory floor, one of those questioning him asked, "Upon what principle do you justify your acts?" He replied: "Upon the golden rule. I pity the poor in bondage that have none to help them; that is why I am here, not to gratify any personal animosity, revenge, or vindictive spirit. It is my sympathy with the oppressed and wronged, that are as good as you and as precious in the sight of God."

He had made a similar point in 1856 in a long conversation with William A. Phillips, a reporter for the *New York Tribune.* Phillips recorded: "One of the most interesting things in his conversation that night, and one that marked him as a theorist, was his treatment of our forms of social and political life." Phillips continued:

He thought society ought to be reorganized on a less selfish basis, for while material interests gained something by the deification of pure selfishness, men and women lost much by it. He said that all great reforms, like the Christian religion, were based on broad, generous, self-sacrificing principles. He condemned the sale of land as a chattel, and thought there was an infinite number of wrongs to right before society would be what it should be, but that in our country slavery was the "sum of all villainies," and its abolition the first essential work. If the American people did not take courage and end it speedily, human freedom and republican liberty would soon be empty names in the United States.[17]

Brown's sense of class was ever with him and he kept returning to it. From his prison cell, he wrote a friend on 1 November 1859: "I do not feel conscious of guilt in taking up arms; and had it been in behalf of the rich and powerful, the intelligent, the great—as men count greatness—of those who form enactments to suit themselves and corrupt others, or some of their friends, that I interfered, suffered, sacrificed, and fell, it would have been doing very well."

It is because this was a thread binding together his whole life that he enunciated it so clearly and so beautifully when called upon by the court to speak before the judge passed sentence upon him. Brown had not expected to be sentenced at that time and had prepared no written statement; so he spoke without notes but without hesitation. He denied treason—especially against the Virginia court that was trying him, for he was

neither a citizen nor a resident of Virginia. He insisted he had not come
to Virginia with the intention of killing anyone and hence was not guilty
of murder. He had planned not insurrection but the freeing of slaves, and
this was his crime. (Many later historians have declared that Brown deliberately lied in saying this; we shall examine that matter later.) He concluded by absolving all others for responsibility in his course, affirming
that it was one he had imposed upon himself and that those who followed
him did so of their own free will. The heart of his final statement lay in
two paragraphs frequently omitted in accounts of what he said:

> I have another objection, and that is it is unjust that I should suffer such a
> penalty. Had I interfered in the manner in which I admit, and which I admit was
> fairly proved—for which I admire the truthfulness and candor of the greater por-
> tion of the witnesses who have testified in this case—had I so interfered in behalf
> of the rich, the powerful, the intelligent, the so-called great, wife or children, or
> any of that class, and suffered and sacrificed what I have in this interference, it
> would have been all right. Every man in this Court would have deemed it an act
> worthy of reward rather than punishment.
>
> This court acknowledges, too, as I suppose the validity of the law of God. I
> see a book kissed, which I suppose to be the Bible, or at least the New Testa-
> ment, which teaches me that all things whatsoever I would that men should do
> to me, I should do even so to them. It teaches me, further, to remember them
> that are in bonds as bound with them. I endeavored to act up to that instruction.
> I say I am too young to understand that God is any respecter of persons. I believe
> that to have interfered as I have done, as I have always freely admitted I have
> done, in behalf of His despised poor, I did no wrong, but right. Now if it is deemed
> necessary that I should forfeit my life for the furtherance of the ends of justice,
> and mingle my blood further with the blood of my children and with the blood of
> millions of this slave country whose rights are disregarded by wicked, cruel, and
> unjust enactments, I say, let it be done.

It was deemed proper that he so suffer; the judge, speaking in the
name of Virginia, sentenced John Brown to be hanged by the neck until
dead on 2 December 1859, one month after these immortal words were
uttered.

The one passage in John Brown's final address to the court that has
been characterized to be a falsehood (as Stephen Oates has done, for
example)[18] occurs where Brown refers to the freeing of slaves in Missouri in 1858 and states that in the Harpers Ferry assault he had "designed to do the same thing again, on a larger scale." He added: "That
was all I intended. I never did intend murder, or treason, or the destruc-

tion of property, or to excite or incite slaves to rebellion, or to make insurrection."

The reader will recall the 1847 conversation between Brown and Douglass in which he laid out his plan of recruiting and arming a limited number of men (one hundred at the outside) and using them to gather fugitives, retreat to mountain fastnesses, set up centers, defy capture, and serve as magnets attracting other slaves. The idea was to set up such centers, or maroon bases, throughout the Alleghenies and thus shake the slaveholding edifice to its foundations.

Oates himself reported that two of the state witnesses at the trial said of Brown that he "had declared his purpose was not to kill whites but to free Negroes and destroy slavery."[19] When Brown's men had come to Col. Lewis Washington's plantation and (as Brown had planned) Washington gave the sword of George Washington to the black liberator Osborne P. Anderson (for, the latter paraphrased Brown, "Anderson being a colored man, and colored men being only *things* in the South, it is proper that the South be taught a lesson upon this point"), Lewis Washington was seized, but otherwise unharmed.[20] Moreover, if it was murder Brown wanted, he had the armory full of townspeople taken prisoner. He harmed none among them—on the contrary, at some trouble, he saw to feeding them. And he overstayed his visit to Harpers Ferry instead of fleeing to the nearby mountains, for, as he stated, he was concerned for the prisoners and their families and had not planned how to dispose of them.

Directly to the point is the account of the interview he had with Frederick Douglass in 1847. And one has the full record, made by Douglass, of his last meeting with Brown, two weeks prior to the attack in 1859. Douglass was summoned by Brown to come to him from his Rochester home. Living with Douglass then was Shields Green, a young black man who had escaped from South Carolina and who had earlier met Brown at Douglass's home. The two men, Douglass and Green, took off at once in response to the call.

They were met in Chambersburg, Pennsylvania, by Henry Watson, a black Underground Railroad operator in that town (he made a living there as a barber). Watson took them to the appointed place, a nearby stone quarry on the Conococheague River. Douglass, after embracing Brown, remembered to give him ten dollars, which a black woman of Brooklyn, New York, Mrs. Gloucester, had given Douglass for Brown. With Brown was his trusted associate, John H. Kagi; both men were armed. Kagi and Green were silent as Douglass and Brown conferred on the best course to pursue; they spent Saturday and part of Sunday on the question. Douglass was surprised to learn that Brown had altered his original plan insofar as he meant first to capture the federal armory at Harpers Ferry, strip it of weapons, and then head to the mountains with his small group of men (and any slaves who may have joined them). Thereafter he meant to carry out the rest of the plan: set up other centers along the mountain ridges, reach deeper and deeper into the South, and attract more and more fugitives.

Douglass pointed out that there were few slaves in the region surrounding Harpers Ferry and that it was not plantation area.[21] He was upset, too, on being informed that Brown had made no effort to let those slaves who were in the area know he was coming—this at a time when slave kidnapping was a common and lucrative undertaking. But, above all, Douglass objected to the idea of attacking Harpers Ferry. This would take time to accomplish and it would mean involving the federal government directly in the assault. This, Douglass thought, was a serious and mistaken change in the original concept; the armory, he warned, would be a steel trap.

Brown pleaded for Douglass to join, pointing out that his participation would add greatly to the attractive power of the effort. But Douglass refused, saying that it would fail, that it was suicide; he, Douglass, was young and had many years before him (actually he lived until 1895). He urged Brown to reconsider. Brown answered that he could not. He had spent years on this plan; he had the men and a good initial supply of weapons. Forbes's treachery had already caused a year's postponement. Furthermore, he, Brown, was old and had not many years before him. If he was to die, this was the way to go.

The men kissed, wept, parted. As Douglass took his leave, Green tarried. "Are you coming, Shields?" he called. "No," said Green, "I believe I'll go with the Old Man." These are the only words we have from the young fugitive, whose own family was still in slavery. He fought bravely, was captured, and was hanged.[22]

Saturday, 16 October 1859, John Brown and eighteen of his comrades set out with horse and wagon (well loaded with pikes and rifles) from the Kennedy Farm in Maryland for Harpers Ferry, four miles down the road across what was then the Virginia border. Brown drove the wagon; the others marched front and rear, two abreast. Three men were left at the cabin on the farm to guard some remaining weapons. They had started three days early: the men were cooped up and restless; the neighbors had become curious. Some had spotted the black men, and the two young women—Martha Brown, the seventeen-year-old wife of Oliver Brown, and Anne Brown, the sixteen-year-old daughter of John—who had provided the cover of "family" for the group—had had to leave. Because of the early departure, others who were scheduled to join—including Harriet Tubman who by 16 October had reached New York City on her way to the farm—were left behind.

Thus did five black men and seventeen whites—all dedicated and ready to die—follow their leader. Of the original twenty-two, ten would be killed in combat, seven captured and hanged, and five make good their escape. In addition, a free black man (servicing the railroad) would be killed, as well as two slaves, among perhaps fifty who had joined the Brown effort.[23]

Brown had telegraph lines cut, but he permitted a local train to come to Harpers Ferry, stopped it, and then inexplicably allowed it to return and spread the alarm. The raiders were soon overwhelmed, caught in the "steel trap" as Douglass had predicted. They were overcome when the trap was sprung by a company of Marines under Lt. J. E. B. Stuart and Col. Robert E. Lee. It was now Monday, 18 October 1859, and the real drama was to begin.

John Brown used to the full the six weeks of life left to him from the date of his capture at the armory until he mounted the scaffold in Charlestown; he particularly used the month from the date of sentence to that of execution. As in the trial he had rejected with indignation the efforts by attorneys to plead insanity for him, so, after being sentenced, he rejected proposals for his rescue from Abolitionist friends. The important thing, he said was not to live long, but to live well; now, he added, at the end of a hangman's noose, he was worth infinitely more to the cause of human emancipation than he would be as a hunted fugitive. He conducted himself with such courage and restraint, consideration and honor, that he all but converted his jailer to Abolitionism, and that person together with the guards wept on the day the Old Man was led away to die.

Meanwhile, in interviews and a steady stream of letters, he attacked slavery as an impermissible evil, as an institution whose corrosive effect was threatening the existence of the Republic. The reports of these interviews and the texts of his letters were published in the *New York Tribune* and in many other papers, magazines, and pamphlets. Public meetings—pro- and anti-Brown—were held throughout the nation; what he said were matters of discussion in households throughout the United

States. It is probably true that never in the history of the country has one man's actions and ideas become for so prolonged a period a matter of such intense interest among so large a proportion of the people.

This is of decisive importance when considering the oft-repeated allegation that the man had "thrown his life away" and that he died as "absurdly" as he had lived. The contrary is the truth. In the life and death of John Brown one finds a marvelous merging of the man's meaning; in living and in dying he struck powerful blows against the "sum of all villainies." As W. E. B. Du Bois wrote, of his "forty days in prison," Brown "made the mightiest Abolition document that America has ever known."

Wendell Phillips, addressing a huge audience in Boston on 18 November 1859, took up this charge of "wasted years." He said: "It seems to me that in judging lives, this man, instead of being a failure, has done more to lift the American people, to hurry forward the settlement of a great question, to touch all hearts, to teach us ethics, than a hundred men could have done, living each on to eighty years. Is that a failure?"[24]

Self-serving rhetoric, perhaps, coming from the lips of a passionate Abolitionist? Well, here is the testimony of Charles Eliot Norton who, soon after Brown's execution, wrote to an English friend:

I have seen nothing like it. We get up excitements easily enough . . . but this was different. The heart of the people was fairly reached, and impression was made upon it which will be permanent and produce results long hence. . . . The events of this last month or two (including under the word events the impression made by Brown's character) have done more to confirm the opposition to slavery, than all the antislavery tracts and novels that ever were written.[25]

The country was ripe for the lessons of Brown's martyrdom; this is proof of the man's genius.

Julia Ward Howe wrote to Anne Mailliard on 6 November 1859: "His death will be holy and glorious,—the gallows cannot dishonor him—he will hallow it."[26] Longfellow, at about the same time, offered the opinion that Brown's death "will be a great day in our history, the date of a new Revolution—quite as needed as the old one."[27] Emerson echoed the words of Julia Ward Howe; in Boston on 8 November 1859 he remarked that Brown's martyrdom "will make the gallows as glorious as the cross." For Thoreau, Brown's behavior and sacrifice constituted "a sublime spectacle"; "he has earned immortality," he concluded. "Few spirits," said Theodore Parker, "have been more pure and devoted than John Brown."[28] Similar sentiments were expressed by Bronson Alcott, and his daughter Louisa May Alcott entered in her diary: "The execution of Saint John the Just took place today."

Lydia Maria Child wrote on 27 November 1859, "Before this affair I thought I was growing old and drowsy; but now I am as strong as an eagle." She offered to go to Brown and nurse him, but Governor Wise would not allow it. She published in one year four pamphlets inspired by Brown. On 20 November 1859 she wrote to friends:

I am astonished at the extent and degree of sympathy manifested for the brave old martyr. It is a remarkable example of the power of a great moral principle to overcome the worst disadvantages of external circumstances. To all outward appearance, all is defeat and ruin. Yet in reality what a glorious success! He is cursed, and scoffed at, and spit upon. Yet how the best intellects, and the largest hearts of the land, delight to do him honor.[29]

Again, because Lydia Maria Child had devoted much of her life to the Abolitionist movement, her words may be construed to reflect her partisanship, but, as in the case of Charles Eliot Norton, there is the countervailing example of an editorial in the *New York Post* by William Cullen Bryant on the day following Brown's execution.

Bryant referred to Brown's hanging as "an event in our national history which warrants every thoughtful man amongst us pondering over it deeply." Bryant was convinced that Brown's "fortitude" and his "hatred of oppression" would move most of "the civilized public" to "lay on his tomb the honors of martyrdom." That martyrdom would "bring recruits to his cause"; Bryant was sure that Brown's "errors of judgment" would be forgotten by history when faced with "his unfaltering courage" and the "nobleness of his aims." His name, Bryant concluded, would surely be included among the "heroes" of humanity.[30]

Abroad, Victor Hugo, from his exile, wrote that Brown "was an apostle and a hero; the gibbet has only increased his glory and made him a martyr"; Garibaldi in Italy spoke in the same breath of John Brown and Jesus Christ; in Czarist Russia, Brown's martyrdom inspired Chernishevsky.[31] Professor Jerzy Jedlicki, of the Polish Academy of Sciences, wrote recently that "the condemnation of John Brown to the gallows," provoked "Cyprian Norwid, the great and somber poet, into writing what is possibly the deepest felt disillusionment with the American myth in Polish literature. In his two memorable poems devoted to 'the citizen John Brown' he wrote in despair that the shadows of Washington and Kosciuszko have been betrayed, and the stars on the American flag proved to be mere fireworks." The poet concluded that "it is America itself which has been hanged in the person of Brown."[32]

It was the hanging of John Brown that moved James Russell Lowell to pen "Truth forever on the scaffold / Wrong forever on the throne," but it was the temper of the times that Brown knew so well that led the poet to continue with the words so often omitted but so pregnant with meaning: "But that scaffold sways the future." That same note of defiance and confidence was struck by the Brown family's black neighbors who sang as his body was lowered into the rocky earth of the Adirondacks:

> Blow ye the trumpet, blow
> The gladly solemn sound.
> Let all the nations know
> To earth's remotest bound
> The year of jubilee has come.

When Brown was offered in jail "the consolation of religion" by Governor Wise's son and a Virginia colonel among others, he rejected it with no note of uncertainty. Apologists for slavery were not Christians, let alone ministers. He wrote to Mrs. George Stearns: "I have asked to be *spared* from having any *mock, or hypocritical prayers made over me,* when I am publicly *murdered.*" He would much prefer "that my only *religious attendants* be poor *little, dirty, ragged, bare headed, and barefooted slave boys, and girls,* led by some *grey headed slave* mother. I should feel much prouder of such an escort, and I wish I could have it."[33]

The artist who depicted Brown as kissing a black child held up to him by a mother did not paint reality but came close to Brown's desire. Benjamin Quarles tells us that as he was on his way to the execution "a slave woman said, 'God bless you, old man; if I could help you, I would.'" If he heard, that surely helped.[34]

Two thousand infantry men, plus cavalry and artillery, surrounded the site of Brown's execution. Seated upon his coffin in the wagon taking him to his death, Brown looked around him and remarked aloud on the loveliness of the Blue Ridge Mountains. He had already said farewell to his weeping jailers and urged them to regain their composure; he handed his final note to a guard foretelling slavery's bloody end.

He had the previous evening said farewell to his much loved and indomitable wife, who had insisted, against his advice, on visiting him. The jailer, John Avis, had provided his own office for the use of the Browns, but when John asked that Mary be permitted to spend his final evening with him, Avis had to deny the request. The Browns discussed his burial and the remaining children's welfare before the final parting. The wife wept softly, but John broke down altogether and cried uncontrollably for some time.

Before leaving the jail Brown went to each of the imprisoned comrades and bade him farewell. And then he was driven to the gallows. At the site among the thousands gathered there were Robert E. Lee and soon-to-be-called "Stonewall" Jackson (who wrote his wife that he feared for Brown's soul) and a well-known actor up from Richmond watching with fascination—John Wilkes Booth. Present, too, among the lines of soldiers was an elderly man clearly not a soldier, whose influence as Virginia's greatest slave owner and leading theoretician of secession earned him his place here—Edmund Ruffin. Shortly, Ruffin's distinction was to gain him the honor of firing the first round against Fort Sumter. Later, hearing of Lee's surrender to Grant, this inveterate defender of slavery (not called either "fanatic" or "mad" by later historians) wrapped his head in the Stars and Bars, put a pistol in his mouth, and blew his life away.[35]

The Old Man mounted the gallows steps quickly and firmly. A white hood was placed over his head and his hands were bound behind him. He was led to the trapdoor. Then he waited, for all the soldiers had to take their correct positions; the two thousand seemed more nervous than the doomed one. An eternity of twelve minutes passed as Brown waited. Did Brown want a handkerchief to release when he was ready? "No, thank you, I am ready, but please do get on with your work." He had nothing further to say.

When all seemed ready, the sheriff called to the executioner to perform his task and spring the trap, but the man either did not hear or did not respond at once, and the call was shouted again. The trap was sprung. The rope was of cotton (purposely, so that slaves' work would choke out his life). The rope slipped, and repeated examinations of his heartbeat were made. After thirty-five minutes, the physician said John Brown was dead.

Mary Brown took the body back by wagon and train on the long journey to North Elba in the mountains of New York. In most villages and cities hundreds and thousands lined the way, mourning; church bells sounded. In black America, in the North, 2 December 1859 was Martyr's Day; all stores and businesses were closed and all churches were open. Those in the churches and black organizations, especially of women, joined many whites in raising money for Mary Brown and her children. Brown's portrait graced the homes and schools of the black folk.

Thoreau, on the morning of Brown's execution, spoke at a church in Concord; he offered a "Plea for Captain John Brown." Brown, he said, would really die for he had really lived, and "in teaching us how to die" he and his men "taught us how to live." The respectable, Thoreau said, called him misguided, vindictive, insane. They mistaked themselves and could not recognize a saint. Thoreau thought, somewhat optimistically, perhaps, that when a painter had caught the glory of his martyrdom, "we shall then be at liberty to weep for Captain Brown."

On 10 December, eight days after Brown was hanged, the young John A. Copeland, his black companion who had joined him from Oberlin, wrote from his cell to his brother: "It was a sense of the wrongs which we have suffered that prompted the noble but unfortunate Captain John Brown and his associates to attempt to give freedom to a small number, at least, of those who are now held by cruel and unjust laws, and by no less cruel and unjust men." Copeland explained "that though shut up in prison and under sentence of death, I have spent some very happy hours here." Why? Because, for his dying in this cause, "true and honest men" would honor him, and surely the very "angels" above would "more readily receive" him to their "happy home of everlasting joy."[36] Copeland went to the gallows six days later, calling out as he mounted the steps (according to the *Baltimore Sun*): "If I am dying for freedom, I could not die for a better cause—I had rather die than be a slave!"

Let the last words on Brown come from one who knew him well and loved him and whose own stature reached that of his. This is Douglass speaking on 1 August 1860:

Our land is too fat with the lost sweat and warm blood of slaves driven to toil and death; our civilization is yet too selfish and barbarous; our statesmen are yet too narrow, base and mobocratic; our press is yet too venal and truckling; our religion is too commercial, too much after the pattern of the pride and prejudices of our times, to understand and appreciate the great character who sacrificed himself for the hated Negroes of this country. With the statesmanship, civilization and Christianity of America, the Negro is simply a piece of property, having no rights which white men are required to respect, but with John Brown and his noble associates, the NEGRO IS A MAN, entitled to all the rights claimed by the whitest man on earth. Brave and glorious old man! Yours was the life of a true friend of humanity, and the triumphant death of a hero. The friends of freedom shall be nerved to the glorious struggle with slavery by your example; the hopes of the slave shall not die while your name shall live, and after ages shall rejoice to do justice to your great history.[37]

Of course, less than two years after Brown's hanging, an army of two million men (at first all white) was beginning the process of crushing both slavery and the slave-owning class. Union troops would go into battle inspired by the strains of "John Brown's body lies a-mouldering in the grave, but his soul goes marching on." And three years later, Frederick Douglass became the first black in history to confer in the White House with the president of the United States. The president was asking the black statesman how best the government might get the news of the Emancipation Proclamation into the heart of the South so that the slaves might learn of it and, acting upon it, cripple the Confederacy. Frederick Douglass tells us:

I listened with the deepest interest and profoundest satisfaction, and at his suggestion, agreed to undertake the organizing of a band of scouts, composed of colored men, whose business should be, somewhat after the original plan of John Brown, to go into the rebel states beyond the line of our army, carry the news of emancipation, and urge the slaves to come within our boundaries.[38]

Surely here is a neatness to historical vindication that has few equals—although we shall see another as we examine the revolutionary character of the war itself, completing the story of the revolutionary nature of Abolitionism.

John Brown's attack shook the foundations of slavery in an immediate and specific sense. Even as he lay in his cell, news came to him—which he noted in letters—of a wave of incendiarism terrorizing Virginia. This arson, of fields, gins, homes, whole towns, shook the entire South for months after Brown was hanged. Southern society was rocked back on its heels and hysteria characterized its leaders. A reign of terror fell upon the South: dozens of suspected whites (native and northern) were driven out, lashed, tarred and feathered; free black people were especially tormented, driven into exile or enslaved.

One episode, told by Ira Berlin, conveys the panic in the region. (The subject merits a book in itself, especially insofar as it helped persuade dominant elements in the slaveholding class that only secession offered the possibility of saving the institution of slavery and perhaps even expanding it.) In Baltimore, white contemporaries were appalled to discover the "enthusiasm with which many free blacks celebrated Brown's assault upon slavery." Citing the *Baltimore Sun* of 14 December 1859, Berlin reports, "When Baltimore police broke into the annual caulkers' ball, they discovered the hall bedecked with pictures of Brown and a bust inscribed 'The martyr—God bless him.' Chalked on the floor was an out-line of Governor Henry Wise [of Virginia] straddled by 'a huge Ethiopian,' surrounded by 'inscriptions unfit for publication.'" Berlin concludes with some understatement: "It was a chilling sight."[39]

That chill symbolizes the hysteria that helped drive a desperate slave-holding class, faced with Lincoln's election, to the course of counter-revolutionary violence—the path of treason, an effort to overthrow the United States government by force.

Chapter Ten

The Civil War as Revolution: Abolitionism's Culmination

James M. McPherson, in a splendid study published in 1964, was nevertheless careless when, at one point, he wrote: "The South did indeed launch a revolution in the winter of 1860–61, but its final outcome was rather different from what the revolutionists hoped."[1] On the contrary, a dominant portion of the slave-owning class in the South—not "the South"—launched a *counter* revolution in that fateful winter. This class, convinced by the election of Abraham Lincoln on the Republican party platform, that it had irrevocably lost control of the national government, decided to resort to force in an effort to sever itself from the government, destroy the Union, and establish its own state founded upon principles precious to it.

McPherson himself, later in the same work, quotes Abolitionists who immediately saw the revolutionary implications of successful resistance to the slave-owners' counterrevolutionary stroke. William Goodell, a leading legal expert of the Abolitionist movement, published an editorial soon after the firing upon Fort Sumter, entitled "The Second American Revolution." Goodell declared that the revolution now had begun; it must, he wrote, "go on to its completion—*a National Abolition of Slavery.*" He added, "What but the insanity of moral blindness can long delay the proclamation inviting [the slaves] to share in *the glorious second American Revolution.*"[2] Indeed the self-exiled Virginian Moncure Conway specifically charged the Confederates with being counterrevolutionists and insisted, in bold type, "WE ARE THE REVOLUTIONISTS."[3]

The dominant components of the slaveholding class chose counter-revolution out of desperation, which was the result of four major developments in the years 1850–60. First was the victory of Lincoln and the new Republican party. Its platform called for national policies antithetical to those desired by the slaveholding class: no further extension of slavery's boundaries; a protective tariff; internal improvements (railroads, canals, turnpikes, bridges) at federal expense to tie together a burgeoning (Free Soil) West; and a homestead act to hasten the populating of the West.

Second was the vast increase in the consequence of the Abolitionist movement as its leaders—especially Wendell Phillips, William Lloyd Garrison, Frederick Douglass, Henry C. Wright, Harriet Beecher Stowe, Elizabeth Cady Stanton, Henry Highland Garnet, and Charles L. Remond—reached through their writings and speeches millions of Americans. The movement experienced not only a quantitative leap but also a qualitative transformation. Once limited to a pacifist, moral secessionist stance, it became committed to political action and militant resistance. The latter phase of that movement was epitomized by John Brown, and the enshrinement of the Old Man in much of the North helped persuade the slave owners that their continued functioning with the new social order was impossible.

The triumph of the Republican party represented, in considerable part, a vindication and a product of the labors of the Abolitionists. In 1856, Garrison had stated that the party embodied "the whole *political* anti-slavery strength of the country—the legitimate product of the *moral* agitation of the subject of slavery for the last quarter of the century."[4] Four years later Phillips exulted: "For the first time in our history, the slave has chosen a President of the United States. . . . Lincoln is in *place,* Garrison is in *power.*"[5] And Douglass had said on 1 August 1860, more than three months prior to Lincoln's election, that although his party was certainly not Abolitionist, nevertheless:

I cannot fail to see that the Republican party carries with it the anti-slavery sentiment of the North, and that a victory gained by it in the present canvass will be a victory gained by that sentiment over the wickedly aggressive pro-slavery sentiment of the country. . . . *The slaveholders know that the day of their power is over when a Republican President is elected.*" (italics added)[6]

James Ford Rhodes acutely observed in 1906:

We cannot resist the conviction that this anti-slavery agitation had its part, and a great part, too, in the first election of Lincoln. . . . by stirring the national conscience, they made possible the formation of a political party whose cardinal principle was opposition to the extension of slavery, and whose reason for existence lay in the belief of its adherents that slavery in the south was wrong.[7]

The antislavery agitation of the Abolitionists became more reasonable to increasing numbers of people in the pre–Civil War generation as the third major development of the period, the socioeconomic transformation of the North, proceeded. The platform of the Republican party—at its creation—reflected the transformation, which was characterized by a split in the mercantile bourgeoisie and banking interests as more and more of each serviced a free-labor economy rather than a slave-based one; the growth of an industrial bourgeoisie with needs—such as protective tariff, vast transportation networks, the populating of the West—that distinguished it from the planter class; and the growth of a working-class and free-farming population, which intensified the antislavery politics of a northern population of "greasy mechanics and filthy operatives" and "small-fisted farmers," as some southerners saw them. Added to these pressures upon the slave owners was the fourth development, the growing unrest of the southern slave population and the intensified class consciousness of an increasingly politicized nonslaveholding white population.

Faced with all these developments, the slaveholding oligarchy decided it had nothing to lose and everything to gain by taking up arms against opposing forces, if necessary, and establishing its own empire. When the oligarchy created its Confederacy—abstaining from submitting the question of secession to a popular vote until after the decision had been made at Montgomery—it made certain to give slavery top priority in its Constitution. By its terms, impairing private property rights in slaves was explicitly forbidden to the Confederate Congress. The Confederacy's vice president, Alexander H. Stephens of Georgia, explained in 1861, as we have seen, that slavery was fundamental to the Confederacy as was racism. He projected also that that institution would yet dominate the entire North American continent.

There were four components to the revolutionary character of the Civil War; all were basically tied to the status of the Afro-American population and thus related to the meaning of Abolitionism. First, there was the question of the actual condition of the black people; this also entailed what the nature of the postwar South would be. Second was the question of remaking the nature of the Union as part of the process of successfully defending it. Third was the question of preserving a government based on the consent of the governed, on equality of rights, on due process of law, of popular sovereignty "of the People, by the People and for the People," with "People" becoming an increasingly all-inclusive concept. Fourth, as a necessary corollary of the third, was the question of amending the Constitution that would entail the most revolutionary changes in social conditions and property relations undertaken anywhere in the nineteenth century.

Since slavery was at the root of the Confederate effort, the undoing of slavery was at the heart of defeating the Confederacy. Slavery's existence had disrupted the Union; slavery's termination was necessary to save it. The reasons for this were manifold and interrelated: (1) a basic source of the Confederacy's strength lay in the labor of the slaves—free the slaves and that source vanished; (2) the black people wanted to fight, work for, and in all possible ways serve the Union—hence, they promised great (indispensable, Lincoln declared in 1864)[8] strength to the Union effort; and (3) a Union policy of emancipation would bring enormous diplomatic advantage to Lincoln's government throughout Europe (especially in vitally important Great Britain, as well as in France where Louis Napoleon had dreams of reestablishing a French-American empire). It would, in fact, make politically impossible pro-Confederate policies among the Great Powers or in the Vatican.

The first break in the wartime status of black people came in May 1861 when Major-General Benjamin F. Butler, in Virginia, announced the "contraband" policy. This was the term he employed in an order welcoming fugitive slaves into his lines, giving them employment, and, in effect, affirming their freedom.[9]

In August 1861, Congress passed what was known as the Confiscation Act. It provided that those masters whose slaves were used for military purposes hostile to the Union were to lose any claim to their labor or payment therefore, with enforcement to be made by federal courts. In this month, also, Congress adopted a resolution "releasing federal officers" from enforcing the Fugitive Slave Law and explicitly authorizing Union commanders to receive and protect escaped slaves. Lincoln, in his message to Congress in December 1861, urged voluntary state emancipation, suggesting that in such cases the federal government might well assist participating states with financial aid. He also recommended U.S. diplomatic recognition of Haiti and Liberia.

The following year, 1862, saw a proliferation of acts tending toward a policy of emancipation, culminating in the issuance, as of 1 January 1863, of the final Emancipation Proclamation. In February, a law was enacted forbidding all U.S. army officers from returning fugitive slaves to their masters. In March, President Lincoln formally submitted to Congress his suggestion that it resolve to help any state that adopted a plan for gradual emancipation with compensation. Congress promptly so resolved, but border-state representatives rejected the proposal. Nevertheless, London sources reported to the White House that this effort had a positive impact upon British public opinion.

On 10 April, Lincoln returned to his proposal of the preceding December, favoring gradual emancipation by individual states, with compensation to such states, but again the congressional delegations from the border states expressed opposition. Six days later a law was passed emancipating at once all slaves in the District of Columbia, with loyal slaveowners receiving $300 per slave. The law carried with it an appropriation of $100,000 for the voluntary colonization of those black people who wished to leave the United States.

Such proposals and efforts by government agencies in the past had always provoked expressions of disapproval from most Afro-Americans; they had never resulted in any appreciable migration. This proposal met with the same result. When Lincoln became aware of widespread opposition to the latest colonization proposal, he took an unprecedented action: he invited a delegation of black people for an exchange of views on the question. Following this came mass meetings and published arguments from blacks rejecting the concept of colonization as flowing out of prejudice, as a hallmark of the slave system, as impractical, as immoral, and as contrary to the real interests of the United States. Rather than colonization, said an "Appeal from the Colored Men of Philadelphia": "We believe that the world would be benefited by giving the four millions of slaves their freedom, and the lands now possessed by their masters. They have been amply compensated in our labor and the blood of our kinsmen."

On 19 June, *Dred Scott* was put to rest when a law was passed abolishing slavery, without compensation, in all the federal territories. Also in June, ministers were appointed to Haiti and Liberia.

In July, perhaps inspired by the anniversary of the Declaration of Independence, Congress authorized the president to "employ persons of African descent for the suppression of the rebellion, and organize and use them in such manner as he may judge best for the public welfare." Although this did not specifically mention service as soldiers, the language certainly did not rule this out. The authorization was, in fact, the root of the policy that eventuated in over 180,000 black soldiers and some 25,000 black sailors as components of Lincoln's army and navy.

In July also, Congress provided for the education of black children in the District of Columbia, the equal administration of the law for black and white people in the district, and for the more effectual suppression by the federal government of the African slave trade.

It was in July 1862 that Lincoln solicited the opinions of his cabinet members as to the wisdom of an emancipation announcement. The response was markedly cool; the least hostile suggested postponement until a notable military victory. Publicly, through the summer of 1862, Lincoln maintained his stance that the major purpose of the war was to preserve the Union, not alter the status of slaves. But in fact the argument of Abolitionists, black and white, that saving the Union required emancipation (and that only a victorious Union would mean emancipation) became more and more persuasive as the war dragged on, casualties among whites mounted, and an absence of an emancipation policy embarrassed U.S. ministers abroad and enhanced the efforts of Confederate emissaries.

On 22 September 1862 was issued the Preliminary Emancipation Proclamation. Here the president took the nearly final step in transforming the war for the Union into a war for freedom, also. Still it gave the rebellious states, and portions thereof—to which alone it applied—one hundred days to stop the fighting and rejoin the nation; if they had not done so at the end of that period, irrevocable emancipation would be announced. Now, too, as he had done several times previously, Lincoln reiterated his preference for gradual, compensated emancipation.

Garrison had written and circulated a petition for emancipation that also called for compensating loyal owners.[10] Black Abolitionists never put forth such proposals. Ralph Waldo Emerson on the announcement, 1 January 1863, of the final proclamation, included this stanza in his "Boston Hymn":

> Pay ransom to the owner,
> And fill the bag to the rim.

> Who is the owner? The slave is the owner,
> And ever was. *Pay him!*

The slave owners, however, remained adamant, and Lincoln issued his final Emancipation Proclamation. This act of confiscation was justified by Lincoln's designating that the proclamation was issued "by virtue of the power in me vested as Commander-in-Chief of the Army and Navy of the United States in time of actual armed rebellion." Lincoln here directed the armed forces of the United States to "maintain the freedom" of persons covered by the proclamation, and—contrary to the provision in the Constitution pledging the nation's military might to suppressing insurrections when requested by states to do so—they here were ordered to "do no act or acts to repress such persons, or any of them in any efforts they may make for their actual freedom." The proclamation expressed the hope that the people now "declared to be free" would "abstain from all violence, *unless in necessary self-defense*" (italics added)—which was much like the position of Henry Highland Garnet and John Brown.

Further, the freed people were urged, where possible, to "labor faithfully for reasonable wages." The proclamation added that persons freed by its provisions, if they were in "suitable condition," would be welcomed into the army "to garrison forts, positions, stations, and other places" and into the navy for all forms of service.

Although Lincoln closed by again citing "military necessity" as warranting the proclamation, he also announced that he "sincerely believed [it] to be an act of justice" for which he felt free to "invoke the considerate judgment of mankind and the gracious favor of Almighty God."

Lincoln's invoking of "the considerate judgment of mankind" reflected no mere rhetorical turn. In the first place, he despised slavery and was delighted to be able to deal it a death blow; in the second place, he knew that vehement opposition to emancipation was by no means absent in the North. Illustrating this latter fact was the resolution adopted by the Illinois State Legislature, whose majority was Democratic. It called the proclamation "a gigantic usurpation," which subverted the Union and constituted "a revolution in the social organization of the Southern States." This description, while troubling these Confederate sympathizers, accurately described the thrust of the proclamation.

It is likely that the proclamation, altering the previously announced purpose of the war, as a war for the Union, into one for a Free Union, provoked some public opposition in the North; certainly it was used to stimulate fearful antiblack—and antidraft—uprisings in several cities, notably New York and Detroit. But on the whole, its impact upon the war from a practical standpoint, let alone a moral one, was positive. By the end of 1862, public opinion in the North had been swung to a considerable degree to an antislavery, if not an Abolitionist, position. Figures like Phillips, Garrison, Stowe, and Douglass had become genuine mass leaders, listened to not by hundreds or thousands, as in the previous generation, but by millions. It certainly inspired the Afro-American population, free and slave, North and South; and it exerted indubitably a positive force upon mass public opinion abroad, not only in Europe, but also in Canada.

The issuance of the proclamation was one of the great dramatic moments in history, eagerly awaited and fervently prayed for by millions for generations. It was an electric moment for them and for their allies. It was, of course, one of the great blows struck for human freedom in all history; it was also, as Du Bois first saw, a historic watershed in the history of working people. Chattel slavery had been dealt a mortal blow: the dignity of all labor had been enhanced; a divisive force in the working class had been lessened; the Bourbon concept that slavery was the proper condition of workers in general had been repudiated; the popular, democratic, essence of the struggle—the "People's War" feature, to quote Lincoln—had been vindicated.

Two immediate results of the proclamation appeared: one was the intensification of the recruitment of blacks for the armed forces of the Union; another was a strong impulse toward further development of the revolutionary quality of the war both in terms of permanently eliminating slavery throughout the nation and improving the status and condition of the Afro-American population.

When news of the proclamation reached the ears of the slaves, tens of thousands acted upon its promise and fled to Union forces. The turmoil, the inevitable antislavery content of the war, and, climactically, the proclamation induced what W. E. B. Du Bois in his *Black Reconstruction* had referred to as a "mobile General Strike."

Black enlistments and recruitment efforts brought over 200,000 black men, with about the same number of black men and women serving the Union forces as fortification builders, draymen, pilots, nurses, cooks, and so on. Because, at first, black soldiers were paid significantly less than white enlisted men, some (the Fifty-fourth and Fifty-fifth Massachusetts Regiments) refused all pay. They stayed with this "work action," until, finally, pay was at first equalized and then in the last months of the war equalized retroactively to the date of enlistment. On land and sea, the black men acquitted themselves very well; testimony to this effect by white officers (there were almost no black officers) seems to have been unanimous. Although black fighters faced especially onerous conditions and duties—they usually were less well equipped, longer on the line, and treated, originally, as insurrectionists rather than war prisoners if taken in combat—they contributed decisively to the victory of Lincoln's forces and therefore to the salvation of the Republic and their own liberation.

Following the issuance of the Emancipation Proclamation, the Abolitionist demanded (1) an immediate termination of slavery in the border states, wherein the proclamation did not apply; (2) the organization of a Freedmen's Bureau to guard the rights and interests of the newly freed people; and (3) the provision, through federal legislation and administration, of properly compensated labor to the freed people, of education for both adults and children, and of land to the tillers, to be either confiscated from or appropriated with compensation from the former major slave owners. Black groups and organizations emphasized in particular the land issue—for "he who owns the land owns the man"; the individuals like Sumner, Thaddeus Stevens, Wendell Phillips, Frederick Douglass, and Lydia Maria Child repeatedly stressed the basic significance of land distribution. Douglass pioneered in emphasizing early on the black man's need as well for three boxes—the ballot box, the jury box, and the cartridge box—or the suffrage, a nonracist judicial system, and a nonracist militia system. Much of this did not come to pass—a matter central to the history of the Reconstruction Era. Nevertheless, these demands were part of the context within which were debated the Civil War amendments, especially the Thirteenth and the Fourteenth.

Abolitionists played a decisive role, also, in fighting for and in some cases winning egalitarian victories in the North. Indeed, by 1860, as a result of strenuous agitation, black people enjoyed full political rights throughout New England, with the exception of Connecticut. The Abolitionist objective as war came was spelled out in an 1861 speech by Susan B. Anthony, quoted by McPherson in his illuminating treatment of this subject:

Let us open to the colored man all our schools, from the common District to the College. Let us admit him into all our mechanic shops, stores, offices, and lucrative business associations, to work side by side with his white brother; let him rent such pew in the church, and occupy such seat in the theatre, and public lecture room, as he pleases; let him be admitted to all our entertainments, both public and private; let him share in all the accommodations of our hotels, stages, railroads and steamboats. . . . Extend to him all the rights of citizenship. Let him vote and be voted for; let him sit upon the judge's bench, and in the jurors' box. . . . Let the North thus prove to the South, by her acts, that she fully recognizes the humanity of the black man. [11]

This program was widely and heroically attempted throughout the North, by black and white people, directly connected with and furthering Abolitionism. Before the 1870s some black men had been elected to public office, as in Massachusetts; jim crow transportation had been terminated in such cities as Philadelphia, New York, and San Francisco. Even in the matter of suffrage for black men, the 1860s saw important challenges to racism. The predominant historical literature, including the work of V. Jacques Voegeli, Eugene H. Berwanger, James A. Rawley, and Phyllis F. Field, takes an opposite point of view and emphasizes the prevalence and persistence of racism. Certainly, in regard to suffrage for black men, the evidence shows racism. Yet there is also evidence of significant and growing rejection of racism, insofar as it was reflected in objecting to black male suffrage. In some cases a majority opinion favored their voting. In Minnesota in 1865 and 1867, the "yes" vote came to 45.2 percent and 48.8 percent. In Wisconsin in 1865 the "yes" vote was 46 percent; in Connecticut the same year, 44.6 percent; in Ohio in 1867, 45.9 percent; in Missouri in 1868, 42.7 percent. In New York State, the affirmative vote in 1846 was 28 percent; in 1860, 36 percent; in 1869, 47 percent. In Iowa and in Minnesota, in 1869, suffrage for black men was *approved* by over 56 percent in each state. [12]

As the war moved toward its termination with spring's approach in 1865, the exhilaration of the Union forces and people was high. There were many dramatic illustrations of the revolutionary potential unleashed by the war. Perhaps the most dramatic was black men fighting white men in the South, with the blessings of the federal government and paid by that government. Frederick Douglass, in his inspired editorial "Men of Color to Arms!" published in 2 March 1863, called on blacks to "smite with death the power that would bury the government and your liberty in the same grave."[13]

The first Union troops to enter the Confederacy's capital, Richmond, Virginia, were those of the Twenty-ninth Connecticut (Colored) Infantry; the date was 1 April 1865. White troops followed and within twenty-four hours the Confederate capital was secured. On 3 April President Lincoln entered the city. A member of the Twenty-ninth recorded the scene:

When the President landed there was no carriage near, neither did he wait for one, but leading his son, they walked over a mile to Gen'l. Weitzel's headquarters at Jeff Davis' mansion, a colored man acting as guide. . . . What a spectacle! . . . As the President passed along the street the colored people waved their handkerchiefs, hats and bonnets, and expressed their gratitude by shouting repeatedly, "Thank God for his goodness; we have seen his salvation." . . . [A black woman] threw her bonnet in the air, screaming with all her might, "thank you, Master Lincoln." . . . He came not with bitterness in his heart, but with the olive leaf of kindness, a friend to elevate sorrow and suffering, and to rebuild what had been destroyed.[14]

A young woman named Charlotte Forten wrote a letter from St. Helena's Island, South Carolina, 20 November 1862. The area had been taken by Union forces led by the pro-Abolitionist Gen. Rufus Saxton. Black men had already formed part of his forces; others were working their own land. Education was now a central hunger and young women—black and white—had come south to answer the need. One such was Forten, a staunch Abolitionist and black granddaughter of James Forten of Philadelphia, one of the founders of the antislavery movement. She was rowed to St. Helena's "from Beaufort by a crew of negro boatmen. . . . they sung for us several of their own beautiful songs. There is a peculiar wildness and solemnity about them which cannot be described, and the people accompanying the singing with a singular swaying of the body, which seems to make it more effective."

She could hardly believe she was in South Carolina, but there she was: "We were in a very excited, jubilant state of mind, and sang the John Brown song with spirit, as we drove through the pines and palmettos. Ah! it was good to be able to sing that *here*, in the very heart of Rebeldom!" Forten wished "some one would write a little Christmas hymn for our children to sing. I want to have a kind of festival for them on Christmas. . . . The children have just learned the John Brown song, and next week they are going to learn the song of the 'Negro Boatman.'"[15]

Charleston itself had been entered on 21 February 1865 by the black Fifty-fifth Massachusetts Infantry. They entered singing "John Brown's Body," and a commander of one of its companies was Lt. George Thompson Garrison—son of the Liberator. Meanwhile, Gen. Robert E. Lee's estate at Arlington, Virginia, had become a freedman's village, and among its streets were two named Garrison and Lovejoy. Former president John Tyler's Virginia home was serving as a school for black children, as was the home of Gov. Henry A. Wise—the man who had seen to the hanging of John Brown. In that latter school one of John Brown's daughters was the teacher; she had adorned the classroom's wall with her father's picture. And a son of Frederick Douglass was teaching a school for black children in Maryland, not far from the place his father had fled as a slave.[16]

After the Fifty-fifth Massachusetts Infantry entered Charleston, the steps of the slave auction market were removed and shipped to Boston and then to Lowell. In March, at both cities, Garrison mounted these stairs and, standing on the auction block, made speeches hailing emancipation. Of the event at Lowell, on 15 March 1865, he wrote that on mounting the block, he "was greeted with the strongest demonstrations of applause, prolonged and repeated, as though there were to be no end to them." Garrison concluded: "What a revolution!"[17]

But the ultimate symbol of a world turned upside down, of the revolution that was the Civil War, came in April 1865—just four years after Capt. Robert Anderson had been forced to surrender Fort Sumter to the Confederacy and the flag of the United States gave way to the Stars and Bars. On 14 April 1865, the Union flag was to be raised over the fort. Ten days earlier Garrison had received a telegram from Secretary of War Stanton inviting him to be present as the guest of the government on that occasion. A similar invitation went to George Thompson, the fiery British Abolitionist who had been obliged to flee the United States thirty years before because of threats to his life. Robert Anderson, now a major-general, was to raise the flag and the orator of the day was to be the Reverend Henry Ward Beecher.

Stanton himself and other dignitaries joined the party and Lt. George T. Garrison was given leave to join his father. On a steamer provided by the government the party proceeded from New York City to the fort and all went well at the ceremony. Adding to the force of the occasion was the news that reached the party: Lee had surrendered to Grant. The celebrants were joined by Robert Smalls, former slave who had taken a Confederate steamer, the *Planter,* through the Confederate guards at Charleston and delivered it to the blockading U.S. Navy two years earlier. He now arrived on the ship—as Capt. Robert Smalls. Aboard, capping the event, were about 2,500 recently emancipated slaves.

On 15 April—the day Lincoln died, an event then unknown to Garrison and the others—Garrison spoke briefly at Calhoun's tomb and then, at some length, at Zion's Church, before a vast assemblage of black and white people. The orator of the day, however, was Samuel Dickerson, a former slave, who, with his two young daughters at his side, thanked Garrison and his comrades for their labors. Pointing to the girls, Dickerson said that a short time before they were not his. But "now, sir, through your labors and those of your noble coadjutors, they are mine, and no man can take them from me." He concluded by pointing to the bouquets held by the youngsters: "Accept these flowers as the token of our gratitude and love, and take them with you to your home, and keep them as a simple offering from those for whom you have done so much."[18]

Although Robert Smalls, Samuel Dickerson, and thousands of former slaves were among those on the vessel chartered by the government and on an accompanying vessel chartered by Henry Ward Beecher's Brooklyn church, not one of the dignitaries was black. How splendid it would have been if Frederick Douglass and Harriet Tubman and Robert Purvis, for example, had been among the visiting dignitaries. That none was present hinted at the poison that remained and was later to help vitiate so much of the revolutionary content of the Civil War.

Symptomatic, too, was the fact that it took organized and public protest by the Afro-American people of New York City to obtain permission for black people to be officially represented among those in the funeral procession of Abraham Lincoln. The City Council voted to have an all-white procession; only demands from black citizens, made public in a letter to the New York *Evening Post,* 24 April 1865, signed by J. Sella Martin, led Charles A. Dana, assistant secretary of war, to order General Dix, who was in command, to rectify the racism of the council. As a result, the procession of 25 April found two thousand black people marching at the rear of the procession behind the Emancipator's coffin.[19]

Slavery had been dealt devastating blows with the final Emancipation Proclamation and the flight from bondage of thousands of slaves. Then late in 1864 and early in 1865 Maryland and Missouri abolished slavery immediately and without compensation. But the culminating event was the passage, on 31 January 1865, of the Thirteenth Amendment by the necessary two-thirds vote of the House of Representatives.

Appropriate mass meetings heralding the passage were widely held in the North. At one such, in Boston on 4 February, Garrison was the featured speaker. Hailing the event with exultant enthusiasm, Garrison declared it had "constitutionalized" the Declaration of Independence; it had made that revolutionary manifesto "the supreme law of the land," its purpose being, he said, "the protection of the rights and liberties of all who dwell in the American soil."[20]

On the face of it, the "protection of the rights and liberties" of all in the United States was the meaning of the Thirteenth Amendment, ratified by twenty-seven states, including eight of those that had been part of the Confederacy. The date of ratification was 6 December 1865. Its text was brief, unambiguous, unequivocal: "Neither slavery nor involuntary servitude, except as a punishment for crime whereof the party shall have been duly convicted, shall exist within the United States, or any place subject to their jurisdiction." This language was a vindication of the arguments of leading Abolitionists—like Theodore D. Weld, Lysander Spooner, William Goodell, and others—who had held that slavery had no legal existence in the United States since those held therein had never been charged or convicted of any crime and therefore were being denied their freedom—a "natural right" of all human beings—without due process of law. That argument was so well known to those who drafted the Thirteenth Amendment that it challenges credulity to believe there was no relationship between the two.

With the passage of the amendment, what then was the legal condition of the Afro-American freed people? That condition could be nothing other than *citizenship.* One draws this conclusion the more readily when recalling that the attorney general of the United States, Edward Bates, affirmed in November 1862 that free persons of color were citizens of the United States—thus contradicting Taney's opinion in *Dred Scott.* Further, the act establishing the Freedmen's Bureau on 3 March 1865 stated in its Section 4 that authority was herewith given to "set apart" abandoned land in the insurrectionary states, title to which was obtained by the United States, to a total of "not more than forty acres, to every male *citizen,* whether [loyal] refugee or freedman" (italics added).

Prior to the coming into force of the Thirteenth Amendment, several southern states—under Johnsonian restoration—had passed so-called Black Codes that went as far as ingenuity allowed to reinstate involuntary servitude without quite instituting chattel slavery. These codes, such as those of Mississippi and Louisiana, instituted peonage for the black population.[21] Given these as instructive illustrations of what might replace slavery, the Thirteenth Amendment outlawed both slavery and involuntary servitude. And for the first time in an amendment, this one carried a second section that states that "Congress shall have power to enforce this article by appropriate legislation."

In the face, however, of President Johnson's hostility, the existence of Black Codes and the reality of the terror practiced against blacks (and anti-Confederate whites), the Congress found it necessary to pass the Civil Rights Act. This first was adopted by both Houses on 13 March 1866, but it was vetoed by Johnson two weeks later. It was then passed over the veto on 9 April 1866. The act described itself as one meant "to protect all persons in the United States [not subject to a foreign power and excluding "Indians not taxed"] in their civil rights"; it also provided penalties of fine and imprisonment for violation of its provisions.

It explicitly affirmed the citizenship of the former slaves and added that they were to possess every right "enjoyed by white citizens" and that this was to prevail despite "any law, statute, ordinance, regulation, or custom, to the contrary notwithstanding." In the punishment section of the law, this formula is repeated, and guilt is affirmed if any person "under color of any law, statute, ordinance, regulation or custom" shall deprive any one of the rights specified in the first section. This act also specifically prohibited any distinction in terms of "punishment, pains, or penalties" because of race or color or previous condition of slavery or involuntary servitude The inclusion of the word *custom* indicated that the Congress that passed the 1866 Civil Rights Act was aiming at the elimination of racist discrimination not only by a state but also by any group or body or individual who, because of custom, practiced such discrimination.

The context of the passage of the Thirteenth Amendment and of the Civil Rights Act is fundamental in comprehending the purposes of the Fourteenth Amendment, passed by Congress slightly more than two months after the Civil Rights Act had been approved over the president's veto. Two years passed before this transforming amendment was ratified by the requisite number of states. Of course, in becoming part of the Constitution, the Fourteenth Amendment supplemented—it did not invalidate—the earlier Civil Rights Act. The latter act was aimed at benefiting the former slaves and preventing "any *person*" from infringing on those benefits. The Fourteenth Amendment is directed at *states,* not persons as such, because its immediate roots were the Black Codes of several states and other discriminatory acts and practices of states. Hence the amendment prohibits states from making or enforcing "any law which shall abridge the privileges or immunities of citizens of the United States"; nor may a state "deprive any person of life, liberty, or property, without due process of law; nor deny to any person within its jurisdiction the equal protection of the law."

The second section of this amendment provided for the reduction of congressional representation to any state in proportion to which such state denied suffrage to any (noncriminal) male citizens of twenty-one years of age or older, thus seeking to void the three-fifths representation provision of the original Constitution which had decisively favored the political fortunes of the slave-owning class. Unfortunately, this section seemed to convey the notion of expecting such disenfranchisement and punishing it in a somewhat abstract manner—made all the worse since in practice even such penalty was not incurred.

The Fifteenth Amendment, passed by Congress in February 1869 and ratified in twelve months, attempted to remedy this defect of the Fourteenth by simply directing that no citizen's right to vote was to be denied or abridged by the United States or by any state "on account of race, color, or previous condition of servitude." Alas, by about 1875, this again was substantially nonenforced and remained so for ninety years.

This amendment says nothing of voting being confined to males, and the leaders of the rising women's rights movement, pointing to this, tried to assert their right to vote. That suffrage, however, was to wait until ratification in August 1920 of the Nineteenth Amendment. But even then, although it enfranchised women, black women in the South remained disenfranchised in practice for another forty-five years.

Before turning to a brief elucidation of the antislavery sources of the Fourteenth Amendment and its intention to federalize the Bill of Rights so far as states were concerned, special note is to be taken of Section 4 of that amendment. Here, claims based on debts accumulated by and for the Confederacy are repudiated; such creditors found their investments, in fact, simply wiped out. But quite extraordinary was the clause in this section that followed the repudiation of such indebtedness. This declared that the U.S. government would not honor "any claim for the loss or emancipation of any slave." On the contrary, said this amendment, "all such debts, obligations, and claims shall be held illegal and void."

Thus was confiscated—without compensation—a very substantial amount of privately held property, including such property held by masters who had *not* been disloyal to the Union. This confiscatory act was revolutionary and may yet, in the future, serve as a precedent for other confiscatory acts should other forms of private property be found to be, by future generations, anachronistic or regressive or socially harmful.

There has been considerable debate as to whether or not the Fourteenth Amendment was meant, by its creators, to extend suffrage to adult black men, including those recently freed, and whether or not it meant to federalize the first eight amendments to the Constitution. The main negative position, recently affirmed, was that offered by Raoul Berger of Harvard in his 1977 book, *Government by Judiciary: The Transformation of the Fourteenth Amendment.*[22] The reviews of this book were generally critical, sometimes intensely so. It is not necessary, here, to repeat the critical evaluation of the Berger thesis, but none of the critics has pointed out a salient distortion in quotation that was basic to Berger's argument. This occurs where Berger calls as his witness Horace E. Flack, whose study of *The Adoption of the Fourteenth Amendment* (Baltimore: Johns Hopkins University Press, 1908) retains its classical quality. Berger wrote:

Flack's canvass of "speeches concerning the popular discussion of the XIV Amendment" led him to conclude: "The general opinion held in the North . . . was that the Amendment embodied the Civil Rights Act. . . . There does not seem to have been any statement at all as to whether the first eight Amendments were to be made applicable to the States or not, whether the privileges guaranteed by those Amendments were to be considered as privileges secured by the Amendment."

But here is the actual statement by Flack, with the words omitted by Berger in italics:

The general opinion held in the North . . . was that the Amendment embodied the Civil Rights Bill *and gave Congress the power to secure the privileges of citizens of the United States.* There does not seem to have been any statement at all as to whether the first eight Amendments were to be made applicable to the States or not, whether the privileges guaranteed by those Amendments were to be considered as privileges secured by the Amendment, *but it may be inferred that this was recognized to be the logical result by those who thought that the freedom of speech and of the press as well as due process of law, including a jury trial, were secured by it.*"

Not only has Berger emasculated the quotation from Flack, but he has misrepresented Flack's conclusions which actually were the opposite of his own. Thus Flack showed that the Civil Rights bills of late 1865 and 1866 meant to include the Bill of Rights within the states (p. 17), and he concluded that Section 1 of the Fourteenth Amendment incorporated the Bill of Rights (p. 54). Further he quoted Sen. John A. Bingham, the main author of that section, as declaring, "It meant nothing less than the conferring upon Congress the power to enforce, in every State of the Union, the Bill of Rights as found in the first eight Amendments" (p. 57). In fact, Flack concludes in very explicit language that Congress "had the following objects and motives in view for submitting the first section of the XIV Amendment to the States for ratification: (1) To make the Bill of Rights (first eight Amendments) binding upon, or applicable to, the States; (2) To give validity to the Civil Rights Bill; (3) To declare who were citizens of the United States" (p. 94).

In addition to misrepresentation on the question of the Fourteenth Amendment and the Bill of Rights, Berger is wrong when he affirms that "the proof is all but incontrovertible that the framers meant to leave control of suffrage with the States, which had always exercised such control, and to exclude federal intrusion" (p. 7). On the contrary, Flack makes clear that to congressmen Bingham of Ohio, George Boutwell of Massachusetts, Thaddeus Stevens of Pennsylvania, Jacob H. Howard of Michigan, and William P. Fessenden of Maine, that is, "to those most influential in framing the Fourteenth Amendment, negro voters seemed the prime objective" (p. 186). Again, Flack concludes his study with this unequivocal passage: "whatever rights were guaranteed against federal interference by the national Bill of Rights were now to be guaranteed by the Fourteenth Amendment against state action," but, he adds, truly, this did not rule out segregation (p. 201).

On the latter point, even the Fifteenth Amendment specifically affirming that race, color, and previous enslavement could not be grounds for disenfranchisement—was defective and was known to be defective by some of those who passed it. Thus, one of its leading sponsors, Oliver P. Morton of Indiana, warned in 1869 that black men, even with the Fifteenth Amendment, "may be disfranchised [by southern states] for want of education or for want of intelligence. . . . They [the states] may, perhaps, require property or educational tests, and that would cut off the great majority of colored men from voting in those States, and thus this amendment would be practically defeated in all those States where the great body of colored people live."[23] Within a few years, and with the cooperation of the U.S. Supreme Court, this came to pass; a century of struggle would be required to undo this betrayal of democracy.

The failure to fully confront racism and the practices of segregation and discrimination was projected by the lily-white delegation at the raising of the flag at Fort Sumter and the original exclusion of Afro-Americans from the procession of Lincoln's funeral. It appeared also even within the American Anti-Slavery Society in the contest between those who, in 1865, wanted the society continued and those who wanted it terminated. Garrison and Edmund Quincy led the latter group; Phillips and Douglass the former. Indeed, it is noteworthy that the left as represented by Phillips and Parker Pillsbury, and the black people as represented by Douglass, and most of the women members, like Lydia Maria Child, Lucretia Mott, and Abby Kelley Foster, wanted the society to continue.

In formal terms the argument revolved between those who insisted that the essential purpose of the Anti-Slavery Society was accomplished with the abolition of the institution and those who pointed out that the original constitution of the society affirmed its purposes to be not only the ending of slavery but also a commitment to combat racism and to strive to improve the conditions of the free black population. The Phillips-Douglass wing did not deny, of course, the primacy of the antislavery struggle, but it warned that racism persisted and that its excision was required to assure an egalitarian and democratic society. This effort was now as vital as had been that against slavery.

In the immediate contest within the society the Phillips-Douglass wing received a majority of the votes. It offered the presidency, again, to Garrison, but he rejected it, reiterating his view that the society's work was done. The society, with Phillips as president, continued for another five years, but the Garrisonian withdrawal and the position that evoked that withdrawal sapped it of strength. Its formal demise in 1870 had little practical impact.[24]

Reconstruction was betrayed and a long period of virulent racism dominated the United States. Always, of course, it met with resistance, but it required another century before *legal* equality became a fact. How long it will be before actual equality brightens the Republic is problematic. Yet this struggle is on today's agenda. That reality testifies to the profound success of the Abolitionist movement. It pioneered in the transformation of this nation from the paradox of a slaveholding Republic to one free of that abomination. Salutary work was left for the ensuing generations. Some was accomplished, but much more remains to be done. We must still create a democracy and undo a racist society that labels itself "democratic." The dedication, courage, and efficacy of the Abolitionist movement of the nineteenth century helped inspire equally noteworthy efforts in the twentieth century and will help inspire those in the decades to come.

Notes and References

Introduction

1. Bernard Bailyn, David Brion Davis, David Herbert Donald, John L. Thomas, Robert H. Wiebe, and Gordon S. Wood, eds., *The Great Republic* (Boston: Little, Brown, 1977), pp. 552–55.

2. Lewis Perry, *Radical Abolitionism: Anarchy and the Government of God in Antislavery Thought* (Ithaca: Cornell University Press, 1973), pp. xxii, 32.

3. James Ford Rhodes, *History of the United States from the Compromise of 1850* (New York: Macmillan, 1906), esp. pp. 53–63.

4. Ulrich B. Phillips developed this view in his "The Central Theme of Southern History," *American Historical Review* (1928), 34:30–43. One of those extending Phillips's theme to the entire United States is Merton L. Dillon, *The Abolitionists: The Growth of a Dissenting Minority* (DeKalb: Northern Illinois University Press, 1974), p. 26. A fuller critique of this view is in my "Resistance and Afro-American History," in Gary Y. Okihiro, ed., *In Resistance: Studies in African, Caribbean and Afro-American History* (Amherst: University of Massachusetts Press, 1986), pp. 18–20.

5. Richard H. Sewell, *Ballots for Freedom: Antislavery Politics in the United States, 1837–1860* (New York: Oxford University Press, 1976), esp. p. viii and chap. 8. See also Herbert Aptheker, *Toward Negro Freedom* (New York: New Century Publishers, 1956), pp. 182–91.

6. Wendell Phillips, *Speeches, Lectures, Letters,* 2d ser. (Boston, 1891) p. 320; quoted by Robert D. Marcus, "Wendell Phillips and American Institutions," *Journal of American History* 61 (1969): 49.

7. Lydia Maria Child, quoted by James M. McPherson, *The Struggle for Equality: Abolitionists and the Negro in the Civil War and Reconstruction* (Princeton: Princeton University Press, 1964), pp. 90–93. On this question of the central importance of racism, especially acute among white Abolitionists was Child. Thus, in the *Liberator,* 20 May 1842, she had written: "Great political changes may be forced by the pressure of external circumstances, without a correspond-

ing change in the moral sentiment of a nation; but in all such cases, the change is worse than useless; the evil reappears, and usually in a more exaggerated form." She is quoted by Aileen S. Kraditor, *Means and Ends in American Abolitionism: Garrison and His Critics on Strategy and Tactics, 1834–1850* (New York: Pantheon, 1967), p. 22. McPherson quotes on p. 431 a remark by Child with similar content made in 1878.

    8. Douglass quoted by John Blassingame, ed., *The Frederick Douglass Papers*. Series One; *Speeches, Debates and Interviews, 1855–1863* (New Haven: Yale University Press, 1985) 3:538; see also pp. 545–46.

    9. Thomas Jefferson to James Monroe, 20 September 1800, in P. L. Ford, ed., *The Writings of Thomas Jefferson,* 10 vols. (New York: G. P. Putnam's Sons, 1892–99), 7:457–58. For the context, see Herbert Aptheker, *American Negro Slave Revolts* (New York: Columbia University Press, 1943; International Publishers, 1987), p. 224.

Chapter One

    1. See Louis Ruchames, ed., *Racial Thought in America: From the Puritans to Abraham Lincoln* (Amherst: University of Massachusetts Press, 1969), esp. pp. 1–250.

    2. Dwight Lowell Dumond, *Antislavery: The Crusade for Freedom in America* (Ann Arbor: University of Michigan Press, 1961), pp. 87–95.

    3. On Lundy, see especially [Thomas Earle], *The Life, Travels, and Opinions of Benjamin Lundy* (Philadelphia: W. D. Parrish, 1847), and Merton L. Dillon, *Benjamin Lundy and the Struggle for Negro Freedom* (Urbana: University of Illinois Press, 1966). Garrison gave the highest praise to Lundy; see his letter to Lucretia Mott, 8 May 1845, in Walter Merrill, ed., *The Letters of William Lloyd Garrison* (Cambridge: Belknap Press of Harvard University Press, 1973), 3:295.

    4. Clarence Gohlen, "Some Notes on the Unitarian Church in the Ante-Bellum South," in David K. Jackson, ed., *American Studies in Honor of William K. Boyd* (Durham: Duke University Press, 1940), pp. 327–66.

    5. Davis in Bailyn, *Great Republic,* esp. pp. 428–43.

    6. Robert H. Abzug, *Passionate Liberator: Theodore Dwight Weld and the Dilemma of Reform* (New York: Oxford University Press, 1980), pp. 53–54.

Chapter Two

    1. Thomas D. Morris, *Free Men All: The Personal Liberty Laws of the North, 1780–1861* (Baltimore: Johns Hopkins University Press, 1974), passim; quotation on p. 41. This is not only a detailed history of the various personal liberty laws; it also is an excellent survey of constitutional law for the period indicated.

2. For the material on Calhoun, see Charles M. Wiltse, *John C. Calhoun,* 3 vols. (Indianapolis: Bobbs-Merrill, 1944–47), 1:188–210; on John Quincy Adams, see Charles F. Adams, ed., *Memoirs of John Quincy Adams,* 5 vols. (Philadelphia: J. B. Lippincott, 1874–77), 4:530–31; 5:10–12, 208–11.

3. Thomas Jefferson to John Holmes, 22 April 1820, in P. L. Ford, ed., *The Writings of Thomas Jefferson* (New York: Putnam, 1892) 10:157.

4. Timothy Fuller is quoted by Dumond, *Anti-Slavery,* p. 104.

Chapter Three

1. The first phrase occurs in a letter from Garrison to *Liberator,* 9 May 1843, in Walter Merrill, ed., *The Letters of William Lloyd Garrison* (Cambridge: Belknap Press of Harvard University Press, 1973), 3:157; the second in a letter of 11 May 1847, 3:479.

2. On Garnet, see Sterling Stuckey, *Slave Culture: Nationalist Theory and the Foundations of Black America* (New York: Oxford University Press, 1987), pp. 169–72.

3. Speech in Boston, 12 April 1852, in Wendell Phillips, *Speeches, Lectures and Letters* (Boston: Lee & Shepard, 1863), pp. 75–89; quotation on pp. 85–86.

4. Douglass's speech, 3 August 1857, in Blassingame, *Douglass Papers,* 3:204.

5. Quoted by James B. Stewart, *Wendell Phillips: Liberty's Hero,* (Baton Rouge: Louisiana State University Press, 1986), p. 153.

6. Quoted in Lowell H. Harrison, *The Antislavery Movement in Kentucky* (Lexington: University of Kentucky Press, 1978), p. 24.

7. J. W. Harris, *Plain Folk and Gentry in a Slave Society: White Liberty and Black Slavery in Augusta's Hinterlands* (Middletown, Conn.: Wesleyan University Press, 1985), p. 36.

8. On Colton, see Alfred A. Cave, *An American Conservative in the Age of Jackson: The Political and Social Thought of Calvin Colton* (Fort Worth: Texas Christian University Press, 1969), esp. pp. 29–38.

9. Charles M. Wiltse, *John C. Calhoun,* 3 Vols. (Indianapolis: Bobbs-Merrill, 1944–51), 2:274.

10. Ibid., 3:334.

11. Hofstadter, *The American Political Tradition and the Men Who Made It* (New York: Knopf, 1948); the chapter on Calhoun is so titled. This theme also appears in Richard Current, *John C. Calhoun* (New York, 1963), esp. pp. 86–102. Clyde N. Wilson's objection is argued in his introduction to volume 13 of *The Papers of John C. Calhoun,* 16 vols. (Columbia: University of South Carolina Press, 1977), pp. xvii–xxi; Wilson repeats his objection in the introduction to volume 15 (1983), p. xii.

12. All quotations from Calhoun come from Wilson, *Papers of Calhoun.*

Most fruitful for this study were vols. 13 (*1835–1837*), published in 1980; 14 (*1837–1839*), published in 1983; and 16 (*1841–1843*), published in 1984.

13. The Randolph speech is quoted in Dumond, *Anti-Slavery,* p. 68.

14. Quoted in Louis Ruchames, ed., *The Letters of William Lloyd Garrison,* vol. 2, *1836–1840* (Cambridge: Belknap Press of Harvard University Press, 1971), p. 239; see also Aileen S. Kraditor, *Means and Ends in American Abolition: Garrison and His Critics on Strategy and Tactics, 1834–1850* (New York: Pantheon, 1967), p. 259. Garrison, in the *Liberator,* 18 March 1837, insisted that "the true secret of all the uproar at the South, is, a *troubled conscience.*" He quoted the influential newspaperman, Duff Green, then editor of the *Washington Reformer* and himself a South Carolinian (and friend of Calhoun): "We believe that we have most to fear from the organized action upon the *consciences* and fears of slaveholders themselves. Our *greatest cause of apprehension* is, from the operation of the morbid sensibility which appeals to the *consciences* of our own people, and would make them the voluntary instruments of their own ruin." This statement was repeatedly quoted in Abolitionist documents and writings—as by Angelina Grimké and William Jay.

15. Wilfred Carsel, "The Slaveholders' Indictment of Northern Wage Slavery," *Journal of Southern History* 6 (1940):504–20.

16. Quoted by Bernard Mandel, *Labor: Free and Slave Workingmen and the Anti-Slavery Movement in the United States* (New York: Associated Authors, 1955), p. 40.

17. Hammond quoted by Kenneth S. Greenberg, "Revolutionary Ideology and the Pro-Slavery Argument," *Journal of Southern History* 42 (1976): 383. The entire essay (pp. 365–84) is relevant.

18. Garrison's letter is in Ruchames, *Letters,* 4:508.

19. See, generally, Harold M. Hyman and William M. Wiecek, *Equal Justice under Law, 1815–1875* (New York: Harper & Row, 1982), pp. 203–31.

20. The quotation from the *Washington Union* is in the *Congressional Globe,* 22 March 1858, appendix, pp. 199–201.

21. For the Stephens speech, see Edward McPherson, *Political History of the Great Rebellion, 1860–1865,* 4th ed., ed. H. M. Hyman and H. Trefousse (1865; New York: J. J. Chapman, 1882; reprint, 1972), pp. 103–4.

22. See Don E. Fehrenbacher, "The Origins and Purpose of Lincoln's 'House Divided' Speech," *Mississippi Valley Historical Review* 46 (1960):615–43. See also Fehrenbacher's *The Dred Scott Case: Its Significance in American Law and Politics* (New York: Oxford University Press, 1978), pp. 485–513.

23. Milton Meltzer and Patricia G. Holland, eds., *Lydia Maria Child: Selected Letters, 1817–1880* (Amherst: University of Massachusetts Press, 1982), pp. 383, 386, 393, 566.

24. Weld is quoted in Merton L. Dillon, *The Abolitionists: The Growth of a Dissenting Minority* (DeKalb: Northern Illinois Press, 1974), p. 266, and Seward, in G. E. Baker, ed., *William Henry Seward: Works* (Boston: Houghton Mifflin, 1884–90), 4:372.

25. Douglass's speech, Rochester, N. Y., 28 April 1861, in Blassingame, *Douglass Papers,* 3:426.

26. Julian quoted in Dillon, *Abolitionists,* p. 266.

27. Phillips quoted in Robert D. Marcus, "Wendell Phillips and American Institutions," *Journal of American History* 56 (1969): 56, 55, 53.

28. Phillips's "war for the Union" speech is in his *Speeches, Lectures and Letters* (1863 ed.), pp. 414–47; quoted matter, pp. 421–428.

Chapter Four

1. Meltzer, and Holland, *Child,* pp. 38–39, 42.

2. Douglass's speech at Salem, Ohio, 23 August 1852, in Blassingame, *Douglass Letters,* 2:396.

3. Hammond quoted in E. N. Elliot, ed., *Cotton Is King* (Augusta, Ga., 1860), pp. 140–41.

4. See P. G. and E. Q. Wright, *Elizur Wright* (Chicago: University of Chicago Press, 1937), p. 84. For a report of a similar conversation held in June 1850 between Sen. John A. Dix of New York with "a merchant" who was "one of the most wealthy and respectable," see W. P. and F. J. Garrison, *William Lloyd Garrison, 1805–1879,* 4 vols. (Boston: Houghton Mifflin, 1894), 3:280.

5. Letter signed "A.B.C. of Halifax City" in *Richmond Whig,* 13 April 1832.

6. Underwood to Sen. Howell Cobb, Clarksville, Ga., 2 February 1844, in U. B. Phillips, ed., "The Correspondence of Robert Toombs, Alexander H. Stephens and Howell Cobb," in *Annual Report of the American Historical Association, 1911* (Washington, D.C.: U. S. Government Printing Office, 1913) 2:54–55.

7. Thornwell quoted by Virginius Dabney in *Liberalism in the South* (Chapel Hill: University of North Carolina Press, 1932), p. 118.

8. On Douai, see W. D. Overdyke, *The Know-Nothing Party in the South* (Baton Rouge: Louisiana State University Press, 1950), p. 18; Morris Hillquit, *History of Socialism in the United States* (1903; New York: Russell & Russell, 1965), p. 191; P. S. Foner, *History of the Labor Movement in the United States* (New York: International Publishers, 1947), 1:264n.

9. See Clement Eaton, *Freedom of Thought in the Old South* (Durham, N.C.: Duke University Press, 1940), p. 228; Overdyke, *Know-Nothing Party,* pp. 17–18, 153; E. W. Dobert, "The Radicals," in A. E. Zucker, ed., *The Forty-Eighters* (New York: Russell & Russell, 1950), esp. pp. 173–79.

10. Congressman Smith's speech is in *Congressional Globe,* 33d Cong., 2d sess., appendix, p. 95.

11. See my "Class Conflicts in the South, 1850–1860," originally published in 1939, reprinted in Bettina Aptheker, ed., *The Unfolding Drama* (New York: International Publishers, 1979), pp. 48–67 and notes on pp. 160–63.

12. Phillips to Purvis, in Stewart, *Wendell Phillips,* p. 333.

13. Theodore M. Hammett, "Two Mobs of Jacksonian Boston: Ideology and Interest," *Journal of American History* 42 (1976): 845–68. esp. p. 864.

14. Letter in Ruchames, *Letters,* 2:618–19.

15. Letter in ibid., 2:696–97.

16. Letter in Merrill, *Garrison Letters,* 3:125.

17. R. J. M. Blackett, *Building an Anti-Slavery Wall: Black Americans in the Atlantic Abolitionist Movement* (Baton Rouge: Louisiana State University Press, 1983), p. 201.

18. Blassingame, *Douglass Papers,* 2:115–16.

19. Letter in Merrill, *Garrison Letters,* 3:292.

20. Letter in ibid., 3:393.

21. Letter in Ruchames, *Letters,* 4:508.

22. Kelley is quoted in Kraditor, *Means and Ends,* 233–95.

23. "Workingmen's Prayer" is in Mandel, *Labor,* p. 70.

24. W. F. Loften, "Abolition and Labor," *Journal of Negro History* 33 (1948): 249–83; the Middlesex County Appeal is on p. 257.

25. The 1849 Resolution is in the *Liberator,* 2 February 1849; see Kraditor, *Means and Ends,* p. 251.

26. Walt Whitman is quoted by Russel B. Nye in *Fettered Freedom* (East Lansing: Michigan State University Press, 1963), p. 249.

27. Louis Filler, *The Crusade against Slavery* (New York: Harper, 1960), p. 70.

28. Thomas Wentworth Higginson, *Cheerful Yesterdays* (Boston, 1898), p. 115; Howard N. Meyer, *Colonel of the Black Regiment: The Life of Thomas Wentworth Higginson* (New York: Norton, 1967), p. 72.

29. Edward Magdol, *The Anti-Slavery Rank and File: A Social Profile of the Abolitionist Constituency* (New York: Greenwood Press, 1986), pp. 36–38, 74. In this work Magdol also treats the antislavery views and activities of such labor leaders as George Henry Evans of New York, George Gunn of Philadelphia, and William West of Boston.

30. Eric Foner, "Workers and Slavery," in Paul Buhle and Alan Dawley, eds., *Working for Democracy* (Urbana: University of Illinois Press, 1965), p. 23.

31. Meltzer and Holland, *Child,* pp. 38–39.

32. Gilbert Hobbes Barnes and Dwight Lowell Dumond, eds., *The Letters of Theodore Dwight Weld, Angelina Grimké Weld and Sarah Grimké, 1832–1844,* 2 vols. (New York: D. Appleton-Century, 1934), 2:891–92.

33. An excellent contemporary account is by Edward Beecher, *Narrative of the Riots at Alton* (New York: E. P. Dutton, 1965), with an illuminating introduction by Robert Merideth. For the impact of Lovejoy's martyrdom, see Stewart, *Wendell Phillips,* pp. 59–60, and Dillon, *Abolitionists,* pp. 93–97. See also Dillon's biography of *Elijah Lovejoy* (Urbana: University of Illinois Press, 1961).

34. Leonard L. Richards, *"Gentlemen of Property and Standing": Anti-Ab-*

olition Mobs in Jacksonian America (New York: Oxford University Press, 1970), passim.

35. Bennett's *Herald* is quoted in the *Liberator,* 10 May 1850; See Ruchames, *Letters,* 4:9n.

36. *Chicago Times* and *New York Tribune* quoted in James McPherson, *Struggle for Equality* (Princeton: Princeton University Press, 1964), pp. 40–44.

37. William Goodell, *Slavery and Anti-Slavery: A History of the Great Struggle in Both Hemispheres: With a View of the Slavery Question in the United States* (New York: Wm. Harned, 1852), p. 407.

Chapter Five

1. See chapter on "Petitions," in Dumond, *Anti-Slavery,* pp. 242–48.

2. Garrison to Benson, 4 November 1836, in Ruchames, *Letters,* 2:182.

3. Mary Grew, in Ira V. Brown, "Cradle of Feminism: The Philadelphia Female Anti-Slavery Society, 1833–1840," *Pennsylvania Magazine of History and Biography* 102 (1978):150.

4. "Schools for agitators" are described in Robert H. Abzug, *Passionate Liberator: Theodore Weld and the Dilemma of Reform* (New York: Oxford University Press, 1980), pp. 151–52.

5. On the *National Era* readership, see Filler, *Crusade,* p. 195. Through 1831, Garrison's *Liberator* had some five hundred subscribers, with about 10 percent of them being white people, but within fifteen months it had increased five times. See Garrison to S. S. Jocelyn in Merrill, *Garrison Letters,* 1:119. The late Professor Russel B. Nye stated that Abolitionists published about thirty-five newspapers between 1831 and 1861. See his *Fettered Freedom,* pp. 86–116.

6. Letter in Ruchames, *Letters,* 2:233.

7. McPherson, *Struggle,* pp. 51, 86.

8. Dillon, *Abolitionists,* p. 91; Garrison to Pease, in Ruchames, *Letters,* 2:324; James G. Birney in Dumond, *Anti-Slavery,* p. 257.

9. Louis Ruchames, ed., *The Abolitionists: A Collection of Their Writings* (New York: G. P. Putnam's Sons, 1963), p. 20.

10. See John L. Myers, "The Beginning of Anti-Slavery Agencies in New York State, 1833–1836," *New York History* 43 (1962):149–81; and his "The Major Efforts of National Anti-Slavery Agents in New York State, 1836–1837," *New York History* 46 (1965):162–86. Quotation is on p. 183. Beriah Green (1795–1874) insisted on the biracial nature of Oneida Institute; at least fourteen black people attended it during Green's presidency. Included were two of exceptional distinction—the already noted Henry Highland Garnet and, later, Alexander Crummell, one of the inspirers of Du Bois. See Milton C. Sernett, *Abolition's Axe: Beriah Green, Oneida Institute, and the Black Freedom Struggle* (Syracuse: Syracuse University Press, 1986).

Chapter Six

1. David Brion Davis, *Problems of Slavery in the Age of Revolution 1770–1823* (Ithaca: Cornell University Press, 1975), pp. 72–73.

2. On Representative William L. Smith of South Carolina denouncing anti-slavery, see Betty Fladeland, *Men and Brothers: Anglo-American Anti-Slavery Cooperation* (Urbana: University of Illinois Press, 1972), p. 150; Howard A. Ohline, "Slavery, Economics and Congressional Politics, 1790," *Journal of Southern History* (1980):335–60, esp. p. 349. Others voiced Smith's sentiments at the time, for example, James Jackson of Georgia. See Stuart E. Knee, "The Quaker Petition of 1791," *Slavery & Abolition* (London) 6 (1985):151–59.

3. Whitman's *Leaves of Grass* (1855), sec. 10.

4. The quotations from advertisements for fugitive slaves are from Lathan A. Windley, comp., *Runaway Slave Advertisements: A Documentary History from the 1730s to 1790*, 4 vols. (Westport, Conn.: Greenwood Press, 1983), 3:345; 4:177; 1:370–71. For an analysis of this remarkable collection, see Herbert Aptheker, *We Will Be Free: Advertisements for Runaways and the Reality of American Slavery*, Occasional Paper no. 1, Ethnic Studies Program, University of Santa Clara, 1984.

5. Solomon Northup, *Twelve Years a Slave* (Auburn, Buffalo, and London: Derby & Miller, 1853), pp. 78ff.

6. *Life and Times of Frederick Douglass Written by Himself* (New York: Pathway Press, 1941), pp. 139–41.

7. On the purchase of freedom, see Herbert Aptheker, *To Be Free* (New York: International Publishers, 1948), pp. 31–40.

8. For Stowe, see ibid., p. 199.

9. The Remond letter is in the *Liberator*, 20 July 1838.

10. Blassingame, *Douglass Papers*, vol. 3 (1985), introduction.

11. On the strenuous speaking tours of the Grimké sisters, see Gerda Lerner, *The Grimké Sisters from South Carolina: Pioneers for Women's Rights and Abolitionism* (New York: Schocken Books, 1971), esp. pp. 183–204.

12. Letter is in the *Liberator*, 30 November 1838.

13. For Remond, see the *Liberator*, 15 February 1842.

14. This story was told by Louis Ruchames, "Race, Marriage and Abolition in Massachusetts," *Journal of Negro History* 40 (1955):250–73.

15. Herbert Aptheker, "The Struggle within the Ranks," *Masses & Mainstream* 3 (February 1950):47–57. On evidences of racism and elitism in Edmund Quincy and Maria Weston Chapman, see Stewart, *Wendell Phillips*, p. 103.

16. Theodore S. Wright, in *The Colored American* (New York), 4 October 1837; reprinted in Herbert Aptheker, *Documentary History of the Negro People in the United States*, 3 vols. (New York: Citadel Press, 1951), 1:169–73.

17. For Garnet, see Aptheker, *To Be Free*, pp. 56, 204–52. It is of great interest that in the massive slave unrest that rocked Jamaica late in 1831, one of the leading insurrectionists, Samuel Sharpe, "did not plan armed rebellion, but

massive passive resistance. . . . The slaves were to sit down and refuse to work until their masters acknowledged that they were free men and agreed to pay them wages." Most of the slaves, however, rejected this concept and armed uprising was the reality; Sharpe seemed to have actually hoped passive resistance by the slaves would continue after the masters did resort to violent repression. Could Garnet have known about this? See Cedric J. Robinson, *Black Marxism: The Making of a Black Radical Tradition* (London: Zed Press, 1983), pp. 216–17.

18. In his newspaper, 5 April 1856, Douglass was compelled to complain: "Opposing slavery and hating its victims has become a very common form of Abolitionism"—quoted in Eric Foner, ed., *America's Black Past* (New York: Harper & Row, 1970), p. 177—quoting an essay (1965) by Leon Litwack. See also Douglass's rage at a very insensitive remark by Garrison in Blassingame, *Douglass Papers*, 3:17–18n5.

19. Garrison to Dole, In Merrill, *Garrison Letters*, 1:155.

20. For Garrison on Beaumont, see Ruchames, *Letters*, 2:312.

21. Dillon, *Abolitionists*, p. 68.

22. Weld on Mrs. Mathews is in Dumond, *Anti-Slavery*, p. 280.

23. Weld to Tappan is in Barnes and Dumond, *Letters of Weld-Grimké*, 1:270–72.

24. Emerson concluded this thought by adding: "America is not civil, whilst Africa is barbarous." See Ralph Waldo Emerson, *Miscellanies* (Boston: Houghton Mifflin, 1884), p. 173. See P. L. Nicoloff, *Emerson on Race and History* (New York: Columbia University Press, 1961), esp. p. 124.

25. Charles Sumner, *Works* (Boston: Lee & Shepard, 1871), 1:160.

26. Gilbert Osofsky, "Abolitionists, Irish Immigrants and the Dilemmas of Romantic Nationalism," *American Historical Review* 80 (1975):889–912.

27. Louis Ruchames, "The Abolitionists and the Jews," *Publications of the American Jewish Historical Society* 42 (1952):131–55.

28. For general estimates of escape, see W. H. Siebert, *The Underground Railroad* (1898; reprint, New York: Russell & Russell, 1967). Siebert thought 60,000 slaves made it to the North from 1830 to 1860 (p. 44). See also, W. B. Hesseltine, *A History of the South*, 2d ed. (New York: Prentice-Hall, 1943, p. 258. See also references in 4 above. For another view, see Larry Gara, *The Liberty Line: The Legend of the Underground Railroad* (Lexington: University of Kentucky Press, 1961).

29. Birney to Lewis Tappan, 27 February 1837, in D. L. Dumond, ed., *Letters of James Gillespie Birney*, 2 vols. (New York: D. Appleton-Century, 1938), 1:376.

30. On black agents of the Underground Railroad, see sources given in Herbert Aptheker, "The Negro in the Abolitionist Movement," *Science & Society* 5 (1941), esp. p. 13n31. See also Henrietta Buckmaster, *Let My People Go* (New York: Harper & Bros., 1941), passim.

31. For Grimes and Burris, see W. H. Siebert, *The Underground Railroad*

in Massachusetts (Worcester: American Antiquarian Society, 1936), pp. 3, 7, 21–24; William Still, *Underground Railroad Records* (Philadelphia: Porter & Coates, 1872), p. 746.

32. John H. Russell, *The Free Negro in Virginia* (Baltimore: Johns Hopkins University Press, 1913), p. 165n, and Helen T. Catterall, ed., *Judicial Cases Concerning American Slavery and the Negro*, 5 vols. (Washington, D.C.: Carnegie Institution, 1926–37), 2:511; 4:200, 232.

33. Kate E. R. Pickard, *The Kidnapped and the Ransomed* (1858; New York: Pathway Press, 1941), and Northup, *Twelve Years.*

34. Still, *Underground Railroad,* preface and p. 329.

35. Odell Shepard, ed., *The Journals of Bronson Alcott* (Boston: Little, Brown, 1938), p. 190.

36. On Nelson Hackett, see Frank Klingberg and Annie Abel, eds., *A Side-Light on Anglo-American Relations, 1839–1858, Furnished by Correspondence of Lewis Tappan and Others with British and Foreign Anti-Slavery Society* (Lancaster, Pa.: Association for the Study of Negro Life and History, 1927), p. 108.

37. See: Still, *Underground Railroad,* p. 368; Carlos Martyn, *Wendell Phillips* (New York: Funk & Wagnalls, 1890), p. 221; Blassingame, *Douglass Papers,* 3:89–90. For William Craft's remarkable speech attacking racism, delivered in England in 1863, see C. Peter Ripley, ed., *The Black Abolitionist Papers,* vol. 1, *The British Isles* (Chapel Hill: University of North Carolina Press, 1985), pp. 537–42. See the biography of the Crafts by Larry Gara in R. W. Logan and M. R. Winston, eds., *Dictionary of American Negro Biography* (New York: Norton, 1982), pp. 139–40; and especially the chapter on them in R. J. M. Blackett, *Beating Against the Barriers: Biographical Essays in Nineteenth Century Afro-American History* (Baton Rouge: Louisiana State University Press, 1986).

38. Still, *Underground Railroad,* p. 81; Lloyd C. Hare, *Lucretia Mott* (New York: American Historical Society, 1937), p. 228. After Samuel A. Smith served his eight-year prison sentence, he moved to Philadelphia. For an account of a mass meeting of black people to welcome him, see *New York Tribune,* 5 July 1856. See also Garrison to Pease in Merrill, *Garrison Letters,* 3:625.

39. For Loguen's remarks in April 1854, see Carter G. Woodson, ed., *The Mind of the Negro as Reflected in Letters Written during the Crisis, 1800–1860* (Washington, D.C.: Associated Publishers, 1926), p. 267.

40. Siebert, *Massachusetts,* p. 5. On Josiah and his son, Edmund, both prominent Abolitionists, see Edmund Quincy, *Life of Josiah Quincy* (Boston: Ticknor & Fields, 1867).

41. The original of this petition is in the Harvard College Library; it is published in Aptheker, *Documentary History,* 1:20–21.

42. Benjamin Quarles, *Black Abolitionists* (New York: Oxford University Press, 1969), pp. 204–5.

43. For a pioneering and still useful study of early antislavery developments, see Mary S. Locke, *Anti-Slavery in America from the Introduction of African Slaves to the Prohibition of the Slave Trade, 1619–1808* (Boston: Ginn,

1901). For a later and more specialized study, see James D. Essig, *The Bond of Wickedness: American Evangelicals against Slavery, 1770–1808* (Philadelphia: Temple University Press, 1982).

44. Eric Williams, *Capitalism and Slavery* (Chapel Hill: University of North Carolina Press, 1940).

45. On Williams's critics, see David Brion Davis, *The Problem of Slavery in the Age of Revolution, 1770–1823* (Ithaca: Cornell University Press, 1975), pp. 63, 347.

46. Thomas L. Haskell, "Capitalism and the Origins of the Humanitarian Sensibility, pt. 2," *American Historical Review* 90 (June 1985): 547.

47. Seymour Drescher, *Econocide: British Slavery in the Era of Abolition* (Ithaca: Cornell University Press, 1977), p. 218.

48. Betty Fladeland, *Men and Brothers: Anglo-American Antislavery Co-operation* (Urbana: University of Illinois Press, 1972), preface.

49. For Davis, see *The Problem of Slavery in Western Culture* (Ithaca: Cornell University Press, 1966); for Genovese, see *From Rebellion to Revolution* (Baton Rouge: Louisiana State University Press, 1979), esp. p. 121.

50. Uprisings in the West Indies are described in Michael Craton, *Testing the Chains: Resistance to Slavery in the British West Indies* (Ithaca: Cornell University Press, 1982).

Chapter Seven

1. Bettina Aptheker, *Woman's Legacy* (Amherst: University of Massachusetts Press, 1982), p. 13.

2. Gerda Lerner, *The Majority Finds Its Past* (New York: Oxford University Press, 1979), p. 34.

3. For the Vermont convention, see Lewis Perry, *Radical Abolitionism: Anarchy and the Government of God in Antislavery Thought* (Ithaca: Cornell University Press, 1973), pp. 228–30.

4. W. R. Waterman, *Frances Wright* (New York: Columbia University Press, 1924); Alice Perkins and Theresa Wolfson, *Frances Wright: Free Enquirer* (New York: Harper & Bros., 1939); Keith E. Melder, "The Beginning of the Women's Rights Movements in the United States, 1800–1840" (Ph.D. diss., Yale University, 1963), pp. 58–61. Important additional material on Wright is in Albert Post, *Popular Freethought in America, 1825–1850* (New York: Columbia University Press, 1943), passim; especially significant here is the attention given to her lectures in cities like Memphis, Louisville, and Baltimore in the 1820s (pp. 141–42). Post also broaches the connection between atheistic and deistic thought and Abolitionism; it deserves full treatment.

5. See Blanche G. Hersh, *The Slavery of Sex: Feminist Abolitionists in America* (Urbana: University of Illinois Press, 1978), pp. 65–67, 197–99. Abner Kneeland, a leader of the free-thought movement of the early nineteenth cen-

tury, attacked the inequality and brutality characterizing the marriage relationship. See Roderick S. French, "Liberation from Man and God: Kneeland's Free Thought Campaign, 1830–1839," *American Quarterly* 32 (1980): 202–21, esp. pp. 205–7.

6. On these marriages, see Hersh, *Slavery of Sex,* pp. 90–91.

7. Anne F. Scott, *The Southern Lady: From Pedestal to Politics, 1830–1930* (Chicago: University of Chicago Press, 1970), esp. pp. 46–79.

8. For the Phelps case, see Katherine Anthony, *Susan B. Anthony* (Garden City, N.Y.: Doubleday, 1954), pp. 156–58, and Bettina Aptheker, *Woman's Legacy,* p. 157n52.

9. For example, by 1822, there was a Female Charity Society in operation in Rochester, N.Y. See Nancy A. Hewitt, *Women's Activism and Social Change: Rochester, New York, 1822–1872* (Ithaca: Cornell University Press, 1984), p. 22.

10. See W. P. and F. J. Garrison, *Garrison,* 1:156–57. Abolitionist women prior to the Civil War conducted petition campaigns on such issues as divorce, child custody, and wages. See, for example, an account of such petitions in New York in Eleanor Flexner, *Century of Struggle,* rev. ed. (Cambridge: Harvard University Press, 1975), pp. 85–86.

11. There is a long obituary on Elizabeth Chandler in the *Liberator,* 29 November 1834, and further notice of her when Garrison visited her grave in Michigan in 1853. Merton Dillon wrote about her in E. T. James, ed., *Notable American Women* (Cambridge: Harvard University Press, 1971), 1:319–20.

12. Weld on Phebe Mathews Weed is in Dumond, *Anti-Slavery,* p. 280.

13. Lillie B. Chace Wyman, "Sojourner Truth," *New England Magazine,* March 1901, p. 84; see Bettina Aptheker, *Woman's Legacy,* p. 24.

14. The 1838 resolution is in Carleton Mabee, *Black Freedom: The Non-Violent Abolitionists from 1830 through the Civil War* (New York: Macmillan, 1970), p. 92.

15. On Mary Putnam, see McPherson, *Equality,* pp. 140–41.

16. Garrison letter, 17 July 1839, is in Ruchames, *Letters,* 2:502.

17. The James Forten, Jr., speech is in Melder, "Beginning of Women's Rights Movement," p. 158.

18. Blassingame, *Douglass Papers,* 2:248.

19. Ibid., 3:39–40.

20. Phillips, in his *Speeches* (1863 ed.), pp. 11–34.

21. On Mott and the Grimké letters, see Lerner, *Grimké Sisters,* chap. 12.

22. Much of Sarah Grimké's argument is reminiscent of Mary Wollstonecraft's *A Vindication of the Rights of Women,* appearing 1792 in the midst of the French Revolutionary upheaval.

23. See Donald H. Maynard, "The World's Anti-Slavery Convention of 1840," *Mississippi Valley Historical Review* 42 (1960):452–71.

24. For the consequence of bazaars, see Betty Fladeland, *Men and Brothers,* p. 358; Jane H. Pease and William H. Pease, *Bound with Them in Chains:*

A Biographical History of the Anti-Slavery Movement (Westport, Conn.: Greenwood Press, 1972), p. 45; and Blassingame, *Douglass Papers*, 1:70–71.

25. On petition campaigns, see, for example, Garrison to Elizabeth Pease, 6 November 1837, in Ruchames, *Letters*, 2:326, and to Isaac Knapp, 6 May 1838, 2:357.

26. See Louis Ruchames, "Race, Marriage, and Abolition in Massachusetts," *Journal of Negro History* 40 (1955):250–73.

27. Lerner, *The Majority Finds Its Past*, pp. 112–28; quotation on p. 128.

28. McPherson, *Struggle*, pp. 125–26; see also Dumond, *Anti-Slavery*, pp. 242–48.

29. Blassingame, *Douglass Papers*, 3:15*n*; 2:461.

30. Ruchames, *Letters*, 2:180, 326.

Chapter Eight

1. *Right and Wrong in Boston* (1836), p. 3.

2. See Filler, *Crusade*, p. 61; Eaton, *Freedom of Thought*, p. 365; Dillon, *Abolitionists*, p. 180.

3. Details are in Aptheker, *American Negro Slave Revolts* (see the 1987 edition) and *We Will Be Free*, passim.

4. David Martin, *Trial of the Rev. Jacob Gruber, Minister in the Methodist Episcopal Church, at the March Term, 1819, in the Frederick County Court, for a Misdemeanor* (Frederickton, Md.: published by the author, George Kalb, printer, 1819). A copy of this rare book of 111 pages was kindly supplied to me by the library of the University of California at Davis.

5. Humphrey Smith in Aptheker, *To Be Free* (1969 ed.), p. 45.

6. On Walker, see my introduction to *One Continual Cry: David Walker's "Appeal to the Colored Citizens of the World" and Its Setting and Meaning* (New York: Humanities Press, 1965) and the sources cited therein. See the essay on Walker in Sterling Stuckey, *Slave Culture* (New York: Oxford University Press, 1987), pp. 98–167.

7. William Pease and Jane Pease, "Walker's *Appeal* Comes to Charleston: A Note and Documents," *Journal of Negro History* 59 (1974):287–92.

8. Samuel J. May, *Some Recollections* (Boston: Fields, Osgood, 1869), p. 124.

9. Garrison's trial and imprisonment may be followed in Merrill, *Garrison Letters*, 1:98–111; and in W. P. and F. J. Garrison, *Garrison*, 1:165–91.

10. Nye, *Fettered Freedom*, p. 154n114.

11. For the Prudence Crandall case, see Edwin W. Small and Miriam R. Small, in *New England Quarterly* 37 (1944):506–29; W. P. and F. J. Garrison, *Garrison*, 1:315–23; Dumond, *Anti-Slavery*, pp. 212–17.

12. Filler, *Crusade*, p. 71; Clarence Gohdes, "Some Notes on the Unitarian

Church in the Ante-Bellum South," in David K. Jackson, ed., *American Studies in Honor of William K. Boyd* (Durham, N.C.: Duke University Press, 1940), pp. 327–66.

13. Merton Dillon, *Elijah Lovejoy, Abolitionist Editor* (Urbana: University of Illinois Press, 1961), pp. 65, 81.

14. Roy Basler, ed., *Works of Abraham Lincoln* (New Brunswick, N.J.: Rutgers University Press, 1953) 1:108–13.

15. Dumond, *Anti-Slavery,* pp. 186, 205; Eaton, *Freedom of Thought,* p. 359.

16. Dumond, *Anti-Slavery,* pp. 234–35.

17. Goodell, *Slavery,* p. 413.

18. Ibid., p. 440.

19. Ibid., pp. 438–39; Nye, *Fettered Freedom,* p. 103.

20. The Birney, Bailey, and Lovejoy cases (and lives) have produced a considerable literature. In particular, see Betty Fladeland, *James G. Birney: Slaveholder to Abolitionist* (Ithaca: Cornell University Press, 1955); Stanley Harrold, *Gamaliel Bailey and Antislavery Union* (Kent, Ohio: Kent State University Press, 1986); and Dillon's *Lovejoy.*

21. Dumond, *Anti-Slavery,* p. 220.

22. The *Amistad* and *Creole* cases evoked great contemporary interest and a substantial secondary literature. See, especially, Bertram Wyatt-Brown, *Lewis Tappan and the Evangelical War against Slavery* (Cleveland: Case Western Reserve University Press, 1969), pp. 205–22; Howard Jones, "The Peculiar Institution and National Honor: The Case of the *Creole* Slave Revolt," *Civil War History* 21 (1975):214–37; Howard Jones, *Mutiny on the Amistad: The Saga of a Slave Revolt and Its Impact on American Abolition, Law and Diplomacy* (New York: Oxford University Press, 1987). Frederick Douglass eulogized the leader, Madison Washington, of the *Creole* uprising; see "The Heroic Slave" in Julia Griffiths, ed., *Autographs for Freedom* (Boston: J. P. Jewett, 1853), 1:174–239. See also Aptheker, *To Be Free,* p. 55.

23. On Giddings, see George W. Julian, *The Life of Joshua Giddings* (Chicago: A. C. McClurg, 1892), esp. pp. 118–19; and Gidding's *Speeches in Congress* (Boston: J. P. Jewett, 1853), esp. pp. 19, 22, 24.

24. Windley, *Runaway Slave Ads.*

25. Ira Berlin, *Slaves without Masters: The Free Negro in the Antebellum South* (New York: Pantheon, 1974), pp. 334–37.

26. Goodell, *Slavery,* pp. 440–41.

27. Lewis Hayden (1815?–89) became a militant Abolitionist and citizen of Boston. He was chief of the Boston end of the Underground Railroad. He was prominent in the Sims and Burns rescue attempts, assisted John Brown, helped recruit black troops in the Civil War (in which his son was killed), and aided in desegregating Boston's schools. After the war, he served as an official of the state government and in 1879 was elected to the state legislature. See the ac-

count of his life by Kenneth W. Porter in the *Dictionary of American Negro Biography*, ed. R. W. Logan and M. R. Winston (New York: Norton, 1982), pp. 295–97.

28. The best source for the astonishing career of Calvin Fairbank is his autobiography, *Rev. Calvin Fairbank during Slavery Times: How He "Fought the Good Fight" to Prepare the Way* (Chicago: R. R. McCabe, 1890). This now rare book contains an appendix by Laura S. Haviland, a close associate of Fairbank's, who organized a rescue attempt that failed. The book is noteworthy in detailing the hellish conditions in Kentucky jails, then operated as privately run businesses, leased from the state. Fairbank's pardon, on 14 April 1864 was ordered by Acting Governor R. T. Jacob. A modern biography of Fairbank is badly needed. See the brief account in Lowell H. Harrison, *The Antislavery Movement in Kentucky* (Lexington: University of Kentucky Press, 1978), pp. 62–64.

29. See *Narrative of Lunsford Lane, Formerly of Raleigh, North Carolina* (Boston: published by the author, printed by J. G. Torrey, 1842).

30. On Rudder, see Merrill, *Garrison Letters,* 3:275n1.

31. Fladeland, *Men and Brothers,* p. 295.

32. J. C. Lovejoy, *Memoir of Charles T. Torrey Who Died in the Penitentiary of Maryland, Where He Was Confined for Showing Mercy to the Poor* (Boston: Jewett & Co., 1847); Merrill, *Garrison Letters,* 3:338; Goodell, *Slavery,* pp. 441-44; Fladeland, *Men and Brothers,* p. 343.

33. *Personal Memoirs of Daniel Drayton, for Four Years and Four Months a Prisoner (for Charity's Sake) in Washington Jail, including a Narrative of the Voyage and Capture of the Schooner "Pearl"* (Boston: Bela Marsh, 1855). See also Ruchames, *Letters,* 4:194n2; and Louise Hall Tharp, *Until Victory: Horace Mann and Mary Peabody* (Boston: Little, Brown, 1953), pp. 234–44.

34. Jonathan Walker, *The Branded Hand: Trial and Imprisonment of Jonathan Walker at Pensacola, Florida, for Aiding Slaves to Escape from Bondage, with an Appendix Containing a Sketch of his Life* (Boston: Anti-Slavery Office, 1845). Slightly enlarged editions were issued by the same source in 1846 and 1850. See also W. P. and F. J. Garrison, *Garrison,* 3:131.

35. Still, *Underground Railroad,* pp. 623–41, 712–19.

36. Aptheker, *American Negro Slave Revolts,* p. 338; Harrison, *Anti-Slavery Movement in Kentucky,* pp. 83–84.

37. *Liberator,* 13 July 1849.

38. Still, *Underground Railroad,* pp. 84–86; *New York Daily Tribune,* 31 July 1856.

39. For note of Grimes, see Aptheker, *Documentary History,* 1:370, 476; and Blassingame, *Douglass Papers,* 2:441n.

40. Meltzer and Holland, *Child,* p. 27.

41. Harold Schwarz, *Samuel Gridley Howe* (Cambridge: Harvard University Press, 1956), pp. 152–54.

42. [Thomas Brown], *Brown's Three Years in the Kentucky Prisons, from*

May 30, 1854 to May 18, 1857 (Indianapolis: Courier Co., 1857). This rare 21-page pamphlet was supplied the author through the kindness of the Library, University of California at Irvine.

43. On the Mexican War and United States expansionism in that period, and the politics surrounding these developments, see esp. Frederick Merk and Lois Merk, *Slavery and the Annexation of Texas* (New York: Knopf, 1972).

44. Edward W. Emerson and Waldo E. Forbes, eds., *Journals of Ralph Waldo Emerson, 1820–1872* (Boston: Houghton Mifflin, 1912), 8:236.

45. On southern developments, 1850–60, see Aptheker, *American Negro Slave Revolts*, pp. 340–59, and "Class Conflicts in the South," in Bettina Aptheker, *The Unfolding Drama*, pp. 48–66, and sources cited therein.

46. Goodell, *Slavery*, pp. 445–46.

47. Clement Eaton, "Mob Violence in the Old South," *Mississippi Valley Historical Quarterly* 29 (1942):364.

48. J. William Harris, *Plain Folk and Gentry in a Slave Society: Liberty and Black Slavery in Augusta's Hinterland* (Middleton, Conn.: Wesleyan University Press, 1985), p. 62.

49. Henry Steele Commager, ed., *Documents of American History*, 4th ed. (New York: Appleton-Century-Crofts, 1948), 1:327–29.

50. Still, *Underground Railroad*, pp. 248–50. Green was a Methodist minister when arrested. After being pardoned in 1862, he moved to Canada. See C. Peter Ripley, ed., *The Black Abolitionist Papers, vol. 1, The British Isles, 1830–1865* (Chapel Hill: University of North Carolina Press, 1985), p. 461n7.

51. *Liberator,* 16 September 1853; Blassingame, *Douglass Papers*, 3:204–5.

52. Ibid., 3:205n, citing *New York Tribune,* 6 June and 9 July 1857.

53. The Sims, Christiana, and Jerry cases have produced a voluminous literature; all general studies of Abolitionism refer to them. Vivid accounts are in Henrietta Buckmaster, *Let My People Go* (New Harper & Bros., 1941). The Christiana case is exhaustively treated in Jonathan Katz, *Resistance in Christiana* (New York: Crowell, 1974). See also Dumond, *Anti-Slavery*, pp. 305–25; and Aptheker, *Documentary History*, 1:299–309, 322–24, 336–41, 368–72.

54. See the 221-page book, *The Trial of Theodore Parker, for the "Misdemeanor" of a Speech in Faneuil Hall against Kidnapping, before the Circuit Court of the U.S. at Boston, April 8, 1855, with the defence by T. Parker* (Boston: for the author, 1855). This examines several cases of the early 1850s, in addition to that involving Parker, including Burns, Christiana, Rachel Parker (1851), Glover (1854), and others.

55. Passmore Williamson, *Case of Passmore Williamson: Report of the Proceedings on the Writ of Habeas Corpus* (Philadelphia: U. Hunt & Son, 1856). Copy in Law Library, University of California, Berkeley. See Still, *Underground Railroad*, pp. 86–97.

56. Julius Yanuck, "The Garner Fugitive Slave Case," *Mississippi Valley Historical Review* 40 (1953): 47–66. See also Harrison, *Anti-Slavery Movement in Kentucky*, p. 91; Blassingame, *Douglass Papers*, 3:128n.

Chapter Nine

1. Du Bois's *John Brown* originally was published in 1909 by the George W. Jacobs Co. in Philadelphia. It has been reprinted many times; significant additional material is in the 1959 edition (New York: International Publishers). See the edition edited by Herbert Aptheker (Millwood, N.Y.: Kraus-Thomson, 1973). The quotation is from the preface; see also p. 99 of the Kraus edition. See also Benjamin Quarles, ed., *Blacks on Brown* (Urbana: University of Illinois Press, 1972), pp. ix–x.

2. Douglass, *Life and Times* (New York: Pathway Press, 1941), pp. 302–6.

3. Brown's "Words of Advice" are in Louis Ruchames, ed., *John Brown: The Making of a Revolutionary* (New York: Grosset & Dunlap, 1969), p. 84.

4. Evidence of this development is in Aptheker, *To Be Free* pp. 41–74, 191–210. The data in the text *supplements* the material in that book.

5. Ann Phillips is quoted from Weston Family Papers, Boston Public Library, by J. H. Pease and W. H. Pease, in "Confrontation and Abolition in 1850," *Journal of American History* 56 (1969); 927.

6. Blassingame, *Douglass Papers,* 3:88; italics added.

7. Smith, W. P. and F. J. Garrison, *Garrison,* 3:440.

8. *Liberator,* 13 August 1858; Aptheker, *Documentary,* 1:406–8.

9. W. P. and F. J. Garrison, *Garrison,* 3:473.

10. The details and history of the Spooner plan (based on papers in the Boston Public Library) are in Aptheker, *To Be Free,* pp. 62–67.

11. On *Ableman* v. *Booth,* see H. M. Hyman and W. W. Wiecek, *Equal Justice under Law: Constitutional Development, 1835–1875* (New York: Harper & Row, 1982), pp. 150–52, 201; and S. I. Kutler, ed., *The Supreme Court and the Constitution* (New York: Norton, 1977), pp. 110–13.

12. W. P. and F. J. Garrison, *Garrison,* 3:436.

13. On Black Jack Creek, see ibid., 3:241.

14. Stephen B. Oates, *To Purge This Land in Blood: A Biography of John Brown* (New York: Harper & Row, 1970), p. 137.

15. On the Oberlin-Wellington rescue effort, see contemporary account by John M. Langston (Charles's brother, and later a representative from Virginia in Congress) in *The Anglo-African* (New York) 1 (July 1859):209–16. The Charles Langston speech is in Aptheker, *Documentary,* 1:423–33. See also Oates, *To Purge This Land,* pp. 266–68.

16. The canard of insanity employed first by court-appointed defense attorneys was immediately and indignantly rejected by Brown. It was reiterated by some proslavery advocates at the time and by many later historians, including Allen Johnson, Allan Nevins, and C. Vann Woodward. This has been effectively refuted by Ruchames, *John Brown,* pp. 37–39, and by Oates, *To Purge This Land,* pp. 330–34, 410–12. Very much to the point of Brown's sanity was the testimony of Frederick Douglass who knew him long and well. This appears in

an essay by him, "Capt. John Brown Not Insane," first published in *Douglass' Monthly,* November 1859; reprinted in P. S. Foner, ed., *The Life and Writings of Frederick Douglass* (New York: International Publishers, 1950), 2:458–60.

17. W. A. Phillips, in Ruchames, *John Brown,* p. 220.

18. Oates, *To Purge This Land,* p. 326.

19. Ibid., p. 325.

20. Osborne P. Anderson, *A Voice from Harper's Ferry* (Boston, 1861), reprinted in Jean Libby, *Black Voices from Harper's Ferry* (Palo Alto, Calif: published by the author, 1979), p. 31.

21. Oates, *To Purge This Land,* p. 274, gives relevant population figures from the 1860 census for the six counties (four in Virginia, two in Maryland) adjacent to Harper's Ferry. These came to 115,449 white people; 9,891 free black people; 18,048 slaves—of whom only 5,000 were male—pointing to the small-farm and domestic character of slavery in the area.

22. Douglass's *Life and Times,* p. 353.

23. On Harriet Tubman being left behind, see Libby, *Black Voices,* p. 148. She had urged that Brown strike on 4 July, but this proved impossible; see Earl Conrad, *Harriet Tubman* (New York: International Publishers, 1942), p. 126.

24. Phillips, *Speeches* (1863 ed.), pp. 278–79.

25. Norton to Mrs. Edward Twisleton, 13 December 1859, in Sara Norton and Mark A. De Wolfe Howe, eds., *Letters of Charles Eliot Norton,* 2 vols. (Boston: Houghton Mifflin, 1913) 1:197–98.

26. Julia Ward Howe to Maillard, in Schwarz, *Samuel Gridley Howe,* p. 236.

27. Longfellow in Oates, *To Purge This Land,* p. 319.

28. Emerson, in Ruchames, *John Brown,* p. 269.

29. Meltzer and Holland, *Child,* pp. 323–29.

30. William Cullen Bryant II and T. G. Voss, eds., *The Letters of William Cullen Bryant* (New York: Fordham University Press, 1984), p. 81.

31. On these statements, see Oates, *To Purge This Land,* p. 356; Frank P. Stearns, *The Life and Public Services of George Luther Stearns* (Philadelphia: Lippincott, 1907), p. 190; Jules Abels, *Man on Fire: John Brown and the Cause of Liberty* (New York: Macmillan, 1971), p. 387.

32. Jerzy Zedlicke, "The Image of America in Poland, 1776–1945," *Reviews of American History* 14 (1986): 673–74.

33. Ruchames, *John Brown,* p. 163.

34. Quarles, *Blacks on Brown,* p. 34.

35. Avery O. Craven, *Edmund Ruffin: Southerner* (New York: D. Appleton, 1932).

36. On Copeland, see Aptheker, *Documentary,* 1:443–45.

37. Douglass, 1 August 1860, in Blassingame, *Douglass Papers,* 3:386–87.

38. Douglass, *Life and Times,* pp. 351–53.

39. For the post-Brown period, see C. L. Mohr, *On the Threshold of Freedom: Civil War Georgia* (Athens: University of Georgia Press, 1986), pp. 3–67; John Cimprich, *Slavery's End in Tennessee* (University: University of Alabama

Press, 1985), chap. 1; Berlin, *Slaves without Masters*, pp. 343–80; Oates, *To Purge This Land*, pp. 321–22; Aptheker, *American Negro Slave Revolts*, pp. 340–59; Bettina Aptheker, *The Unfolding Drama*, pp. 48–66.

Chapter Ten

1. McPherson, *Struggle*, pp. 29, 65–68.
2. William Goodell, in *Principia* (New York), 4 May 1861.
3. Moncure Conway, *The Rejected Stone* (Boston: Walker, Wise & Co., 1861), pp. 75–80, 110.
4. W. P. and F. J. Garrison, *Garrison*, 3:445.
5. Phillips in 1860—see ibid., 3:505.
6. Blassingame, *Douglass Papers*, 3:381.
7. Rhodes, *History of United States*, p. 63; see McPherson, *Struggle*, p. 24.
8. For Lincoln remark, see Basler, ed., *Works of Lincoln*, 7:499–500. See also Lincoln to James Conkling, 26 August 1863, ibid., 6:408–10.
9. On federal action relative to slavery during the Civil War, see W. P. and F. J. Garrison, *Garrison*, vol. 4, passim; McPherson, *Struggle;* Herman Belz, *Emancipaiton and Equal Rights: Politics and Constitutionalism in the Civil War Era* (New York: Norton, 1974), passim; and several of my own works, especially *The Negro in the Civil War* (New York: International Publishers, 1938), passim; *To Be Free,* pp. 73–135; and *Documentary History,* 1:459–98.
10. W. P. and F. J. Garrison, *Garrison*, 3:69.
11. McPherson, *Struggle*, pp. 221–37.
12. These books are V. Jacques Voegeli, *Free But Not Equal* (Chicago: University of Chicago Press, 1967); Eugene H. Berwanger, *The Frontier against Slavery* (Urbana: University of Illinois Press, 1967); James A. Rawley, *Race and Politics* (Philadelphia: University of Pennsylvania Press, 1969); Phyllis F. Field, *The Politics of Race in New York* (Ithaca: Cornell University Press, 1982). See my essay in G. Y. Okihiro, ed., *In Resistance* (Amherst: University of Massachusetts Press, 1986), pp. 10–20.
13. Aptheker, *Documentary History,* 1:477–80.
14. Ibid., 1:488–90.
15. Ibid., 1:491–93.
16. W. P. and F. J. Garrison, *Garrison*, 4:133.
17. Ibid., 4:134–35.
18. Ibid., 4:143–45.
19. Aptheker, *Documentary,* 1:499, 507.
20. W. P. and F. J. Garrison, *Garrison*, 4:129–30.
21. The texts of these codes may be examined in Commager's *Documents,* 2:2–7.
22. On the Berger book, there is a considerable literature. See, as exam-

ples, E. R. Larsen in the *Nation,* 10 December 1977, and the exchange between Berger and Larsen in the *Nation,* 25 February 1978. See also the review of Berger by Robert Kaszorowski in *American Historical Review* 83 (1978): 811–12. In particular, see R. Kaszorowski's essay in *American Historical Review* 92 (1987): 45–68, and sources cited therein. In general, see Bernard Schwarz, ed., *The XIV Amendment: A Century in American Law and Life* (New York: New York University Press, 1970); and Jacobus ten-Broek, *Equal under Law* (New York: Collier Books, 1965).

23. On Morton and the Fourteenth Amendment, see J. R. Pole, *The Pursuit of Equality in American History* (Berkeley: University of California Press, 1978), esp. pp. 172–74.

24. W. P. and F. J. Garrison, *Garrison,* 4:153–62.

Bibliographic Essay

The literature on Abolitionism is abundant. In this brief bibliographical essay, attention will be centered on (1) bibliographies of the movement; (2) collections of contemporaneous writings by Abolitionists; and (3) compilations of relevant essays by historians. Also, in the Notes and References of this volume will be found the outstanding interpretive writings on the movement.

Antislavery Bibliographies

Preeminent is Dwight Lowell Dumond's *A Bibliography of Anti-slavery in America* (Ann Arbor: University of Michigan Press, 1961). This oversized, double-column volume of 119 pages lists "the literature written and circulated by those active in the anti-slavery movement" including its "seeding time" in the 1790s. It is a monument to a scholar who devoted his life to studying antislavery in the United States.

The late distinguished librarian, Dorothy B. Porter, who assisted a generation of students (including myself), compiled a bibliography of *The Negro in the United States* (Washington, D. C.: Library of Congress, 1970). Porter wrote in the preface that the volume "is selective rather than exhaustive," and she called attention to several other bibliographical sources. But hers is authoritative up to the date of publication. For the antislavery struggle, the titles listed on pages 117–42 are especially pertinent.

A year after the publication of Porter's volume appeared a book of equal consequence with additional listings and some evaluation: James B. McPherson, Laurence B. Holland, James M. Bonner, Nancy J. Weiss, Michael D. Bell, *Blacks in America: Bibliographical Essays* (Garden City, N.Y.: Doubleday & Co., 1971). Especially important for Abolitionism are pages 73–98.

Merton L. Dillon, whose work has been noted in the text, published "The Abolitionists: A Decade of Historiography, 1959–1969," *Journal of Southern History* 35 (1969): 500–522. Some more recent listings are in Dillon's *The Abolitionists* (DeKalb: Northern Illinois University, 1974), pp. 277–86.

David Brion Davis's "The Emergence of Immediatism in British and American

Antislavery Thought," *Mississippi Valley Historical Review* 49 (1962): 209–30, contains seventy-two extended footnotes that serve as a good bibliographical source for the period from the middle of the eighteenth century to 1830.

Don E. Fehrenbacher's *The Dred Scott Case: Its Significance in American Law and Politics* (New York: Oxford University Press, 1979), reflects the author's conviction that the case "studied in breadth and depth . . . becomes a point of illumination, casting light upon more than a century of American history" (p. 7). The book contains a section of notes (pp. 597–723) which is a very full guide to political and, especially, legal history involving slavery in the United States.

Collections of Contemporaneous Documents

Pioneering in documentary work in Afro-American history—as in that subject as a whole—was Carter G. Woodson. Two of the many books he produced are especially pertinent: *Negro Orators and Their Orations* (Washington, D.C.: Associated Publishers, 1925), and *The Mind of the Negro as Revealed in Letters Written during the Crisis* (Washington, D.C.: Associated Publishers, 1926).

I spent about seven years searching archives, newspapers, and other original sources for the first volume of my *A Documentary History of the Negro People in the United States* (New York: Citadel Press, 1951); much of it deals directly with the antislavery movement. Devoted entirely to that movement is *And Why Not Every Man? The Documentary Story of the Fight against Slavery in the United States* (New York: International Publishers, 1970).

There are several good collections of writings by Abolitionists; all make exciting reading. Among these are two edited by Louis Ruchames: *The Abolitionists: A Collection of Their Writings* (New York: G. P. Putnam's Sons, 1963) and *Racial Thought in America: From the Puritans to Abraham Lincoln* (Amherst: University of Massachusetts Press, 1969). Note also Ruchames's *John Brown: The Making of a Revolutionary* (New York: Grosset & Dunlap, 1969). The last title calls to mind Benjamin Quarles, ed., *Blacks on John Brown* (Urbana: University of Illinois Press, 1972) with contemporary accounts on pages 3–44. Important is William H. Pease and Jane H. Pease, eds., *The Anti-Slavery Argument* (Indianapolis: Bobbs-Merrill, 1965). Note also Donald G. Mathews, ed., *Agitation for Freedom: The Abolitionist Movement* (New York: Wiley, 1972).

Special attention must be called to Garrison's *Liberator* which was published each week from the beginning of 1831 to the close of 1865. Many major libraries have bound volumes of the complete run. There is no more single illuminating source of the movement than this newspaper; it also remains a vibrant periodical that holds the reader.

The writings of black women during the epoch of enslavement make up the first 258 pages of the fascinating book edited by Dorothy Sterling, *We Are Your Sisters: Black Women in the Nineteenth Century* (New York: Norton, 1984). Broader in coverage but equally exciting, with much of it directly relevant to Abolitionism, is Gerda Lerner, ed., *Black Women in White America: A Docu-*

mentary History (New York: Pantheon, 1972), esp. pp. 47–72. Supplementing Lerner's book is that edited by Bert J. Loewenberg and Ruth Bogin, *Black Women in Nineteenth Century Life* (University Park: Pennsylvania State University Press, 1976), esp. pp. 181–280.

The letters and other writings of several leading Abolitionists have been published; these constitute an invaluable source and, again, are stimulating, sometimes inspiring. Good collections include Gilbert H. Barnes and Dwight Lowell Dumond, eds., *The Letters of Theodore Dwight Weld, Angelina Grimké Weld and Sarah Grimké, 1822–1844*, 2 vols. (New York: D. Appleton Century, 1934); and D. L. Dumond, ed., *Letters of James Gillespie Birney, 1831–1857*, 2 vols. (New York: D. Appleton Century, 1938).

Milton Meltzer, Patricia G. Holland, and Francine Krason edited *Lydia Maria Child: Selected Letters, 1817–1880* (Amherst: University of Massachusetts Press, 1982). The nearly six hundred pages of this book are a mine of information.

The Letters of William Lloyd Garrison, edited alternately by Walter M. Merrill and Louis Ruchames, 5 vols. (Cambridge: Harvard University Press, 1971–75) is an indispensable work. Supplementing it are the four volumes produced by his sons, Wendell Phillips Garrison and Francis Jackson Garrison, *William Lloyd Garrison, 1805–1879* (Boston: Houghton Mifflin, 1894).

The three volumes (available as of this writing) of John W. Blassingame, ed., *The Frederick Douglass Papers* (New Haven: Yale University Press, 1979–85) constitute a basic resource. Not to be overlooked, however, are the four volumes produced by Philip S. Foner on the *Life and Writings of Frederick Douglass* (New York: International Publishers, 1951); this effort, while containing some errors noted in Blassingame, remains very helpful and is a tribute to its indefatigable producer.

Badly needed is a modern full collection of the letters, speeches, and papers of the indomitable Wendell Phillips. Available are two volumes collecting some of them (Boston, 1891).

Essays by Historians

Collections of essays on Abolitionism by historians include Hugh Hawkins, ed., *The Abolitionists: Immediatism and the Question of Means* (Boston: D. C. Heath, 1964); Richard O. Curry, ed., *The Abolitionists: Reformers or Fanatics?* (New York: Holt, Rinehart & Winston, 1965); Martin Duberman, ed., *The Antislavery Vanguard* (Princeton, N.J.: Princeton University Press, 1965); John H. Bracey, Jr., August Meier, and Elliott Rudwick, eds., *Blacks in the Abolitionist Movement* (Belmont, Calif.: Wadsworth Publishing Co., 1971); and Robert H. Abzug and Stephen E. Maizlish, eds., *New Perspectives on Race and Slavery in America: Essays in Honor of Kenneth M. Stampp* (Lexington: University Press of Kentucky, 1986).

Index

Ableman v. *Booth* (1859), 128
Adams Express Co., 73, 113
Adams, John, 1
Adams, John Quincy, xv, 9–12, 24, 106, 107
Adoption of the Fifteenth Amendment (Flack), 159–60
Africa, 74, 85, 106
African Methodist Episcopal Church, 62
Alabama, 2, 4, 6, 24, 40, 102, 105
Albany, N.Y., 70, 81, 110
Alcott, Bronson, 71–72, 136
Alcott, Louisa May, 137
Akron, O., 84
Allan, William T., 2
Allegheny Mountains, 125, 133
Allen, Richard, 62
Allen, William, 95
Alton, Il., 47, 106
American and Foreign Anti-Slavery Society, 54, 87
American Anti-Slavery Society, xii, 2, 3, 48, 52, 54, 57, 62, 66, 67, 87, 104, 105, 112, 127, 160
American Committee for Promoting Abolition of Slavery, 3
American Home Missionary Society, 5
American Negro Slave Revolts (H. Aptheker), 75
American Revolution, 74
American Society for the Promotion of Temperance, 5
Amherst College, 54, 94

Amistad, mutiny aboard, 106
Anderson, Osborne P., 133
Anderson, Robert, 154
Andover Seminary, 94, 110
Anglo-African (a magazine), 85
Anthony, Susan B., 79, 81, 83, 92, 151–52
Antigua, 76
Anti-racism, 4, 51, 64, 67–69, 72–73, 82, 83, 84, 85, 92, 151–52, 161
Anti-Semitism, 69
Anti-Slavery Bugle (a newspaper), 55, 82, 106
Appeal in Favor of that Class of Americans Called Africans (Child), 68, 82
Appeal to the Colored Citizens of the World (Walker), 98–99
Aptheker, Bettina, 76–77
Arkansas, 6, 72
Asia, 74
auction, slave, 61
Augusta, Ga., 98
Augusta, John, 70
Austin State Times (a newspaper), 38–39
Autobiography (Douglass), 14
Avis, John, 138–39

Bahamas, 27, 72, 107, 111
Bailey, Gamaliel, 106
Baldwin, Henry, 11
Ballard, John, 120
Ballou, Adin, 32, 94

Baltimore, Md., 3, 37, 39, 70, 100, 108, 110, 111, 141
Baltimore Sun (a newspaper), 140, 141
Baptists, 4
Barbados, 76
Barrow, David, 1
Bates, Edwin, 156
Bayard, James A., 112
bazaars, anti-slavery, 51, 91
Beardsley, Samuel, 48
Beaumont, Gustav de, 67
Beecher, Catharine, 68, 89
Beecher, Henry Ward, 89, 154
Beecher, Lyman, 89
Bennett, James Gordon, 47–49
Benson, George W., 55
Benson, Henry G., 52, 55
Berger, Raoul, 158–60, 181–82n22
Berlin, Ira, 107–8, 141
Berwanger, E. H., 152
Bessick, Thomas, 70
Bill of Rights, 85, 158–60
Bingham, John A., 159, 160
Birmingham, England, 16, 82
Birney, James G., 48, 53, 56, 70, 106
Bishop, Antoinette, 79
Blackburn, Gideon, 2
Black Codes, 156
Blackett, R. J. M., 42–43
Black Reconstruction (Du Bois), 150
Blackwell, Henry, 80
Blackwell, Lucy Stone. *See* Stone, Lucy
Bond, Samuel, 70
Book and Slavery Irreconcilable, The (Bourne), 2, 68
Booth, John Wilkes, 139
Booth, Sherman M., 128
Boston, 16, 33, 47, 49, 55, 62, 64, 70, 73, 82, 84, 98, 99, 100, 114, 118, 136, 154, 155
Boston Female Anti-Slavery Society, 52, 90, 94
Bourne, George, 2, 68
Boutwell, George, 160
Bowditch, Henry J., 94
Bowdoin, Me., 63
Boyer, Henry, 109
Braddock, James P., 120

Branch, Julia, 78–79
Breckinridge, John, 18
Brice, Nicholas, 100
Brief and Candid Answer (Saffin), 18
Bristol County Anti-Slavery Society, 45
British West Indies, 13, 18, 27, 69, 74, 76
Bronson, Asa, 45
Brooklyn Eagle (newspaper), 45
Brooklyn, N.Y., 62, 133, 155
Brown, Anne, 135
Brown, Antoinette, 79
Brown, Henry ("Box"), 73, 113
Brown, John, xi, xvi, 17, 106, 116, 122, 123–42, 144, 149, 153, 179n16
Brown, John L., 109
Brown, Martha, 135
Brown, Mary, 123, 138–39
Brown, Oliver, 135
Brown, Thomas, 114–15
Brown, William Wells, 55
Bryant, William Cullen, 137
Buchanan, James, 26, 30, 130
Buffalo, N.Y., 65, 127
Buffum, Arnold, 56
Burns, Anthony, 114, 118, 119
Burr, James E., 108
Burris, Samuel D., 70
Burritt, Elihu, 99
Burritt, Elijah, 99
Bushnell, Simon N., 129
Butler, Benjamin, 146

Cadre-training school, 53–54
Calhoun, John C., xvi, 9–10, 19–29, 31, 38, 103, 154
Campbell, Alexander, 2
Canada, 28, 63, 70, 72, 128, 150
Canadaigua, N.Y., 17
capitalism, 75
Capitalism and Slavery (Williams), 74
Carman, Joshua, 2
Carsel, Wilfred, 29
Carter, Landon, 60
Carter, Robert, 60
Centre College, 113
Chambersburg, Pa., 133
Chandler, Elizabeth, 82, 83, 174n11

Chapel Hill, N.C., 99
Chaplin, William L., 117
Chapman, Maria Weston, 35, 53, 66, 82, 91, 94, 112
Charleston, S.C., 24, 30, 47, 59, 95, 99, 103, 154
Charlestown, Va., 135
Chartist Movement, 43
Chase, Samuel P., 106, 121
Chernishevsky, Nikolai, 137
Chicago, 49, 73
Chicago Times (a newspaper), 49
Child, Lydia Maria, xi, xv, 32–33, 35–36, 46, 55, 68, 82, 91, 92, 114, 137, 151, 167, 163–64n7
Choate, Rufus Jr., 49
Christiana, Pa., 118
Cincinnati, 47, 48, 54, 68, 70, 83, 103
Cincinnati Ladies Anti-Slavery Circle, 93
Cinque (slave rebel), 106
citizenship of Afro-American, 156, 157, 159
civil liberties, xvi, xviii, 25, 105
Civil Rights Act (1866), 156–57, 159
Civil War, 32, 98, *143–62*
Clapp, Henry, 79
Clapperton, Hugh, 85
Clay, Henry, 19, 25
Cleveland, O., 84, 130
Coffin, Joshua, 2, 62, 70, 94
Cole, Thomas, 62
Coles, Edward, 2
Coles, Lester B., 117
Collins, John A., 32
colonialism, 20, 28
colonization (of Afro-Americans), 82, 89, 98, 147
Columbia, Pa., 70
Columbia, S.C., 117
Colton, Calvin, 19
Concord, Mass., 72, 140
Confederacy, 31, 33, 141, 145, 146, 148
Confiscation Act, 146
confiscation of property, 158
Connecticut, 32, 101, 102, 151, 152
Considerations on Negro Slavery (McDonnell), 18

Constitution, U.S., xvii, 8, 10, 12, 13, 21, 74, 120, 146, 149, 158
Conway, Moncure, 143
Copeland, John A., 130, 140
Cornutt, John, 117
Covey, slave-breaker, 61
Craft, Ellen, 72, 83
Craft, William, 72–73
Crandall, Prudence, 83, 101–2
Crandall, Reuben, 104
Crawford, William, 114
Crittenden, John J., 109
Cuba, 76, 106
Curti, Merle, 99
Curtis, William, 120

Daily Dispatch (a Richmond newspaper), 117–18
Dana, Charles A., 155
Danders, Jacob, 95
Davis, David Brion, xi, 4–5, 58, 74, 75
Davis, Jefferson, xvi, 29, 92
Davis, Paulina, 79
Day, William H., 112
De Baptist, George, 70
Declaration of Independence, 21, 26, 50, 52, 91, 107, 110, 147–48
Delany, Martin R., 70, 123
Delaware, 112
Demerara, 76
Democratic Party, 149
Denham, Dixon, 84
Detroit, 73, 150
Deutsche Zeitung (a newspaper), 39
Dickenson, Anna, 83
Dickerson, Samuel, 154–55
Dillon, Merton, 56, 67, 163n4
discrimination, racist, 64
District of Columbia, 21, 26, 50, 52, 91, 107, 110, 147, 148
Dix, John A., 155, 167n4
Doak, Samuel, 2
Dominica, 76
Douai, Adolph, 38, 39
Douglas, Margaret, 117
Douglas, Stephen, 31

Douglass, Frederick, xi, xv, xvi, 15, 17, 32, 33, 35, 43, 55, 61, 63, 66–67, 70, 80, 84, 85, 87, 93, 119, 123, 125–27, 133–34, 140–41, 144, 150, 151, 152, 154, 155, 160–61, 177n18
Doyle, Patrick, 112–13, 115
Drayton, Daniel, 110–11
Dred Scott case, 23, 30, 120, 128, 147, 156
Drescher, Seymour, 75
Dresser, Amos, 103–4
Du Bois, W. E. B., xvi, 75, 123, 136, 150
Dumond, Dwight Lowell, 1

Econocide: British Slavery in the Era of Abolition (Drescher), 75
Eden, Joshua, 59
Edmundsen, Emily, 62
Edmundsen family, 111
education, demand for, 151
Elkins, Stanley, 59
Emancipation Proclamation, xv, xvi, 141, 147–49, 156–59
Emancipator (a newspaper), 3, 89
Embree, Elihu, 3
Emerson, Ralph Waldo, 69, 115, 118, 136, 148, 171n24
Engels, Frederick, 76
England, 2, 67, 90, 109, 114
Enterprise (a ship), 27
Essay on Slavery and Abolitionism (Beecher), 68, 89
Europe, 14, 15, 28, 32, 41, 55, 150
Evans, George Henry, 168n29

Fairbank, Calvin, 108–9, 114, 115, 117n28
Fall River, Mass., 45
Fay, Richard, 49
Fee, John G., 94
Fessenden, William P., 160
feudalism, 75
Field, Phillis F., 152
Fifteenth Amendment, 158, 160
Filler, Louis, 45
Fillmore, Millard, 11

Finney, Charles G., 5
Fitzhugh, George, 30
Flack, Horace E., 159–60
Fladeland, Betty, 75, 109
Florida, 4, 6, 72, 111–12
Follen, Charles, 94
Foner, Eric, 46
Forbes, George, 128, 134
Forsyth, John, 98
Forten, Charlotte, 83, 153
Forten, Harriet, 83
Forten, James, 35, 153
Forten, James Jr., 86
Forten, Marguerite, 83
Forten, Sarah, 83
Fort Sumter, S. C., 138, 143, 154, 160
Foster, Abby Kelly, 43, 54, 81, 83, 85, 87, 161
Foster, Stephen S., 66, 79
Fourteenth Amendment, 151, 157–60
France, 5, 28, 43, 146
Frances, Convers, 46, 114
Franklin, Benjamin, 1
Free Black people, xiv, 7, 8, 98, 99, 109, 110, 113, 141, 156, 161
Freedmen's Bureau, 151, 156
Freedom's Journal (a newspaper), 65
Freeman, Theophilus, 61
Free Soil Party, xv, 56, 121
Fremont, John C., 39, 94
French Revolution, 74
Fugitive Slave Act (1793), 6, 8, 71, 73
Fugitive Slave Law (1850), 25, 71, 115, 118, 122, 128, 146
fugitive slaves, 7, 12, 43, 59–60, 69–74, 107, 110–11, 112, 113, 115, 117, 118–20, 121, 128, 129, 147, 171n28; *See also* individual cases
Fuller, John E., 53
Fuller, Timothy, 13

"gag rule" in Congress, 24, 25, 105
Gaines, Archibald K., 121, 122
Galliland, James, 2
Garibaldi, Guiseppi, 137
Garner, Margaret, 119, 121–22

Garner, Simon Jr., 121

Garnet, Henry Highland, 15, 65–66, 123, 127, 144, 149

Garrett, Thomas, 112

Garrison, George T., 153

Garrison, Helen Benson, 42

Garrison, William Lloyd, xi, xvi, 1, 2, 3, 4, 10, 11, 15, 16, 21, 30, 32–35, 40, 41–42, 43, 52, 53, 54, 55, 56, 67, 79, 81, 85, 86, 91, 93, 98, 99–101, 112, 119, 126, 127, 144, 148, 150, 154, 155, 160–61

Gay, Sidney Howard, 56

General, a runaway slave, 60

Genius of Universal Emancipation (a newspaper), 3, 81, 82, 99

Genovese, Eugene D., 75

Georgetown, S.C., 98

Georgia, 4, 6, 9, 24, 60, 72, 96, 98, 99, 104, 105, 118, 145

Germany, 38

Gibbons, Abby Hopper, 81

Giddings, Joshua, 107

Glanding, E. T., 112

Gloucester, J. M., 123

Gloucester, J. M., Mrs., 123, 133

Glover, Joshua, 128

Gohlen, Clarence, 4

Goodell, William, 15, 21, 49, 57, 143, 156

Goodrich, William, 70

Government by Judiciary (Berger), 158

Grant, Ulysses S., 138, 154

Great Britain, 5, 10, 14, 17, 20, 27, 42, 60, 63, 67, 74, 75, 81, 146; *See also* England

Greece, 5

Green, Beriah, 57, 169n10

Green, Duff, 166n10

Green, Mary, 83, 84

Green, Samuel, 117

Green, Shields, 133, 134

Grenada, 76

Grew, Mary, 53

Griffiths, Julia, 93

Grimes, Leonard, 70, 113–14

Grimké, Angelina, 53, 63–64, 68–69, 82, 89–90, 93; *See also* Weld, Angelina Grimké

Grimké, Sarah, 53, 63–64, 82, 84, 89, 90–91, 93

Gruber, Jacob, 96–97

Gunn, Lewis, 44

Hackett, Nelson, 72

Haiti, 74, 75, 147

Hamilton, Alexander, 1

Hammett, Theodore M., 41

Hammond, James H., 29, 30, 36–37, 109

Hancock, John, 73

Harper, William, 30

Harpers Ferry, 124, 129, 130, 132, 133, 134–45

Harris, Elijah, 117

Harris, Sarah, 101

Harris, William, 101

Harvard College, 94, 117, 158

Haskell, Thomas, 75

Hatfield, John, 70

Haviland, Laura, 83

Hawks, Martha, 46

Hayden, Harriet, 108

Hayden, Lewis, 70, 108, 176n27

Hayes, Rutherford B., 122

Hedrick, Benjamin, 94

Heinzen, Karl, 39

Herold des Westens (a newspaper), 39

Heyrick, Elizabeth, 3, 81

Hickman, William, 2

Higginson, Thomas Wentworth, 45, 46, 80, 118

Hildreth, Richard, 55

Hillsborough, Ga., 104

Hillsborough, N.C., 99

Hofstadter, Richard, 19

Hogsmire, Jonas, 96

Howe, Julia Ward, 136

Howe, Samuel Gridley, 114

Hugo, Victor, 116, 137

Hunn, John, 112

Hyde, Udney H., 118

Ignashias, John, 95
Illinois, 2, 31, 47, 83, 102, 108, 149
Immediate, Not Gradual Emancipation
(Heyrick), 3, 82
Independent, The (a magazine), 56
India, 28, 74
Indiana, 2, 70, 109, 114, 115, 160
"Indians". *See* Native Americans
insurrection, of slaves, 65, 75, 95, 98,
107, 112, 116, 125, 127
Iowa, 152
Ireland, 14, 15, 16, 28, 91
Isaac, a slave, 108–9
Ithaca, N.Y., 102

Jackson, Andrew, 11, 24, 47, 103
Jackson, Francis, 52
Jackson, Thomas J. ("Stonewall"), 139
Jacksonian era, 5
Jamaica, 76, 170–71n17
Jay, John, 1
Jay, William, 94
Jedlicki, Jerzy, 137
Jefferson City, Mo., 108
Jefferson, Thomas, xvii, 1, 13, 28, 75,
97, 107
Johnson, Andrew, 156
Johnson, Jane, 119–20
Johnson, Miriam B., 46
Jones, George, 71
Jones, Jane E. Hitchcock, 82
Julian, George W., 32, 33

Kagi, John Henry, 130, 133
Kane, John K., 120
Kansas, 25, 30, 102, 128–29
Kelly, Abby. *See* Foster, Abby Kelly
Kentucky, 2, 4, 18, 38, 105, 108, 112,
114–15, 117, 121, 122
Key, Francis Scott, 104
Key to Uncle Tom's Cabin (Stowe), 111
Kimball, John S., 53
King, Rufus, 9
Kitchell, Aaron W., 104
Knapp, Isaac, 53
Kneeland, Abner, 173n5

Know-Nothingism, 69
Kosciuszko, Thaddeus, 137

Labor and Abolitionism, xiv, xvi, 23, *35–
49*, 168n29
land distribution, 15, 147, 151, 156
Lane, Lansford, 109
Lane Seminary, 2, 68, 94, 106
Langston, Charles, 129–30
Latin America, 13, 55
Lawrence, Kansas, 129
League of Gileadites, 126
Leary, Lewis S., 130
Leavitt, Joshua, 64
Lecompton Constitution, 30
Lee, Robert E., 124, 135, 138, 153, 154
Lerner, Gerda, 78, 92
Letters on the Equality of the Sexes (Sarah
Grimké), 90
Letters to Catharine E. Beecher (Angelina
Grimké), 68
Lewis, Thomas, 99
Lexington, Ky., 108, 113
Liberalist (a newspaper), 101
Liberator, The (a newspaper), 10, 52,
54–55, 66, 67, 71, 80, 82, 83, 85, 89,
90, 99, 101, 169n5
Liberia, 147
Liberty Party, 56
Limus, a fugitive slave, 59–60
Lincoln, Abraham, xvii, 12–13, 103, 106,
109, 141, 142, 143, 144, 145, 146,
147, 152, 155
Lind, Jenny, 62
literacy, seeking, 117–18
Loguen, J. W., 12, 70
London, 18, 43, 91
London Prison Discipline Society, 114
Loring, Ellis, 52
Louisiana, 4, 6, 38, 94, 156
Louisiana Purchase, 6
Louisville, Ky., 39
Lovejoy, Elijah, 2, 47, 102, 106, 110,
153, 168n33
Lowell, James Russell, 62, 84, 94, 138
Lowell, Mass., 44, 154

Lundy, Benjamin, 2, 3–4, 82, 98, 99–100, 111, 164n3
lynching, 103, 106
Lynn Female Society, 46
Lynn, Mass., 45, 55, 83, 84

McBride, Jesse, 117
McDonnell, Alexander, 18
McIntosh, Francis J., 102–3
McPherson, James B., 55, 143, 151
Madison, James, 2
Magdol, Edward, 45–46
Mahan, John B., 105
Maillard, Anne, 136
Maine, 8, 9, 24, 62–63, 109, 160
Manchester, England, 16
Mann, Horace, 111, 114
Marines, U.S., 124, 135
Marion College, 102
maroons, 76, 116, 125
marriage, 64, 78–80
Marshall, James, 121
Martin, David, 96
Martin, James, 120
Martinique, 73, 76
Marx, Karl, xvi, 19, 39, 75
Marxists, 38
Maryland, 3, 9, 38, 72, 96, 97, 117, 134, 154
Massachusetts, 8, 9, 12, 27, 36, 44, 45, 47, 56, 62, 63–64, 69, 72, 73, 92, 110, 111–12, 120, 127, 152, 160
Massachusetts Abolition Society, 86
Massachusetts Anti-Slavery Society, 44, 54, 69, 86
Mathaus, Edward, 117
May, Samuel J., 37, 42, 55, 99
Methodists, 4, 96, 105
Mexican War, xvii, 50, 115
Mexico, 6, 130
Michigan, 49, 83, 160
Middlesex County Anti-Slavery Society, 44
Miller, Stephen D., 18
Miner, Charles, 107
Minnesota, 152
Mississippi, 4, 6, 103, 156

Missouri, 6, 7, 8, 9, 10–12, 39, 98, 102, 108, 128, 132, 152
Missouri Compromise, 8, 11, 26
Mitchell, George, 100
Mobile, Ala., 102
mobs, anti-slavery, 24, 39, 47–49, 105
Monroe, James, xvii
Montesquieu, Baron, 68
Montgomery, Ala., 145
Moore, Isaiah, 120
More, Hannah, 81
Morris, Thomas, 2, 21
Morris, Thomas D., 7
Morton, Oliver P., 160
Mott, James, 113
Mott, Lucretia, 35, 88, 91, 112, 113, 120, 160
Mott, Lydia, 81
Mowrer, Milo, 101
Mumford, James Hall, 96
Myers, John L., 56–57
Myers, Stephen, 70

Napoleon, Louis, 146
Nashville, Tenn., 103
National Anti-Slavery Standard (a newspaper), 34, 55, 82, 91
National Anti-Slavery Tract Society, 3
National Council of the Colored People, 127
National Era (a newspaper), 55, 106
National Leader (a newspaper), 44
National Women's Convention, 79, 87
Native Americans ("Indians"), xiii, xiv, 81, 99, 157
Nelson, David, 102
New Bedford, Mass., 69, 109, 127
Newburyport, Mass., 45, 100
New England, 38
New England Anti-Slavery Society, 54, 56
New England Spectator (magazine), 90
New Hampshire, 105
New Haven, Conn., 62
New Jersey, 3
New Orleans, 39, 61, 99, 101, 102, 107, 108, 114

New York (City), 37, 42, 47, 48, 49, 53, 55, 65, 70, 82, 104, 127, 130, 135, 150, 155
New York (State), 9, 32, 38, 49, 56, 57, 63, 108, 113, 125, 138, 152
New York Anti-Slavery Society, 54, 65
New York Courier and Enquirer (a newspaper), 48
New York Herald (a newspaper), 47, 48–49, 124
New York Post (a newspaper), 137, 155
New York Sun (a newspaper), 71
New York Times (a newspaper), 55
New York Tribune (a newspaper), 49, 55, 130, 135
New York University, 9
Nicaragua, 119
Nixon, Sam, 70
non-slaveholding whites, 116
Norfolk, Va., 70, 109, 117
Norristown, Pa., 70
North Carolina, 1–2, 4, 62, 70, 71, 99, 105, 117, 128
North Elba, N.Y., 138
North Star (a newspaper), 14, 66
Northup, Solomon, 61, 71
Northwest Ordinance, 5–6
Norton, Charles Eliot, 136, 137
Norwid, Cyprian, 137
Nye, Russell B., 105, 169n5

Oates, Stephen, 129, 132, 133
Oberlin College, 54, 108, 129
Oberlin, Ohio, 104
Oberlin-Wellington Case, 129–30
Observer (a newspaper), 106
Ohio, 2, 3, 21, 49, 56, 83, 104, 105, 106, 107, 108, 121, 122, 129, 130, 152, 160
Ohio Anti-Slavery Society, 54, 129
Oneida Institute, 57, 169n10
Oppie, Amelia, 81
Osborn, Charles, 2
Osofsky, Gilbert, 69
Otis, Harrison Gray, 98

pacifism, 86
Park, Mungo, 85
Parker, Joel, 102
Parker, Mary, 90
Parker, Theodore, 94, 118, 136
Patriot (a newspaper), 110
Paul, Nathaniel, 67
Pearl (a ship), 110–11
Pease, Elizabeth, 17, 42, 56, 93
Pease, Jane H., 99
Pease, William H., 99
Pennsylvania, 2, 11, 38, 70, 96, 107, 118, 119, 133
Pennsylvania Anti-Slavery Society, 54
Pensacola, Fla., 111
peonage, 156
Perry, Lewis, xi
Personal Liberty Laws, 7, 9, 13, 121
petitions, anti-slavery, 21, 22, 23, 27, 50, 52, 53, 64, 91–92, 93, 174n10
Philadelphia, 37, 39, 47, 70, 73, 84, 113, 153
Philadelphia Female Anti-Slavery Society, 53, 86
Philleo, Calvin, 102
Phillips, Ann, 127
Phillips, Wendell, xi, xv, 16–17, 17–18, 32–34, 35, 40, 46, 47, 54, 55, 66, 79–80, 81, 85, 87–88, 91, 106, 112, 118, 119, 127, 136, 144, 150, 151, 160–61
Phillips, William A., 131
Pickens, F. W., 29
Pierce, Franklin, 121
Pillsbury, Parker, xv, 84, 160
Pinkney, William, 9
Pittsburgh, 70, 73, 81
Planter (a ship), 154
Poland, 5, 137
political activity, question of, 86
Political Economy of Slavery (Ruffin), 32
Porter, Susan F., 93
Portland, Me., 62
Pottawatomie, Kansas, 128–29
Potter, George, 62
Potter, Rosella, 62
Price, John, 129, 130
prisons, conditions in, 114–15

Pro-Slavery Argument (Harper), 30
Providence, R.I., 41, 54, 64, 110
Puerto Rico, 76
Pugh, Sarah, 120
purchasing freedom, 62, 69
Purvis, Harriet, 83
Purvis, Robert, 35, 40, 66, 155
Putnam, Mary, 84–85

Quakers, 34, 56, 81, 101
Quarles, Benjamin, 73, 138
Quincy, Edmund, 14, 55, 65, 160
Quincy, Illinois, 108
Quincy, John

Racism and Abolitionism, xiv, 63, 64–65, 83, 125
Raleigh, N.C., 109
Randolph, Thomas Mann, 22
Rankin, John, 2, 68
Rapp, Wilhelm, 39
Rawley, James A., 152
Rayado, Joseph, 96
Reconstruction era, 151, 161
Record of an Obscure Man (Putnam), 84–85
Religion and Abolitionism, xvi, 20
Remond, Charles Lenox, 62–63, 64, 127, 144
Republican Party, xv, 56, 143, 144, 145
Rhode Island, 41, 56, 96, 110
Rhodes, Andrew, 95
Rhodes, James Ford, xii, 144–45
Richards, Leonard L., 47–48
Richmond, Va., 39, 70, 71, 73, 99, 108, 113, 117, 152
Richmond Enquirer (a newspaper), 30, 108
Ricketson, Gilbert, 109
Roane, Spencer, 9
Robinson, C. W., 113
Robinson, Marius R., 106
Rochester, N.Y., 54, 66, 70, 87, 133
Rochester Ladies' Anti-Slavery Sewing Society, 93
Rockenberg, George, 95
Rome, N.Y., 45

Rose, Ernestine, 79
Ross, David, 70
Ruchames, Louis, 56, 69
Ruffin, Edmund, 32, 138
Ruggles, David, 70, 71
Ruggles, John, 24
Russia, 5, 16
Rye, George, 105

Saffin, John, 18
St. Louis, Mo., 39, 47, 102–3, 106
Saint Lucia, 76
sailors, Afro-American, 148, 151
Salem, Mass., 83
San Antonio Zeitung (a newspaper), 38
Sarge, John, 96
Saugus Female Society, 46
Savannah, Ga., 60, 98
Sayres, Edward, 110–11
Schenectady, N.Y., 45
Schnauffer, Carl H., 39
schools, public, 64, 92
Scotland, 109
Scott, Anne F., 81
Scudder, Rev., 64
Seamen's Acts, 25
Secession movement, 117
segregation, 160
Seneca Falls Convention, 87, 91
Seward, Frederick, 31
Sewell, Richard H., xv
Sewell, Samuel, 18
Sewell, Samuel H., 53
Seymour, Horatio, 49
Shelby, Isaac, 18
Simmons, George F., 102
Sims, Thomas, 118, 119
sit-in, 84
Slavery and Anti-Slavery (Goodell), 16
slave-trade, 10, 50, 73, 74, 91, 100, 148
Smalls, Robert, 154
Smith, Edward, 99
Smith, George, 2
Smith, Gerrit, xv, 35, 117, 127
Smith, Humphrey, 98
Smith, James, 99
Smith, Samuel A., 73, 113

Smith, W. R., 40, 59
Socialists (and Socialism), xvi, 19, 32, 38–40
Sociology for the South (Fitzhugh), 30
soldiers, Afro-American, 148, 150–51, 152–54
South Carolina, 2, 18, 29, 38, 59, 98, 99, 105, 109, 117, 127, 128, 133, 153
Southwick, Joseph, 53
Spain, 6
Spartacus, 116
Spooner, Lysander, 21, 128, 156
Springfield, Il., 103
Springfield, Mass., 45, 126
Stanton, Edwin M., 154
Stanton, Elizabeth Cady, 79–80, 91, 92, 144
Stanton, Henry B., 52, 67, 94
Stearns, George, Mrs., 138
Stephens, Alexander, 31–32, 145
Stevens, Thaddeus, 118, 151, 160
Stewart, James B., 40
Still, Peter, 71
Still, William, 70, 71, 73, 113, 119–20, 123
Stone, Lucy, 79, 80, 121
Storrs, George, 105
Stowe, Harriet Beecher, 14, 33, 55, 62, 81, 82, 89, 111, 144, 150
Stuart, Charles, 57
Stuart, J. E. B., 135
suffrage, for Afro-Americans, 152
Sumner, Charles, xv, 69, 74, 111, 114, 128, 151
Supreme Court, U.S., 11, 30, 97, 106, 128, 160
Sutton, John, 2
Syracuse, N.Y., 70

Tait, Charles, 9
Tallmadge, John, 9
Taney, Roger B., 47, 97, 112, 128, 156
Tappan, Arthur, 3, 5, 100
Tappan, Lewis, 35, 68, 87, 100
Tarrant, Carter, 2
Taylor, John W., 9
Ten Commandments, 124

Tennessee, 2, 3, 4, 103, 128
Tennessee Manumission Society, 3
Texas, 6, 38
Thirteenth Amendment, 151, 155–56, 157
Thomas, William, 18
Thome, James, 2
Thompson, George, 108
Thompson, George (of England), 154
Thoreau, Henry David, 118, 136, 140
Thornwell, James H., 38
Tilton, Theodore, 56
Todd, Frances, 100
Torrey, Charles T., 109–10
Tortola, 76
trade-unions, 43–44
Trinidad, 76
Truth, Sojourner, 35, 83, 84
Tubman, Harriet, 83, 123, 135, 155, 180n23
Turner, E. N., 112
Turner, Nat, xvi, 38, 59, 126
Tyler, John, 153

Uncle Tom's Cabin (Stowe), 14, 55, 117
Underground Railroad, 62, 70, 83, 112, 133, 171n28, n30
Underwood, John W., 38
Unitarians, 4, 45, 102
Utica, N.Y., 45, 47

Van Buren, Martin, 56
Van Renselaer, Thomas, 64
Vatican, 146
Vermont, 43, 78, 79, 108
Vesey, Denmark, 62, 95
vigilance committee, 71
Virginia, 2, 4, 9, 22, 38, 60, 68, 70, 96, 99, 107, 113, 116, 126, 128, 131, 138, 141, 146, 153
Voegeli, V. J., 152

Walker, David, xvi, 1, 82, 98
Walker, Jonathan, 111–12
Washington, D.C., 104, 106, 117
Washington, George, 1, 107, 116, 119, 133, 137

Washington, Lewis, 133
Washington, Madison, 107
Washington Union (a newspaper), 31
Watson, Henry, 123, 133
Webb, James Watson, 48
Webster, Daniel, 27, 36
Webster, Delia A., 108–9
Weed, Phebe Matthews, 68, 83
Weld, Angelina Grimké, 47, 55; *See also* Angelina Grimké
Weld, Theodore D., 5, 24, 32, 47, 52, 53, 55, 57, 68, 83, 85, 102, 106, 156
West Virginia, 3
West, William, 168n29
Wheedon, D. D., 94
Wheeler, John H., 119–20
Whipper, William, 70
White, Addison, 118
Whitman, Walt, 45, 59
Whittier, John Greenleaf, 52
Williams, Eric, 74
Williamson, Passmore, 119–21
Wilmington, N. C., 99
Wilson, Benjamin, 60
Wiltse, Charles M., 19
Wisconsin, 152
Wise, Henry A., 137, 138, 142, 153

Women and abolitionism, *77–93*
Women and petitions, 46, 64
Women slaves, fleeing of, 60
Women's Anti-Slavery Society (in England), 82
Women's Loyal National League, 92
Women's movement, xvi, 51, 54, 64, 68, 74, 105, 158
Wood, Joseph, 45
Woolfolk, Austin, 100
Worcester, Mass., 45, 87
Work, Alanson, 108
workers and slavery, 10
Workingmen's Association (of England), 44
World and Africa, The (Du Bois), 75
World Anti-Slavery Convention, 91
Wright, Elizur, 94
Wright, Frances, 79, 173n4
Wright, Henry C., 144
Wright, Lucy, 83
Wright, Silas, 48
Wright, Theodore S., 65

Yale University, 57, 94, 110
Yanuck, Julius, 122
York, Pa., 70